D0204656

The Government Policy of Protector Somerset

Endpapers: 'King Edward the Sixth' from the original of Holbein, in the collection of The Ear of Egremont, drawn by William Derby and engraved by T. A. Dean (left). 'Edward Seymour, Duke of Somerset, Lord Protector' from the original of Holbein, in the collection of The Marquis of Bath, drawn by William Hitton, R.A., and engraved by H. Meyer (right). Both engravings are reproduced by courtesy of The Mansell Collection.

To my parents

The Government Policy of Protector Somerset

M. L. Bush

McGill-Queen's University Press

MONTREAL 1975

© M. L. Bush 1975
First published 1975 by
Edward Arnold (Publishers) Ltd, London
Published in North America 1975 by
McGill—Queen's University Press, Montreal

ISBN: 0 7735 0260 2
Legal Deposit 4th Quarter 1975
Bibliothèque Nationale du Québec

All Rights Reserved. No part of this publication may be reproduced,
stored in a retrieval system, or transmitted in any form or by any
means, electronic, mechanical, photocopying, recording or otherwise,
without the prior permission of the publishers.

Printed in Great Britain by
Butler & Tanner Ltd, Frome and London

Contents

Conclusion   160

Index   163

Preface

This book attempts both to demolish an interpretation erected by A. F. Pollard and renovated latterly by W. K. Jordan,[1] and to construct a new framework for the study of politics in Edward VI's reign. The subject is not so much the impact and enforcement of government policy as its creation and character. The consequences of government decisions and the effectiveness of the machinery of government are beyond the scope of the book unless they contribute to the making and the characterization of policy by serving as its subject, by influencing its evolution, or by determining its success and failure. Primarily the book studies the way the various strands of government policy interacted, and analyses the role of principles, personalities, social pressures and changing circumstances in the policy's formulation. It is also a study of a government's mentality and conduct in a time of crisis, the outcome of royal minority, unprecedented inflation, peasant uprisings, reformation and war. Finally, since the beliefs and attitudes of Protector Somerset are conceived as typical of those held by Tudor statesmen, the book is about Tudor government in its policy-making capacity.

This work cannot pretend to be either pioneering or definitive. Most of the evidence it uses has been considered before although differently interpreted; and others have questioned the standard interpretation, but not so comprehensively.[2] Furthermore, the broadness of the subject has inevitably left certain loose ends which require a more intensive and individual treatment than this book can provide without losing its balance. Nevertheless, there seems an urgent need to regard the government's policy as a unity, both as a complete corrective of the old view and in order to provide something which earlier works on the subject lacked, largely because they tended to examine the various aspects of the policy in isolation without any real attempt to establish an order of importance or degree of interaction, and because they imposed a coherence only by insisting on the dominant influence of Protector Somerset. Justifying this study is the importance of a unifying conception of the policy as a whole, as well as the undeserved durability of the standard interpretation.

[1] See A. F. Pollard, *England under Protector Somerset* (London, 1900) and W. K. Jordan, *Edward VI: The Young King* (London, 1968).

[2] E.g. M. W. Beresford, 'The Poll Tax and Census of Sheep, 1549', *Agricultural History Review* 2 (1954), pp. 21*f*; C. S. L. Davies, 'Slavery and Protector Somerset: the Vagrancy Act of 1547', *Econ. HR* ser. 2, 19 (1966), pp. 533*ff*; G. R. Elton, 'Government by Edict?' *Historical Journal* 8 (1965), pp. 266*ff*, and Elton, 'The Good Duke', *Historical Journal* 12 (1969), pp. 702*ff*.

The book rests upon the assistance of a large number of people, particularly the initial guidance of H. E. Howard, J. H. Plumb and G. R. Elton. The colleagues at Manchester University whom I would like to thank for discussing the subject of Somerset with me are P. W. J. Riley, T. S. Willan, J. R. Western, I. J. Prothero and C. R. Lucas. I am grateful to C. R. Day for reading the typescript and for his penetrating criticisms of it, to R. S. Schofield for providing me with information concerning the relief on sheep and cloth, to M. H. Merriman for reading chapter two, to G. R. Elton for helping me to structure chapter four, and to A. Knox for helping me with that part of chapter three which deals with the court of requests. Parts of the book were given trial runs as talks to the special subject seminars of M. H. Merriman and L. Beier at Lancaster University, to the Liverpool and Huddersfield branches of the Historical Association and to the history department of the North London Polytechnic. In each case I must express gratitude for the opportunity to express my views in public and to learn from the response which they received. The research behind the book depended upon many visits to London, the cost of which was relieved by an award from the Raleigh Fund of the British Academy. The book also owes a great deal to the services of a number of libraries and record offices, particularly the British Museum, the Public Record Office, the House of Lords' Record Office, the Norwich Record Office, the Northampton Record Office, the Library of the Inner Temple and the University and Central Reference Libraries in Manchester. In addition, I must thank the Marquises of Anglesey and Bath for allowing me access to their family papers. I am also grateful to C. Rawcliffe of the Royal Commission on Historical Manuscripts for answering my enquiries. Most of all, the book is indebted to my own family who sacrificed holiday time to study with me the sites of Somerset's Scottish garrisons, and particularly to my wife. Needless to say, the book owes a large debt to A. F. Pollard, without whose work on Protector Somerset this book would never have been written.

Didsbury, Manchester   M.L.B.
August 1974

Abbreviations

APC	*Acts of the Privy Council of England*, ed. J. R. Dasent (London, 1890–1907)
Alexander	G. M. V. Alexander, *The Life and Career of Edward Bonner, Bishop of London until his Deprivation in 1549* (unpublished London University Ph.D. thesis, 1959)
BM	British Museum
Burnet	G. Burnet, *The History of the Reformation of the Church of England* (Oxford, 1829)
CPR	*Calendar of the Patent Rolls*
DNB	*Dictionary of National Biography*
EETS	Early English Text Society
Econ. HR	*Economic History Review*
Engl. HR	*English Historical Review*
Foxe	*The Acts and Monuments of John Foxe*, ed. J. Pratt (London, 1877)
Ham.	*The Hamilton Papers*, ed. Joseph Bain (Edinburgh, 1890–92).
HMC	*Historical Manuscripts Commission*
Holdsworth	W. S. Holdsworth, *A History of English Law* (London, 1922–52)
Hughes and Larkin	*Tudor Royal Proclamations*, I, ed. P. L. Hughes and J. F. Larkin (New Haven, 1964)
Jordan I	W. K. Jordan, *Edward VI, The Young King* (London, 1968)
Jordan II	W. K. Jordan, *The Threshold of Power* (London, 1970)
Lamond	*A Discourse of the Common Weal of this Realm of England*, ed. E. Lamond (Cambridge, 1893)
LP	*Letters and Papers, Foreign and Domestic, of the Reign of Henry VIII*, ed. J. S. Brewer, J. Gairdner and R. H. Brodie (London, 1864–1932)
Lodge	*Illustrations of British History . . . from the MSS of Howard, Talbot and Cecil*, ed. E. Lodge (London, 1838)
Muller	*Letters of Stephen Gardiner*, ed. J. A. Muller (Cambridge, 1933)

Original Letters	*Original Letters Relative to the English Reformation . . . chiefly from the Archives of Zurich,* ed. Hastings Robinson (Parker Society, Cambridge, 1846–7)
PLB	Paget Letter Book, Northamptonshire Record Office
Pocock	*Troubles Connected with the Prayer Book,* ed. N. Pocock (Camden Society, new ser., 37 (1884))
Pollard	A. F. Pollard, *England under Protector Somerset* (London, 1900)
PRO	Public Record Office
Scottish Correspondence	*Scottish Correspondence of Mary of Lorraine, 1543–60,* ed. A. I. Cameron (Scottish Historical Society, 3rd ser., 10 (1927))
Selve	Odet de Selve, *Correspondance Politique, 1546–9,* ed. G. Lefevre-Pontalis (Paris, 1888)
SP Dom.	*Calendar of State Papers Domestic, Elizabeth I, 1601–1603, with Addenda, 1547–1565*
SP For.	*Calendar of State Papers, Foreign*
SP Scot.	*Calendar of State Papers, Scottish,* ed. Joseph Bain
SP Span.	*Calendar of State Papers, Spanish*
St.P	*State Papers, published under the Authority of His Majesty's Commission, King Henry VIII* (London, 1830–52)
Strype	J. Strype, *Ecclesiastical Memorials relating chiefly to Religion, and its Reformation under the Reigns of King Henry VIII, King Edward VI and Queen Mary* (London, 1816)
TED	*Tudor Economic Documents,* ed. R. H. Tawney and E. Power (London, 1924)
Thesis	M. L. Bush, *The Rise to Power of Edward Seymour, Protector Somerset, 1500–1547* (unpublished Cambridge University Ph.D. thesis, 1964)
TRHS	*Transactions of the Royal Historical Society*
Tytler	*England under the Reigns of Edward VI and Mary,* ed. P. F. Tytler (London, 1839)

Throughout the book, the spelling and punctuation of quotations from original sources have been modernized.

1

Government Policy

This study departs from the standard view in four basic respects. First, it regards Scotland as the government's main concern and the hub around which the rest of the policy revolved. Secondly, it questions the decisiveness of new principles in the making of policy and elevates the importance of circumstance. Thirdly, it disagrees with the established assumption that Somerset differed profoundly from his colleagues in his basic political and social beliefs. Finally, while accepting a close connection between the policy of the government and the force of Somerset's personality, it attaches importance to the influence of his obsessional nature and his desire to appear virtuous rather than to his alleged idealism, gentleness and magnanimity.

Scotland was much more than one aspect of the government's foreign concerns. It was an overriding force which pervaded its whole policy. Without the Scottish war the character of the policy and the behaviour of the protector would have been very different. After the resumption of the war in late 1547 Somerset spent most of his time and most of the government's resources on the Scottish matter. The Scottish war was the area of policy in which the government proceeded most singlemindedly, making no concessions to the rest of its policies, foreign and domestic, until peasant insurrections intervened in 1549. Furthermore, the Scottish war directed most of the government's major decisions and plans. It helped to determine the government's social programme. Not only did the Scottish war quickly consume the wealth of the chantry lands, taking away the social purpose which was originally proposed for them, but, in addition, as a result of its ambitions in Scotland, the government completely overlooked the responsibility of war when it sought to remedy the economic and social problems of the time. The Scottish war encouraged the government to attribute inflation not to the debasement of the coinage upon which the financing of the war-effort relied, nor to war itself, but mainly to factors such as sheep-farming and covetousness which could be remedied without restricting the government's military designs. The Scottish war also made sheep the target for the government's wrath because of the supposed connection between sheep-farming as a cause of depopulation and the country's military incapacity, particularly since the latter weakness was exposed by the exhausting warfare of the 1540s. The Somerset government needed to act because of the spectacularly high rate of inflation, but its military ambitions produced a social policy which aimed to sustain rather than to interfere with the war effort. The priority of the Scottish war also explains, in part, Somerset's apparent leniency towards the peasant rebellions of 1549. Military action was delayed against the rebels not out of sympathy for them but because Somerset needed all available resources for an imminent campaign against Scotland. The Scottish war was certainly a major influence in the religious settlement. The government's wish to maintain the domestic peace upon which the foreign war depended, and its eagerness not to antagonize Emperor Charles V whose support or neutrality was essential to the Scottish war, created the ambivalent character of the settlement which did not reflect the beliefs of Somerset or his colleagues but what they thought to be unobjectionable to Charles V and likely to preserve harmony at home. The Scottish war dominated foreign affairs. In the context of early Tudor foreign policy the Somerset government was remarkable because it made its relations with France secondary to its relations with Scotland. For the sake of success in Scotland Somerset seemed prepared to undo the achievement of Henry VIII's closing years, even to the extent of surrendering Boulogne prematurely in return for the withdrawal of French aid from Scotland and the possession of the Scottish queen. Holding a position of top priority in the government's mind, the Scottish matter exerted a dominant influence over the whole range of its main concerns.

The Scottish war was of outstanding importance in a second sense. It represented an area of government policy which was undeniably the direct result of what was for the Tudors a new outlook. This did not rest upon the idea of national consolidation, but of controlling Scotland through a network of garrisons. There was nothing idealistic, lenient or farsighted about this approach. Although it quickly proved unworkable, in origin it stemmed from practical considerations, particularly the costliness of having to invade Scotland frequently with armies royal for the purpose of calling the Scots to order; and while designed to offer protection to friendly Scots, the garrisons were also meant to apply force. What is more, they were an essentially new device for realizing an ancient goal. Garrisoning was something which seized Somerset's imagination and eventually ruled his mind. So potent was its appeal that it also figured in his plans for governing the Irish and for withstanding peasant rebellion.

In contrast, the distinguishing features of the rest of the policy were largely the outcome of circumstances and necessity. The rigour of Henry VIII's reign compelled a reaction upon his death. The repeal act must be seen in this light, not as an 'experiment in liberty'. Somerset supported the act as a protestant seizing the opportunity to erase the measures from which his kind had suffered in the past and as a governor needing by an act of popularity to establish rapport with the realm. He did not act because of a belief in political liberalism or religious toleration. The considerations of the repeal act were eminently practical. The preamble was merely the froth on an otherwise down-to-earth, realistic and inevitable measure.

Similarly, inflation and the requirements of war made the social programme a necessity, and its character was the product of circumstance, as conditions and the government's needs closed off the options. Although the standard interpretation regarded as exceptional the principles upon which the programme was based, there is no certainty that the Somerset government's social concern was anything but the familiar paternalism of the monarchical-aristocratic state. Instead of springing from an ideology of social welfare alien to the age, Somerset's social programme was moved by the need to dispense impartial justice and to maintain the security of the state against revolution and foreign conquest, aims which aristocratic society had no difficulty in accepting as worthy and politic. The conventionality of the regime's social outlook is confirmed by its treatment of peasant rebellion in 1549. This did not denote a sympathy for the rebels' cause, except in the minds of those who misinterpreted it. Somerset and his colleagues abhorred rebellion and acted in response to military considerations, particularly the priority of its Scottish designs and the military tactics which Somerset's considerable military experience caused him to favour.

The religious changes were again basically the product of necessity and circumstance. A government of protestants had no choice but to carry out a reformation in a catholic state. Under Somerset's direction, circumstances seemed to determine the specific character of that reformation. The standard account explains the ambiguity of the settlement as the result of Somerset's own moderate and tolerant protestantism. Yet in view of his patronage of Hooper, Becon, Turner and Pollanus, it is clear that throughout the protectorate Somerset was far from moderate in his religious beliefs. Moreover, in view of his government's insistence upon religious uniformity, and of Somerset's participation in the persecution of Gardiner, Bonner and Princess Mary, he cannot be regarded as an apostle of toleration, or as remarkably tolerant. The discrepancy between his religious affiliations and the settlement itself can only be explained by circumstantial considerations such as the government's unwillingness to offend Charles V and to arouse the realm by too blatant a breach with the past.

Circumstances again seemed to dictate the changes made to the personnel of government, except possibly for the exclusion of bishops from further areas of the government which seemed to reflect the protestant insistence that bishops should devote themselves to their dioceses. Certain new peers dominated the government, not because of a prejudice against the old aristocracy but because of the legacy of Henry VIII; certain old noble families were restored during the protectorate in accordance with a traditional formula of compassion and because the king who had felled them was dead. Changes in the machinery of government likewise occurred without any deep and novel design and largely in response to the situation, except for the garrisoning of midland Ireland. The abolition of the proclamations act derived from the practical need to free proclamations from the restrictions imposed by the act; and the government's creation of proclamations in remarkably large numbers—a spectacular feature of the regime—was a normal response to the emergencies of war, rebellion, religious change and inflation. Proclamations were frequently made because circumstances provided a multitude of occasions which needed them. Some were harsh and others of dubious legitimacy, but the impression given is of a government coping with crises rather than planning to rule by edict.

The masterful role of circumstance in the formulation of policy is exemplified by the distinction between the policies of the Somerset and Northumberland regimes. Dictating the differences was not a conflict of principle, but a change of circumstance brought about by the termination of war, the collapse of the Antwerp market, the fall of Somerset and the repeated failure of the harvest.

Somerset had serious differences with his colleagues on the council which eventually culminated in his fall from power. Yet these differences were not the result of an ideological conflict but of disputes over the details of policy and reactions against the personal obnoxiousness of the protector. While Somerset dominated policy, he did so because his views largely coincided with his colleagues. Thus, although much of the direction and dynamism stemmed from him, the responsibility can be said to have lain with a governing group which shared a common attitude. On several occasions Somerset acted without the council's consent. Haddington, according to the charges brought against him in October 1549, was a device which he forced upon the government; and he certainly negotiated for the cession of Boulogne behind the government's back in 1548; and the enclosure commissions of 1549 were issued without the council's approval. But these examples of private initiative expressed either his arrogance or obstinacy, not a social or political outlook which differed from that of his colleagues. As evidence of the elementary agreement in attitude, the Northumberland regime pursued a policy which, in changed circumstances, promulgated roughly the same beliefs.

The Scottish policy owed much to Somerset, and was very much under his command and direction. Nevertheless, he allowed the rest of the council to have some say in it, and it would be wrong to think that in conducting the Scottish war Somerset was acting autocratically. As captain-general of the king's forces against Scotland, Somerset possessed an executive command of Scottish affairs in the situation of war, but this was subject to the advice and consent of his colleagues. Disagreements arose, but not over establishing a network of garrisons in Scotland or over going to war with the Scots. For this reason the fall of Somerset did not occasion the abandonment of the garrisoning system which was carefully maintained until its nagging impracticability made it an acceptable concession in the treaty of Boulogne.

The rest of the government's policy substantiates this impression. His agrarian programme was criticized at his trial, but not because it was totally alien to the other councillors. He established the 1548 commission with the consent of the council. Opposition was voiced to it only after it had come into operation and because it appeared to be causing disorder. In contrast, the 1549 commissions were opposed before they were issued, essentially because the time was not ripe. According to the surviving evidence, opposition in the council to the social measures favoured by Somerset was because of their inopportunity, impracticability or illegitimacy. The objection was to the means, not to the aims. Much the same can be said of the government's treatment of peasant risings. Again, Somerset seemed chiefly responsible for it, but in conjunction with other councillors. While failing to act as quickly or as harshly as some wished, and divided from some of them by his preference for initial pacification rather than immediate chastisement, the differences in the council seemed to be over tactics and priorities rather than social attitudes. Somerset was certainly not on the side of rebellious peasants, and the tactics he advocated for subduing them were eventually applied with success by the earl of Warwick in Norfolk. The religious settlement was less clearly the product of Somerset's individual direction; but, while differing from some in his advanced protestant beliefs, he seemed at one with his colleagues over the policy to be pursued. He was certainly not divided from them by an appreciation of liberal principles. He was as responsible as the rest of the government for the persecution of Gardiner and Bonner and for refusing to tolerate permanently Mary's non-conformity. Mary was treated more harshly by the Northumberland government, as was religious dissent, and the settlement itself became more overt in its protestant standpoint, but this seemed to be the consequence of the termination of war and the earlier changes in religion, not of the removal of Somerset from the centre of power. The policy towards the means of government followed the general pattern. Somerset provided the direction, but proposed no radical departures, and basically the council was in agreement. Opposition was voiced to the use of proclamations, but only in certain circumstances and if contrary to the law. The criticism related to detail, to certain proclamations, not to the general use made of proclamations, and in response to critical circumstances the Northumberland regime resorted to the same device with a similar frequency and for the same purposes. The traditional interpretation exaggerated the radicalism of Somerset's beliefs and the conservatism of the rest of the council. The evidence suggests that, while there were differences on a wide range of matters, there was also a broad band of agreement on the basic aims of the policy: the garrisoning of Scotland, the establishment of religious change, the control of inflation and the maintenance of political security.

The government's policy was heavily influenced by Somerset and bore the imprint of his personality. It expressed his obsessive stubbornness. In addition to the pressure of circumstance, Protector Somerset's political behaviour was directed not by ideals, but by *idées fixes*, particularly the garrisoning of Scotland and the issuing of enclosure commissions. The policy of the protectorate acquired its distinct character as Somerset lost all sense of reason and persisted with such devices in an attempt to make them work. The government's policy also expressed Somerset's desire to appear virtuous and to be held in esteem. In temperament Somerset seemed harsh and acquisitive as his activities against the Scots and his massive accumulation of estates revealed. Nevertheless, he clearly craved the reputation of a virtuous ruler in order to achieve popularity and renown. This helped to set the tone of the policy. But it tended to lead to a concern only with appearances. His government made frequent declarations of clemency and justice, so much so that neither the Scots, the peasant rebels nor the poor could accuse it of being totally inconsiderate and unmerciful. However, clemency and justice were not at the heart of the realized policy. With Somerset's encouragement the Scots and the peasant rebels were chastised for their disobedience. Moreover, because of his determined concentration on the Scottish matter, only token action could be taken to relieve the lot of the poor. What distinguished his policy was his avid desire to subscribe to what was traditionally expected of a good prince, and not an unusual concern of a ruler for his subjects. This ambition helped to sugar the government's policy with a benevolence which neither broke with the past nor penetrated very deeply, and which, when seen within the context of the government's actions as a whole, appeared to have a self-justificatory rather than an altruistic aim.

2
The Policy towards Scotland

Basic Aims

In the closing years of Henry VIII's reign the war against the Scots had a profound effect upon Somerset's career. It revealed his exceptional talents as a military leader: after his spectacular invasion of Scotland in 1544 and his brutally efficient and effective border raid of 1545, men could no longer appreciate him merely as a relative of the king. His final rise to power undoubtedly owed much to his military triumphs in the north since they brought him close to the king, rendered the Howards expendable as military leaders and therefore disposable as subjects and provided Somerset with a reputation which must have clinched his bid for the protectorship.[1] As the war became not only a source of personal satisfaction for Somerset, but also a habit with the English, not one year passing between 1541 and 1547 without some device for the chastisement of the Scots, it was not surprising that upon Henry VIII's death and with Somerset in charge of the government, the war against the Scots should be resumed.

Edward VI's Scottish war continued the one Henry VIII had waged since 1542. They shared the same circumstances of a Scotland weakened by a royal minority and drawn towards union with France. Initially, the minority had raised English hopes that Scotland would be united with England; but these hopes were dashed by a Franco-Scottish alliance, already declared by James V's marriages to French princesses in the late 1530s, and finally fulfilled in 1548 when his successor, Mary Stuart, removed to France and was betrothed to the Dauphin. The two wars also possessed a similar aim, principally the English Crown's dynastic desire to take complete possession of the realm of Scotland, and similar means which consisted of enforcing Edward VI's marriage to Mary Stuart, and of asserting the English king's ancient claim of suzerainty over the Scottish kingdom. By means of the marriage both Henry VIII and Somerset had hoped to annex the Crown of Scotland and thus to eliminate a vassal who, as James V had demonstrated, could be intolerably troublesome because of his French and papal connections.[2] With the

---

[1] See Thesis, chs. 4 and 5.

[2] For the motivation, causes and course of the Scottish war, see G. Donaldson, *James V–James VII* (Edinburgh, 1965), ch. 5; A. J. Slavin, *Politics and Profit: a Study of Sir Ralph Sadler, 1507–47* (Cambridge, 1966), chs. 5 and 6; J. J. Scarisbrick, *Henry VIII* (London, 1968), ch. 13; W. B. Wernham, *Before the Armada: the Growth of English Foreign Policy, 1485–1588* (London, 1966), chs. 12 and 13; and Jordan I, ch. 9.

failure of the marriage, both resorted to military action, but not to take immediate possession of the Scottish kingdom. Both, in the circumstances, undoubtedly intended the forceful imposition of direct rule as their ultimate
objective, if union was otherwise unattainable. Both rested their case for possession upon the broken promises of the Scottish Crown and the consequent right of
forfeiture invested in the English king's claim of suzerainty over the kingdom of
Scotland. Paget expressed the underlying aim and its continuity when he wrote in
1549: 'We have been in war with the Scots these eight years, and yet continue
still intending conquest of the realm upon pretence of forfeiture.'[3] But because of
a preference for a union by marriage, this intention was played down. It featured
as a declared aim in the preamble to a statutory grant of supplies in 1542, before
Mary's birth provided another means of union.[4] It was put to certain Scots in
January 1543, but in a secret article;[5] it appeared in a draft of instructions to the
diplomat Ralph Sadler in August 1543, but was omitted from the final version.[6]
Moreover, because of his involvement with France, Henry was in any case prepared to postpone indefinitely his design of annexing Scotland.[7] Somerset
certainly had a freer hand because of the peace with France, and also a greater need
to take possession when the marriage plans collapsed completely in August 1548.
Frequently his government referred to the Scots as rebels, and therefore as subjects, not as enemies,[8] and the claim to Scotland was one of propriety, not mere
superiority.[9] But Somerset likewise held his hand. Although he possessed a means
of imposing direct rule upon the Scots through the garrisons which had been
established in the country, and although in the past he had regarded garrisons as a
means of compelling the Scots to serve as subjects of the English monarchy,
Somerset resisted all suggestions to use them for that specific purpose during the
protectorate.[10] Instead, with the marriage unrealized, both Henry and Somerset
applied force only to ensure obedience and to provide punishment, while continuing to believe their aims of possession would be eventually fulfilled through a
party of friends among the Scots who would agree to the union. Both laid great

[3] PLB, Paget to Somerset, 17 April 1549.

[4] 34/5 Henry VIII, c. 27.

[5] Henry reported to Sir Richard Southwell that ten of the prisoners taken at Solway Moss 'have
subscribed an article that in case of the death of the daughter, the king's highness will take upon him
the crown and government of the realm of Scotland, they will serve his majesty to their powers in
that behalf' (*Ham.* I, pp. 367f (*LP* XVIII (1), 22)).

[6] The deleted passage read that if the young queen were abducted and the governor remained loyal
to the English 'whereby his highness may have the whole dominion on this side the Firth, his highness
will not fail to aid and assist him . . . till he make him king of all the rest beyond the Firth.' Substituted
was simply the promise to make Arran king of the Highlands by force of his (Henry VIII's) title of
superiority' (*Ham.* I, 439).

[7] See *LP* XIX (1), 314, 319 and 348; see Somerset's struggle in the circumstances of a French
priority in 1545 (*LP* XX (1), 837).

[8] The enemy Scots were being referred to as rebels in 1547 (*CPR* 1547–8, p. 170 and 1 Edward VI,
c. 13), but not consistently until late 1548. A turning point seemed to be reached in May 1548 when
in Clinton's instructions the phrase 'our ancient enemies' was deleted and replaced by 'his highness'
rebels' (PRO SP10/IV/9).

[9] BM MS Cotton Caligula B VII, I. 343b.

[10] *LP* XIX (1), 319, and see below, p. 19.

store in encouraging the Scots to assure their support for the English cause.[11] But they also regarded force as a crucial inducement of friendship.[12]

Nevertheless, the two wars were far from identical in approach. Henry VIII's and Somerset's Scottish policy differed first in the importance each attached to the question of Scotland, and secondly in their appreciation of how best to apply effective pressure and control.

J. J. Scarisbrick regarded Henry's war aims against France as the principal cause of his war against Scotland.[13] If this was so, Henry's Scottish policy is sharply distinguishable from Edward VI's which took place when England was keen to leave France at peace.[14] But Henry VIII's war against Scotland did not simply derive from his war against France. The two theatres of war were undoubtedly connected since James V proved himself a nuisance by his association with the French, and the French proved themselves a nuisance through furnishing the Scots with military assistance. Yet connection did not mean encapsulation. It is far from certain that Henry's last Scottish war would not have occurred in the absence of his war with France. The Scottish war had a life and existence of its own. It stemmed as much from the lack of cooperation of James V and his French and papal connections and, after his death, from the Scottish repudiation of the marriage agreement contained in the treaty of Greenwich, as it did from the English need to hamstring a potential northern intruder before warring across the channel. To regard the Scottish war as contained within the French war is to commit the error of the interpretation which saw Henry's war against France as resulting from his designs against Scotland.[15] The basic difference between the two policies lay in priority not motive. Henry's approach towards Scotland was heavily influenced by his tendency to regard the Scottish problem as secondary to his quarrel with France, while Somerset's attitude towards Scotland was coloured by his view of the French problem as secondary to the quarrel with Scotland. In the matter of priority, and because of it, their policies are poles apart.

Unlike Henry VIII Somerset shied away from open conflict with France in order to concentrate whole-heartedly upon winning Scotland. To prevent the struggle for Boulogne from bursting into official war, he tolerated the provocation of the French, particularly their failure to pay the pension, their provision of martial aid to the Scots, their encouragement of piracy and the persistence of their reprisals against the English continental fortifications. Needled constantly by the struggle for Boulogne, Somerset desisted from declaring war, only accepting it when the French finally declared it upon the English.[16] He and his colleagues even regarded the removal of the Scottish queen to France and her betrothal to the

11 The system of assurance is described by M. H. Merriman, 'The Assured Scots', *Scottish Historical Review* 47 (1968), pp. 10ff; for Somerset's appreciation of friends, see below, pp. 19, 31 and 27f.

12 For Henry VIII, see *LP* XIX (1), 314; for Somerset, see below, pp. 29f.

13 Scarisbrick, *op. cit.*, pp. 426f.

14 War was finally declared by the French in August 1549, but for three years the two countries were technically at peace.

15 See Wernham, *op. cit.*, pp. 153f, of whom Scarisbrick is critical (*op. cit.*, p. 424 n. 1).

16 Jordan I, pp. 264f, 280–82 and 292f, and Pollard, pp. 137–41.

French Dauphin as the responsibility of the Scots, as a breach of contract on their part, rather than an act of theft committed by the French.[17] Moreover, to isolate Scotland and gain possession of Mary Stuart, Somerset was keen before October 1548 to negotiate for the immediate cession of Boulogne, the trophy of Henry's French war, instead of waiting for its scheduled cession in 1554. This deal only collapsed because the French desired the English to yield Calais as well. Somerset stuck on this point, refusing to abandon part of 'the king's majesty's patrimony which his ancestors hath so long possessed', although he and his colleagues seem to have considered a further plan for ceding Boulogne in 1549.[18] Generally he was prepared to comply with France in order to have his way with Scotland. As protector his first concern was not to extend or uphold England's possessions in France, but to solve the ancient problem of sharing an island with an alien power.

This prime appreciation of the Scottish war did not rest upon a novel programme of political or social reform, as A. F. Pollard and W. K. Jordan have suggested.[19] Somerset's mentality, like Henry VIII's, was strictly dynastic. His concept of union basically concerned one royal family's acquisition of another royal family's possessions. He was moved by the need for national security and the satisfaction of honour,[20] but not by any theory of national consolidation. His political concept of the union was a loose federation in which the laws, customs and institutions of Scotland were to stand untouched.[21] Equally without foundation is Jordan's belief that, along with James Henrison, Somerset regarded the union of England and Scotland as an instrument of social reform.[22] In his dealings with Scotland Somerset's social concern was minimal. In November 1548 the council ordered the goods and houses of the laird of Millerstoon's poor tenants to be spared, but this was a rare instance of intervention and seemed conditional on assurance.[23] Thomas Holcroft, writing from Scotland in August 1549, informed Somerset that he wished that the poor inhabitants would be spared, but only 'for the maintenance of the king's majesty's forts and pieces, and paying of their meals and rents to the same which will raise his highness much of his charges.'[24] Somerset showed little interest in the welfare of the Scots, and none of the English officials engaged in the war felt themselves restrained by any philanthropic bent in their master. Furthermore, James Henrison's work, 'The Godly and Golden Book for Concord of England and Scotland', which outlined a social programme

[17] See BM MS Harley 523, f. 28b.

[18] BM MS (Harley 249, f. 24b; and BM MS Cotton Galba B XII, ff. 42*f* (incompletely printed in Strype II (2), CC).

[19] See Pollard, pp. 148*f*, and Jordan I, p. 270.

[20] His feelings are clearly expressed in his instructions to Wotton of October 1548 (BM MS Harley 249, ff. 18*ff*.).

[21] Evident in the terms offered to the Scottish magnates Huntley, Argyle and George Douglas (Selve, pp. 268*f*; PRO SP50/III/60 (*SP Scot.* I, 177); and SP50/II/19 (*SP Scot.* I, 69)). The only change envisaged was the use of the name 'Great Britain' for the united kingdoms' which is no new name but the old name to them both' (SP50/III/60).

[22] Jordan I, p. 270.

[23] *SP Scot.* I, 330.

[24] BM MS Cotton Caligula B VII, f. 384b.

of eliminating distress and of instituting agrarian reform in both countries, was so ignored by Somerset that in 1549 Henrison wrote him a bitter complaint and then produced a second tract which severely criticised Somerset's Scottish policy.[25]

Neither did Somerset's prime regard for Scotland mean a complete break with previous foreign policy, since it did not imply the abandonment of the traditional English ambition to hold parts of France. He was merely paving the way for its future realization. As he saw it the English acquisition of the Crown of Scotland and the cession of Boulogne to the French would produce a peace by means of which 'his highness should be so enriched that when the sword shall come into his hands, he shall be able to get as much as ten Boulognes be worth with that or some other quarter of France more. . . .'[26] Somerset connected the priority of Scotland only with the minority of Edward VI, and saw it as a preparation for his majority. In the short term Somerset's foreign policy was quite distinct from Henry VIII's; but in the long term they resembled each other closely.

Henry VIII had valued large-scale military expeditions as the best means of dealing with the Scots; in sharp contrast, Somerset and his advisers preferred the presence in Scotland of garrisons manned either by Englishmen or foreign mercenaries in English pay.[27] This does not mean that Henry and his privy councillors had had little regard for garrisons. In 1545 the privy council reported to the earl of Shrewsbury, then engaged in the Scottish war: 'His grace never thinketh to come to his purpose of keeping the country in subjection until he shall lay garrisons amongst them, which shall also be a present aid to them that shall come in to serve him.'[28] Garrisons were actually established in the reign—temporarily at Jedburgh and Coldingham in 1542 and also in several places in the southwest in 1544 and 1545—many more were proposed, but the priority of the French war prevented their establishment.[29] As funds and supplies were required principally for the siege and relief of Boulogne, the government tended to regard garrisons not as the solution to the Scottish problem, but as a temporary standby until it could concentrate the full resources of the English Crown upon the conquest of Scotland. Following the failure to fortify Leith and to take Edinburgh Castle in 1544, the privy council advised Somerset, for example, to possess Hume Castle and other forts, 'the keeping whereof may serve to better purpose against the time of a further invasion to be made at leisure, than any fortification that in so short time may be made at Leith or Edinburgh.'[30] Somerset echoed the same idea in 1545 when he informed Paget that, as invasion was momentarily out of the question, garrisons should be temporarily erected at Kelso and Hume to harass the

[25] *SP Scot.* I, 285, 352, 357.
[26] BM MS Harley 249, f. 23b.
[27] In this respect, Somerset was certainly not 'implementing a manifestly bankrupt Henrician policy' (Jordan I, p. 244).
[28] *LP* XX (1), 129.
[29] *LP* XVII, 1090 and 1249; M. H. Merriman, 'The Platte of Castlemilk, 1547', *The Transactions of the Dumfriesshire and Galloway Natural History and Antiquarian Society*, 3rd ser., 44 (1967), p. 176; see below, pp. 23f.
[30] *Ham.* II, 217 (*LP* XIX (1), 348).

Scots.[31] Only with the treaty of Campe, which terminated the war with France, and with the accession of Edward VI could the government look upon garrisons as its main instrument of military action.

By 1547 Somerset was acutely aware of how little Henry VIII's military operations against the Scots had achieved. What is more, the matter had troubled him for some time. In 1544 he had pondered on an alternative to the usual expensive invasion which noticeably had little effect on 'a small country which they shall be able to recover in short time'.[32] It was clear to him that once the army returned Scotland recovered its independence. A defeat in battle was a blow to its pride but no impediment on its future actions. So deep was his concern, the problem figured in his dreams. While on the battlements at Berwick waiting to invade Scotland in September 1547, he recounted a dream in which he returned in triumph from an expedition against the Scots and received the generous compliments of the king, yet knew that he had accomplished nothing.[33] However, his awareness of Henry VIII's military ineffectiveness did not dissuade him from seeking in a similar manner to subject the Scots by force. It only convinced him of the error of Henry VIII's approach. He therefore invaded Scotland in September 1547 partly as a reprisal for an act of Scottish aggression, but essentially to render unnecessary the future invasion of Scotland.

In November and December 1547 Somerset discussed his Scottish designs with the imperial and French ambassadors and revealed his views on the garrisons established in the course of the Pinkie campaign. He regarded them as the solution to the problem of the past when armies, sent into Scotland at great expense, crushed the opposition but failed to subdue the country. With garrisons planted on Scottish soil, he informed the imperial ambassador, 'they had been able to win not a battle alone, but a country.'[34] He told the French ambassador how the existence of the garrisons would remove the need for armies royal and solve the old problem of keeping what had been conquered.[35] Somerset planned, then, not to crush Scotland periodically with an impressive and expensive army in the traditional manner, but to hold Scotland in permanent subjection, if necessary, by means of garrisons: in this respect, his military aims differed considerably from those of the Henrician government. Somerset's preoccupation with garrisoning Scotland gave his foreign policy a unique character since garrisons not only provided him with a means of action, but also eventually determined his objective. By 1549 the basic aim of his Scottish policy had degenerated into the defence, maintenance and extension of the garrisons, although by this time most of them served no practical purpose.

The novelty of his policy lay in the priority which he allowed the Scottish war and in his obsession with garrisons, not in being the work of a dreamer, a pacifist

---

[31] *St.P* V, pp. 451*f* (*LP* XX (1), 837).

[32] *St.P* V, pp. 371–3 (*LP* XIX (1), 319).

[33] See W. Patten, 'The Expedition into Scotland . . .', in *Tudor Tracts, 1532–1588*, ed. A. F. Pollard (London, 1903), p. 82.

[34] *SP Span.* 1547–9, p. 196.   [35] Selve, 262.

or of an idealist totally unaware of reality, as Pollard originally asserted and Jordan and Wernham upheld.[36] In the first instance his garrisoning of Scotland was the realistic product of an enthusiastic and experienced soldier who believed that, in the circumstances, the art of persuasion lay not with the word but with the sword. Garrisoning for Somerset and his colleagues was the practical alternative for maintaining some control and influence, the Scots having proved treacherous and invading armies having failed to provide a remedy. In view of the well-known and often demonstrated inability of the Scots to maintain an army for long in the field, it was subtly conceived.[37] However, one event rendered it futile—the arrival of the French in Scotland. Somerset's failure to adapt his policy to this change in circumstance turned his garrisons into castles in the air as a feasible form of controlling Scotland.

Basic Method

Either immediately before or after the battle of Pinkie the English established garrisons at Hume Castle, Roxburgh Castle, Eyemouth, Castlemilk and Moffat on the Scottish Borders, at Broughty Craig in the Tay and on the island of Inchcolm in the Firth of Forth.[38] The idea of establishing military bases in Scotland had been in the government's mind for some time. In March for example, it had required the Scottish rebels in St Andrews Castle, the murderers of Cardinal Beaton, to assist the English in the erection and maintenance of garrisons in return for financial and military assistance.[39] In June Adam Otterburn, the Scottish ambassador resident in England, reported home the English plan to found forts in Fife and Lothian.[40] The French ambassador reported similarly after a conversation with the protector in the same month.[41] Somerset's keen interest to apply the idea was evident in July when he commented upon a suggestion of the earl of Glencairn for using a fortress to control the traffic of the Clyde: 'this advice is very good and upon further occasion it may be used.'[42] Shortly before leaving for the north in August 1547, Somerset revealed to the imperial ambassador his warm attachment to a project for controlling Scotland by means of two strategically placed forts.[43] Clearly, the forts erected in 1547 were not the fortuitous outcome of victory, but the fruit of long-term planning; and without a doubt the main aim

[36] Pollard, pp. 148f; Jordan I, p. 268, and Wernham, *op. cit.*, p. 167.

[37] Described by Jean de Beaugué in his *The History of the Campagnes, 1548 and 1549* (Edinburgh, 1707), pp. 28f, and clearly revealed, for example, in 1545 (*LP* XX (2), 169).

[38] See Jordan I, p. 261. He wrongly includes Blackness and omits Eyemouth. For an account of the expedition and the garrisons it established, see W. Patten, *op. cit.*, pp. 81, 137–41, 145 and 148. For the southwest garrisons established at the same time but independently by Thomas Wharton, see Merriman, 'The Platte of Castlemilk', *op. cit.*, p. 177.

[39] *Foedera, Conventiones, Litterae . . .*, ed. T. Rymer (London, 1704–35), XV, p. 144.

[40] *Scottish Correspondence*, cxxxvi.

[41] Selve, 176 (p. 154).

[42] PRO SP50/I/33 (*SP Scot.* I, 26).

[43] *SP Span.* 1547–9, p. 147.

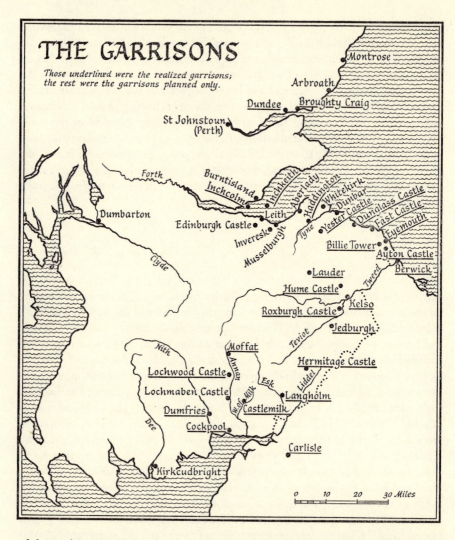

THE GARRISONS

*Those underlined were the realized garrisons;
the rest were the garrisons planned only.*

of the Pinkie campaign which seemed occasioned by the loss of England's only garrison in Scotland,[44] was to replace it with a number of garrisons.[45]

[44] The connection is made clear in Norroy Herald's announcement to the Scots delivered before the battle (PRO SP50/I/53 (*SP Scot.* I, 50)), in the earl of Warwick's military instructions (SP50/I/35 (*SP Scot.* I, 28)), and in a statement made by Somerset to the Scottish ambassador (*Scottish Correspondence*, cxliv).

[45] Significantly, Somerset's first task in entering Scotland in September 1547 was to view Eyemouth and assess its worth as a garrison, and he took with him on the campaign 1,400 pioneers, presumably for the purpose of instant fortification. After the battle his first concern was to consider a garrison at Leith, and most of his time in Scotland was spent in supervising the establishment of English forts (Patten, *op. cit.*, pp. 79ff). In view of this, Jordan's judgement that Somerset 'had naively assumed that only a decisive military defeat would be required to persuade Scotland of the virtues of the treaty of Greenwich' is plain nonsense (Jordan I, p. 263).

These garrisons provided a foundation which was built and elaborated upon in the following two years. First and foremost in the government's mind in the winter of 1547 and the following spring was the need to consolidate its hold on Scotland by erecting further garrisons. Some of the plans failed. The proposal to garrison Kirkcudbright with 1,000 men was dropped in April because of the provisioning difficulties.[46] An ambitious plan to take Edinburgh Castle in January failed, and so did an attempt to take Dunbar Castle in May.[47] In March the idea of garrisoning Dundee was considered for a second time but abandoned because of the large numbers of troops required to man it.[48] Early in 1548 the government thought of placing garrisons in the houses of loyal Scotsmen, also without result.[49] Of the garrisons actually established, some owed everything to the initiative of northern officials acting within the framework of general instructions; companies of light horse and foot thus came to be stationed at Jedburgh, Kelso, Billie Tower and Ayton Castle in the Merse and Teviotdale, and at Cockpool, Lochwood Castle and Dumfries in the southwest, and for a very short time in January at Dundee.[50] Others were founded under Somerset's close direction by special military expeditions. In February Somerset decided to establish garrisons in the heart of the Scottish Lowlands.[51] This led to the fortification and garrisoning of Yester Castle in March and April, of Lauder in April, both manned with Spanish troops,[52] and of Haddington in June. Somerset had first appreciated Haddington in January 1548 as a possible base for distracting an invading enemy force.[53] Then in February it became a base for Lord Grey's military operations in Lothian.[54] Gradually the government evolved the plan of fortifying the town and of installing there not the usual small garrison force but an army. Haddington was not the only place considered for this purpose. Both Dunbar and the church at Inveresk ('the church above Musselburgh') near the site of the battle of Pinkie were reviewed, but had been ruled out by the end of April.[55] The government therefore selected Haddington as its major garrison in the Lowlands, fortified it hurriedly, manned it with 2,500 troops, some of them foreign mercenaries, and protected it against a siege by burning and pillaging the surrounding countryside.[56]

[46] *SP Dom.* I, 44; ibid., II, 7, 8, 27 and 59.

[47] *SP Scot.* I, 120, 124 and 125; Selve mentions the siege of Dunbar Castle on 7 May and its termination by 27 May (364 and 384).

[48] *SP Scot.* I, 184 and 196 and BM MS Harley 353, f. 95b.

[49] PRO SP50/III/57 (*SP Scot.* I, 174).

[50] *SP Scot.* I, 129, 143, 146 and 155, and PRO SP50/II/7 (*SP Scot.* I, 58); *SP Dom.* I, 59 and Merriman, 'The Platte of Castlemilk', *op. cit.*, p. 177; *SP Scot.* I, 127 and 129 (1).

[51] See PRO SP50/III/44 (*SP Scot.* I, 161). The plan seemed to be a garrison at 'Daussy', unidentifiable but presumably close to Edinburgh (see SP50/III/39 (*SP Scot.* I, 156)).

[52] *SP Dom.* II, 33 and 39; PRO SP50/III/76 (*SP Scot.* I, 193), *SP Scot.* I, 220 and see SP50/III/87 and 88 (*SP Scot.* I, 214 and 215).

[53] *SP Scot.* I, 135.   [54] *SP Scot.* I, 149 and 168.

[55] PRO SP50/III/87 and 88 (*SP Scot.* I, 214 and 215), SP50/III/58 (*SP Scot.* I, 175) and SP50/III/62 (*SP Scot.* I, 179); *SP Dom.* II, 59 and *SP Scot.* I, 228. Momentarily considered was a plan to turn the Lauder garrison into a camp for 1,000 men (*Ham*, II, 444).

[56] *SP Scot.* I, 251 and 269, Selve, 398, BM MS Harley 289, f. 33, and *SP Scot.* I, 240.

Garrisons remained a chief concern of the government for the rest of the year not only because of its preoccupation with the defence and provisioning of Haddington during the town's siege by the French, but also because of its search for further forts, particularly one on the coast to serve as a feeder for Haddington. Basically the government aimed to remedy Lord Grey's failure to take Dunbar Castle in May. Dunbar had been quickly dismissed as a possible base for an army camp, but the government seems to have persisted in wanting it as an entry for victuals and other supplies for the Haddington garrison, that is until, having despaired of taking its castle, Grey burnt the town to the ground on 12 June.[57] In August under government instructions, Shrewsbury and Grey sought to establish an equivalent coastal fort either at Aberlady, Musselburgh or Whitekirk, all within provisioning distance of the besieged Haddington garrison.[58] Somerset seemed particularly keen on a fort at Musselburgh, possibly as a replacement for Haddington.[59] However, the task of relieving Haddington thwarted this part of the mission. The only garrison which Grey and Shrewsbury succeeded in establishing was at Dunglass Castle, on the coast but too distant from Haddington to serve it adequately.[60]

Also in August 1548, a naval expedition under Lord Clinton tried and failed to establish further garrisons in Fife. Somerset directed Clinton to fortify Burntisland in the Forth, then to establish a new fort in the Tay estuary near to Broughty Craig, as well as other garrisons possibly at Perth (St Johnstoun), Montrose, Arbroath or Dundee, and to place 1,000 troops in Fife for the winter.[61] Somerset wanted the Tay project to have top priority, and for the sake of it the scheme to fortify Burntisland was ditched.[62] In the Tay, troops were landed, and Dundee reoccupied;[63] but this was the sum of the achievement. Finally, in mid-September rough weather scattered Clinton's fleet and the Master of Ruthven failed to keep his promise to yield Perth, while in November Dundee fell again to the enemy.[64] The government shelved the Tay project when a shortage of supplies forced a choice between persisting in the Tay where nothing had been as yet achieved and completing the fortification of Dunglass Castle which at least was under way.[65]

In this second winter the enthusiasm of England's Scottish policy flagged. Dispirited and on the defensive, the English essentially aimed to hold on and to avoid risks, 'to keep fast the key in hand', as Somerset put it.[66] The government ordered the Broughty Craig garrison 'to lie there as you were dead', and the

---

[57] *SP Scot.* I, 242.

[58] See Lodge I, pp. 120f (misdated), and *SP Scot.* I, 309 and 321.

[59] Selve, 500, and PRO SP50/IV/104 (*SP Scot.* I, 321).   [60] *SP Scot.* I, 262.

[61] For the plan see Clinton's May instructions (PRO SP10/IV/9), Fisher's July instructions (PRO SP50/IV/44 and 45 (*SP Scot.* I, 262 and 263)), and *Scottish Correspondence*, clxxx.

[62] *Ibid.*, and *SP Scot.* I, 313.

[63] Their arrival in late 1548 is indicated by their recall in January 1549 (*SP Dom.* III, 23); *SP Scot.* I, 336, and Selve, 515.

[64] *Scottish Correspondence*, clxxxiv, and *SP Span.* 1547-9, p. 297; *SP Scot.* I, 239; Selve, 515, and *SP Scot.* I, 336.

[65] See Lodge I, pp. 121f, and *Scottish Correspondence*, cxciv.

[66] PRO SP50/IV(120) (*SP Scot.* I, 338).

Haddington garrison 'to keep well at home'.[67] But this loss of aggressiveness and buoyancy did not persuade the government to abandon the garrisons, nor to withdraw from any of them, nor even to terminate its plans for new ones. Its main aim in 1549 was to take reprisals for lost garrisons, to revictual existing garrisons and even to extend the network. New garrisons came into being; in February, without specific direction, at Fast Castle, and in July, with government encouragement, on the island of Inchkeith in the Firth of Forth. Both were short-lived, the first disbanded voluntarily in November, the second terminated by conquest in July.[68] In addition the government half-heartedly revived the Tay project in March when John Luttrell and Thomas Fisher, who had been authorized to treat with the earl of Argyle, were instructed to keep an eye open 'for any place meet to be fortified'.[69] It also revived the project for a coastal garrison in Lothian. In January it commissioned Thomas Holcroft and Francis Leek to take reprisal for the loss of Hume Castle, to enlarge the fortress at Lauder and also 'to view the place by the church, what hill or ground were meet for fortification': in all likelihood a further attempt to implement a proposal originally suggested a year earlier for a garrison near the site of the battle of Pinkie.[70] Within a month this latter plan was quashed when the French proceeded with 'the fortification at Musselburgh church'.[71] In April the Scots queen dowager talked of an English plan to fortify Aberlady, another of the previous year's plans.[72] If ever conceived by the English in 1549, it was anticipated in August by the French who garrisoned that town also.[73] The English persisted with their intention to found a coastal garrison in Lothian, now no longer as a feeder but as a replacement for Hadding-ton. In July the earl of Warwick received this task, but the outbreak of peasant risings in England thwarted the operation.[74] The government of the protectorate made its final attempt to establish a garrison in July when Italians and Spaniards were dispatched to man the Hermitage, a fortress in Liddesdale ceded by agree-ment with the earl of Bothwell.[75]

Some of these garrisons had a very short life. Those at Dumfries, Cockpool and Yester Castle had fallen to the enemy by mid-1548; those at Jedburgh, Inchkeith

[67] *Scottish Correspondence*, cxciv, and PRO SP50/IV/120 (*SP Scot.* I, 338).

[68] *HMC* Rutland IV, p. 192, and PRO AO 1/283/1067; *SP For.* 1547–53, 180, and BM MS Cotton Titus B V, f. 33.

[69] PRO SP50/V/13 (*SP Scot.* I, 345).

[70] *SP Dom.* III, 23, and *Ham.* II, 463. The clue to the whereabouts of the proposed garrison lies in the phrase 'the place by the church'. Earlier there had been talk of a garrison in connection with the church above Musselburgh which featured in the battle of Pinkie (e.g. PRO SP50/III/88 (*SP Scot.* I, 215) and *SP Dom.* II, 59, and see above, p. 15).

[71] *Ham.* II, p. 459.

[72] *Relations Politiques de la France et de l'Espagne avec l'Ecosse au XVIe siècle*, ed. A. Teulet (Paris, 1862), I, p. 192.

[73] *HMC* Rutland I, p. 42.

[74] See PRO E351/215. Warwick's instructions have not survived, but the purpose can be pieced together. In June Paget and Hoby informed Somerset that the emperor had been told that 'my lord of Warwick shall be shortly sent thither to take a further fort' (PRO SP68/III/169). In August Somerset informed the imperial ambassador that the peasant revolts had prevented him from building a coastal fort to replace Haddington (*SP Span.* 1547–9, p. 432).

[75] BM MS Cotton B VII, f. 385 and *SP Scot.* I, 354.

and Hume Castle, by early 1549.[76] Others were abandoned for reasons of impracticability—Inchcolm in February 1548, Haddington in September 1549 and Fast Castle in November.[77] The garrison at Broughty Craig was picked off by the enemy early in 1550.[78] Nevertheless, the rest survived until 1550 when they were surrendered in the negotiations leading to the treaty of Boulogne.[79]

The garrisons had a number of functions. The government intended the Broughty Craig, Inchcolm, Inchkeith and the abortive Burntisland garrisons to dominate the traffic and hinterlands of Scotland's great rivers, the Tay and the Forth, and also, like the unrealized garrison at Kirkcudbright, to allow the English an effective means of providing protection and reprisal in normally inaccessible parts of Scotland. In addition, Broughty Craig was regarded as a springboard for further garrisons, and like Burntisland, as a haven for the fleet.[80] The garrisons at Castlemilk, Roxburgh Castle, Hume Castle, Jedburgh, Kelso, Billie Tower, Ayton Castle, Lochwood Castle, Dumfries, Cockpool, Moffat and the Hermitage were designed to push the line of border defence into the Scottish Marches, and thus to protect the English borders, and to extend the reach of English raiding parties in the southwest, Teviotdale, the Merse and Lothian. The garrisons at Haddington, Lauder, Yester Castle and the unrealized garrison on the site of Pinkie were meant to extend the penetration of English raiding parties even further, and in the case of Lauder to establish a blockage on the pass between the Moorsfoot and Lammermuir hills, and in the case of Haddington, in view of its size, possibly to distract an army otherwise intent on invading England.[81] Finally, the coastal garrisons of Eyemouth, Fast Castle, Dunglass Castle and the unrealized garrison at Aberlady or Musselburgh were planned as victualling ports for sustaining the English presence in Scotland, and also, along with the Tay and Forth garrisons, as a means of excluding outside assistance.[82]

[76] *SP Dom.* II, 22 and 27, and PRO SP50/IV/21 (*SP Scot.* I, 239); BM MS Cotton Caligula, B VII, f. 330; for Inchkeith, see above, p. 27, and *Scottish Correspondence*, cxciii and cxciv. It seems that Jedburgh was taken by the French in October 1548, soon retaken by the English, taken by the French again in February 1549 and recovered by the English in April (MS Cotton Caligula B VII, f. 330, and *A Diurnal of Remarkable Occurrents . . .*, ed. T. Thomson (Bannatyne Club, 1833), pp. 47f). After two very brief tenures by the English, a garrison at Dundee twice fell to the enemy in 1548 (see above, pp. 15 and 16).

[77] *SP Scot.* I, 184, and Selve, 310; *SP Scot.* I, 310; for Fast Castle, see above, p. 17.

[78] Jordan II, pp. 147f.   [79] *Ibid.*, p. 148.

[80] Inchcolm: Patten, *op. cit.*, pp. 137 and 139, *SP Scot.* I, 76; Broughty Craig: Patten, *op. cit.*, p. 141, PRO SP50/I/56 (*SP Scot.* I, 46), and *SP Scot.* I, 74 and 119; Inchkeith: presumably complied in purpose with Somerset's earlier advocacy which arose from a spy's report that such a garrison could control the traffic of the Firth (*HMC Bath* IV, pp. 46f (1 (11) and 2), and *Ham.* I, App. to Introduction, vii) (*LP* XVII, 1100 (3)); Burntisland: PRO SP10/IV/9 and SP50/IV/44–5 (*SP Scot.* I, 262 and 263).

[81] Southwest garrisons: *SP Dom.* I, 29, 34, 44, and PRO SP15/II/15; southeast garrisons: *SP Scot.* I, 129, 151 and PRO SP50/III/26 and 29 (*SP Scot.* I, 143 and 146); also see Somerset's remarks in 1545 on the establishment of such garrisons (*St.P* V, pp. 451f (*LP* XX (1), 837)); Lothian garrisons: *SP Scot.* I, 228, and SP50/IV/4 (*SP Scot.* I, 221). The idea of involving a Scottish army, which happened in practice with Haddington, was proposed as a possible function of a garrison in 1545 by Somerset and Wharton (*LP* XX (1), 867, and *LP* XX (2), 685).

[82] Eyemouth: Patten, *op. cit.*, p. 81; Fast Castle: *HMC Rutland* IV, p. 203; Dunglass: BM MS Cotton Caligula B VII, 473 f. and *SP Scot.* I, 168. For the idea of coastal garrisons as a means of excluding an enemy, see *SP Span.* 1547–9, p. 393.

At the same time, all of them shared the common purpose of bringing the Scots to obedience without the need for an army royal. This did not mean immediate obeisance. The English government did not regard the garrisons as an instrument of direct rule, even after the removal of Mary Stuart to France. Somerset regarded the garrisons as 'a foot and entry' or as 'the key', as a means of admission and presence 'in the bowels . . . of the realm'; not as a means of collecting rents, taxes or customs dues, nor of administering law and order.[83] Implicit in Somerset's Scottish policy was the firm belief that Scottish friends existed and the desire not to alienate them by acts of tyranny.[84] For this reason the suggestions which northern officials frequently made for annexing church property and of collecting rents in Scotland were never authorized,[85] and the government did not even insist on making the Scots pay for the English presence. It is true that with Somerset's approval a proclamation was issued forbidding assured Scots to pay rents to un-assured Scots and, what is more, the assured Scots were encouraged by English garrison officials to pay these dues to the English Crown.[86] But the government did not call upon the garrisons to enforce nor even to insist upon these require-ments.

Somerset did not conceive the garrisons as instruments of government. Nor did he regard them, as Pollard thought, as 'a centre for missionary efforts to convert Scotland to the virtues of protestantism'.[87] Essentially they were meant to secure the Scots' acceptance of Edward VI as the husband of their queen and as overlord of their kingdom. Their immediate purpose was to offer protection to the assured Scots and to apply military repression to the remainder as an incentive to assure.[88] In practice, because of their limited ability to offer proper protection, the garri-sons' general function was to punish, and thus to play the identical role of border raiding parties, fleets patrolling northern waters and other military expeditions.[89] By 1549, bottled up by the enemy and paralysed by a lack of supplies, the garri-sons had lost even this faculty and became simply a diversion to an enemy which otherwise might have threatened the English border.

The military approach was not the only arrow in Somerset's quiver. He and his advisers also resorted to methods which did not involve their own direct military intervention, particularly by working through several great Scottish magnates and by promoting the protestant cause in Scotland. However, the ineffectiveness of these other methods, Somerset's lack of faith in them and his firm insistence on a military presence left garrisoning the most central and durable element of his Scottish policy.

[83] See *St.P* V, p. 372 (*LP* XIX (1), 319), Selve, 176 (p. 154) and PRO SP50/IV/120 (*SP Scot.* I, 338).
[84] See Grey's rejoinder to Somerset (PRO SP50/III/26 (*SP Scot.* I, 143)).
[85] See e.g. *Ham.* II, 455 and 461; *SP Scot.* I, 74, 117, 329 and 351. Wharton proposed that the garrisons should maintain law and order (*SP Dom.* II, 65).
[86] PRO SP50/II (22 and 24) (*SP Scot.* I, 70 and 72); *Ham.* II, 461 and *SP Scot.* I, 329.
[87] Pollard, pp. 149f and 162.
[88] For the function of protection, see *SP Span.* 1547–9, p. 196, and the *Epistle* despatched to the Scots by Somerset and the council in February 1548 (printed by EETS extra ser., 17 (1872), p. 244).
[89] See below, p. 30.

His dealings with the Scottish magnates belonged mainly to late 1547 and early 1548 when advances were made to the earls of Huntley, Argyle, Bothwell and Lennox, the Douglases and Lord Maxwell. Meeting with almost complete failure, this proved to be no viable alternative to military repression. Somerset's scepticism about Sir George Douglas, because of his frequently broken promises in the early 1540s, soon proved fully justified.[90] In October 1547 Lord Grey, on instructions from the government, required Douglas to support the marriage, to pledge to the English the castles of Dunbar and Edinburgh, to persuade the governor to comply with the English, and, if he turned contrary, to place the governor and the Douglas fortress of Tantallon in English hands.[91] Not unreasonably in view of the demands made of him, Douglas temporized until June when the patience of the English snapped and his family's possessions were burnt and pillaged.[92] In January 1548 the government sought similar terms with the captive earl of Huntley. Somerset insisted that Huntley bring pressure upon the governor to permit Mary Stuart to take up residence in England in three years' time.[93] He also insisted upon Huntley binding himself with his signature to certain articles. After some delay Huntley signed the articles, but upon entering Scotland joined the enemy.[94] Similar proposals were put to the earl of Argyle who came to be regarded as an ally when he called off the siege of Broughty Craig.[95] While Douglas was offered unspecified rewards, and Huntley, his release, Argyle was promised a pension of 2,000 crowns and a reward of 4,000 crowns either for the immediate delivery of Mary Stuart or her delivery within one month of her tenth birthday. Somerset expected Argyle to take action against the governor if he could not win him over by persuasion. Argyle was approached in October 1547, in July 1548 and in March 1549, but without result.[96]

The government's lack of success with the other magnates was not so complete, but was still a fact. The earl of Lennox was a willing accomplice, but after a period of exile seemed to have lost his effective authority in Scotland. Aided by English funds, he hoped in February 1548 to lead the assured Scots of Annandale against the governor. But when the time arrived all the support he could muster came from six of his own servants. At the end of February the government dispensed with his services and he retired to the company of his blue-blooded wife, Margaret Douglas, at Wressel Castle.[97] Lord Maxwell in October 1547 promised the delivery to the English of his fortress at Lochmaben, but nothing came of this plan.[92] Only the earl of Bothwell appeared to keep his promises, and he was well paid for his services.[99] Presumably Hales, Saltoun and Wroughton Castles fell to the

---

[90] PRO SP50/II/19 (*SP Scot.* I, 69); *SP Scot.* I, 213.   [91] PRO SP50/II/19 (*SP Scot.* I, 69).

[92] *SP Scot.* I, 57, *SP Dom.* II, 1, and *SP Scot.* I, 149 and 175; BM MS Harley 289, f. 33.

[93] Selve, pp. 268f.

[94] Selve, 294, 302 and 310; *APC* II, p. 544, *SP Scot.* I, 197, and Selve, 379; and *Scottish Correspondence*, cxciv.

[95] PRO SP50/III/60 (*SP Scot.* I, 177).

[96] See *SP Scot.* I, 263 (misdated and belongs to late July), and 345.

[97] *SP Dom.* II, 11 and 22.

[98] *Ibid.*, I, 38.

[99] He received £1,225 between October 1548 and June 1550 (PRO AO 1/283/1067).

English in February 1548 because of an arrangement with him. The Hermitage may likewise have entered English hands in 1549.[100]

A number of Scottish aristocrats, notably Lord Gray and the lairds Ormiston and Brunstane, were attracted to the English cause and served faithfully at great danger to themselves, their families and possessions.[101] But in spite of their hatred of the governor, the great magnates remained ambivalent towards the English. In return for rewards or pardons they made promises but, with the exception of Bothwell, did not commit themselves by open deeds. Dealing with Scottish magnates had been an unrewarded experience for Somerset in the early 1540s.[102] It was an approach in which he had learnt to have little faith and upon which as protector he was not keen to rely to achieve his ends. In 1549 he continued to approach Argyle, and as late as October 1548 he was dispatching letters to Scottish earls 'for the more encouragement towards the king's majesty's service';[103] but otherwise, the effort to operate through Scottish magnates was confined to a brief and abandoned trial in the closing months of 1547 and early 1548.

The other non-military approach, the encouragement of protestantism in Scotland, was equally fruitless and unsustained. Some demand existed in Scotland for preachers and testaments. In February 1548 Thomas Wharton informed Somerset that in response to their request he had sent a great bible to the citizens of Dumfries.[104] In November 1547 Andrew Dudley claimed that the people of Angus and Fife urgently required 'preachers, bibles, testaments and other good English books of Tyndale and Frith's translation'.[105] In his opinion 'a good preacher and good books . . . would do more good than fire and sword.'[106] Without a doubt, the most committed and loyal of the assured Scots were keen protestants. The situation in Scotland seemed ripe for a mission, and a mission seemed likely to favour the English cause. The government responded by ordering John Rughe to Dumfries to preach to the inhabitants.[107] Somerset also planned to send two or three preachers into the eastern Lowlands.[108] A number of Scottish preachers received pensions, and some of the oaths of assurance administered to Scotsmen required a renunciation of the bishop of Rome.[109] But his government appeared to be in no hurry to exploit this opportunity to win Scotland over. There was the difficulty of persuading preachers to enter Scotland. Moreover, Scottish protestants could remain neutral for safety's sake.[110] Whilst prepared to proselytize in order to increase the allegiance of the Scots, Somerset probably did not attach much importance to this approach or value its feasibility very highly.[111] When he

---

[100] *SP Scot.* I, 168; after long negotiation which began in October 1547, see *SP Scot.* I, 69 (3) and n. 75, p. 17.

[101] Merriman, 'The Assured Scots', *op. cit.*, pp. 23f.

[102] See Thesis, pp. 415–19. [103] BM MS Cotton Caligula B VII, f. 443.

[104] *SP Dom.* II, 11. [105] PRO SP50/II/26 (*SP Scot.* I, 74).

[106] PRO SP50/II/60 (*SP Scot.* I, 107). [107] *SP Dom.* II, 2.

[108] *SP Scot.* I, 239.

[109] In the declared account relating to Scottish matters for the period 1548–50 only three received rewards or pensions (PRO AO 1/183/1067); e.g. *SP Dom.* I, 45.

[110] *SP Scot.* I, 56 and 239.

[111] For the opposite view, see Pollard, pp. 149, 152 and 162.

talked of 'the godly purpose', it is not certain that the phrase had strong evangelical implications for him. For him 'the godly purpose' appeared to be the marriage of Edward VI and Mary Stuart and the consequent union of the two realms.[112] Like his dealings with magnates, evangelism was a marginal detail of his general Scottish policy.

This was the extent of the measures which did not involve direct military intervention. It is true that Somerset and his colleagues also issued several declarations urging the Scots to accept the union of the two kingdoms in order to secure peace and to realize the will of God, which was thought to be explicitly stated in the coincidence of an unmarried Scottish queen and English king who were roughly of the same age. As with the garrisons, Somerset conceived this device in Henry VIII's reign, first in 1544 when he planned to nail a proclamation of his own composition to a number of church-doors in Scotland.[113] He employed the same device in August 1547.[114] In February 1548 copies of a printed letter addressed to the Scots from Somerset and the council were circulated in Scotland.[115] Finally in late 1548 or early 1549 the English government issued a second printed plea to the Scots.[116] However, this verbal persuasion was not a self-contained measure. It was, in fact, part of the military approach. As well as applauding the benefits of union, each declaration issued a warning of extreme punishment for those who rejected the union and thus opposed God, reason and the common good. To make this warning real, each declaration, with the possible exception of the last one, accompanied a military expedition into Scotland. The proclamations of 1544 and 1547 were composed in connection with the invasion of Scotland by armies royal. Each promised mercy for the submissive and the sword for the rest. The *Epistle* of February 1548 also coincided with a military expedition, the massive border raids of Wharton and Grey. Again the declaration justified the depredations of the English and warned that resistance would suffer. The declarations did not express the government's faith in words or in the goodness of human nature.[117] Because of the circumstances in which they were issued, they were forms of self-righteous propaganda, aimed not simply to convince the Scots of the virtues of union, but to justify the military activities of the English. Somerset himself admitted that they were ruses.[118] They were clearly no more than a component of the military approach.

[112] The *Epistle* suggested that the union was termed 'the godly purpose' because the coincidence of an unmarried heir and heiress was thought to indicate the will of God (EETS extra ser., 17, pp. 239f).

[113] BM Add. 32, 654, f. 48 (*LP* XIX (1), 231).

[114] The surviving proclamation is owned by the Society of Antiquaries. I am thankful to the librarian for allowing me to inspect it. Summaries occur in the *Warrender Papers*, A. I. Cameron, ed., Scottish History Society, 3rd ser., 18–19 (1931–2), I, xxvi, and in *Tudor and Stuart Proclamations, 1485–1714* (Oxford, 1910), I, 312.

[115] See EETS extra ser., 17, pp. 238–46.

[116] See *SP Span.* 1547–9, pp. 297f. The letter was probably 'An Epitome of the Title that the King's Majesty of England hath to the Sovereignty of Scotland, continued upon the Ancient Writers of Both Nations from the Beginning' (EETS extra ser., 17, pp. 247ff).

[117] For this point of view, see Jordan I, pp. 253 and 268.

[118] *SP Span.* 1547–9, pp. 268 and 298.

In default of a union by marriage and in view of the intransigence of the Scots, Somerset's Scottish policy rested essentially on military action. The other measures were peripheral to the main instrument of policy, the garrisons.

Conditioning circumstances

The Scottish policy of the Somerset regime owed much to an obsession with garrisons. This obsession was the outcome of long-held plans and the frustration of failing to implement them. In particular, it derived from Somerset's own failure to establish garrisons in the previous reign, and to realize fully his original scheme during the protectorate. A second major influence on the government's Scottish policy was the arrival of the French in Scotland, their generous assistance of the Scots and the tenacity of their presence in the country, which must have far exceeded English expectations. Finally, the policy applied was due to the garrisons' failure to perform their expected function of offering protection to the assured Scots.

The garrisons which came into being belonged to a history of schemes which reach back to the beginning of the war in 1542. In that year an estimate for the invasion of Scotland had mentioned the possibility of extending the English frontier to the banks of the Forth 'by building of fortresses and establishing of garrisons'.[119] In the same year Somerset himself, as a result of a brief experience as warden of the Marches, had toyed with planting a garrison on an island in the Firth of Forth.[120] In 1544 he had passionately advocated a garrison at Leith. He even went northwards on government instructions to establish such a garrison, as well as two others 'in the heart of that realm', but before he could achieve anything the government changed its mind and ordered him to 'put all to fire and sword' instead.[121] Somerset vigorously objected to this change of plan, believing the advantage of fortifying Leith to exceed by far the gain of burning it to the ground, but without effect.[122] In the same year he also advocated the establishment of garrisons at Dumbarton and on the island of Inchkeith. The importance he attached to the latter gave him a sleepless night when he omitted it from a letter justifying the garrisoning of Leith. The government had argued that Leith would be difficult to victual; Somerset rejoined—not with a garrison on Inchkeith dominating the Firth.[123] His arguments, however, failed to move the king and the council, and Somerset followed a policy of devastation in accordance with his instructions.[124]

The garrisoning idea reappeared in the following year, again with Somerset's enthusiastic support. It took a somewhat different form. Instead of garrisons to threaten Edinburgh the plan was to extend the frontier northwards by founding garrisons in the Scottish Marches. Somerset suggested garrisons at Hume and

[119] PRO SP1/174 (*LP* XVII, 1034).
[121] *LP* XIX (1), 314.
[123] *Ibid.*, 327.
[124] *Ibid.*, 348 (3), and see Thesis, pp. 364f.

[120] See n. 80, p. 18 (Inchkeith).
[122] *Ibid.*, 319.

c

Kelso, and secured the government's approval, but this was later withdrawn.[125] For the remainder of the year Somerset enthused over installing a garrison at Roxburgh Castle, and proposed a start on it in the new year, although nothing happened until he became protector.[126]

The purpose and function, as well as the extent of the garrisoning system, were worked out in the closing years of Henry VIII's reign. Garrisons to interfere with river traffic, to serve as economical and effective alternatives to the normal invasion of armies royal, to protect the assured Scots, to safeguard against the arrival of the French, to extend the reach of raiding parties, to relieve the border garrisons of their burden of defence, to act as feeders for other garrisons: all of this was proposed and supported by Somerset as he struggled to solve the Scottish problem in 1544 and 1545.[127] Both the garrisoning idea and nearly the full extent of its function were thus formulated long before the system came into operation. In the interval and because of it, Somerset's advocacy of almost realized but continually thwarted plans left him with a determined attachment for garrisons and a diminished ability to see the idea in the light of reality.

Somerset's frustration did not end with the death of Henry VIII; in this respect his obsession with garrisons also derived from his failure as protector to implement his garrisoning scheme. The Pinkie campaign established a network of garrisons, but failed to realize the earlier schemes largely because of an accidental fire which razed Leith and rendered it useless.[128] A major aim of England's Scottish policy in 1548 and 1549 was to overcome this setback. Military expeditions led by Lord Grey in February and May, by Shrewsbury and Grey in August, by Leek and Holcroft in January 1549 and by Warwick in the following July stemmed from the original burning of Leith and the vital need, in accordance with the plans of 1544, for a garrison in Lothian close to Edinburgh.[129] The failings of the established garrisons drove the government in the same direction. The failure of the garrisons on islands in the Firth of Forth meant that only the fleet could control the river traffic unless a coastal garrison was erected in the vicinity of the Firth. The founding and the siege of Haddington made a controlled port a vital necessity. Early in 1548 the government created some of its own major difficulties first by deciding to base its army camp at Haddington and not Inveresk, and then by failing to take Dunbar Castle which would have allowed for the easy victualling of Haddington by sea.[130] Afterwards the concentrated effort to establish a coastal garrison was due to the problem of provisioning Haddington, a problem spotlighted by Sadler when he commented: 'I see not . . . how we can keep Haddington unless we be able to bear the charge to victual it twice a year with an army.'[131]

Somerset's main military problem in Scotland was not the Scots but the French.

[125] *LP* XX (1), 837, and *LP* XX (2), 128 and 328.   [126] *LP* XX (2), 347 and 359.
[127] *LP* XIX (1), 319 and 327, *LP* XX (1), 129, 837 and 867, *LP* XX (2). 685, and M. L. Bush, 'The Problem of the Far North: A Study of the Crisis of 1537 and its Consequences', *Northern History* 6 (1971), p. 62.
[128] Patten, *op. cit.*, p. 140.   [129] See above, pp. 15 and 17.
[130] See above, pp. 15*f*.   [131] Lodge I, p. 120.

With their arrival in large numbers the garrisoning of Scotland became completely unworkable. A new policy was required—a naval blockade and the dispatch of an army royal to flush them out. However, Somerset's obsession dictated affairs; the garrison policy was maintained and armies were employed only to relieve and provision the garrisons. The French presence caused no reversal of policy, but it heavily influenced the government's attitude towards the garrisons.

For years the English had feared a French occupation of Scotland would result from the Anglo-Scottish war. Nevertheless, before June 1548 actual French aid for the Scots was infrequent and meagre.[132] On 19 June the worst fears of the English were realized when the French landed a force of 10,000 men in the Firth of Forth.[133] Within little more than a year they had firmly entrenched themselves in Scotland with garrisons situated in places which the English had coveted, at Musselburgh, Aberlady, Dunbar and Leith.[134] For allowing this to happen Somerset must take the blame. In 1547 an English fleet under Andrew Dudley and Thomas Wyndham had patrolled northern waters maintaining an effective blockade of the Forth.[125] At the close of the year Somerset tried to recall it, was persuaded to let it remain in Scottish waters a while longer, but then had his way in March when the fleet returned to Newcastle to be re-equipped and was discharged.[136] It is true that a much larger fleet under Admiral Clinton was commissioned to sail northwards to intercept the French, but when the French reached Scotland Clinton's fleet still lay at Harwich. Only in late July did Clinton's fleet set sail.[137] Even then Somerset had other than a blockading role for it. Accepting the presence of garrisons in Scotland as a better means of resistance than a blockade of the Firth by the fleet, Somerset regarded Clinton's fleet first and foremost as an instrument for establishing forts in Fife.[138] Because of this miscalculation, the French gained unimpeded access to Scotland.

The French had influenced the Scottish policy of the Somerset regime before their arrival in Scotland in June 1548. Somerset's plans to garrison Kirkcudbright aimed 'to impeach the French men of their passage along the western seas for relief of the Scots',[139] and his encouragement of a programme of devastation in January and February 1548 was his reply to the news of the arrival of French aid.[140] The May–June expedition of Lord Grey, which aimed to establish an army

---

[132] Before June 1548 no more than three French convoys had managed to reach Scotland, and only by the western route—in June 1545 when 3,500 troops were landed in the Clyde (*LP* XX (1), 909), in March 1547 when two ships with powder and ordnance arrived at Dumbarton (*SP Scot.* I, 9), and in December 1547 when a further two ships with troops, money and supplies again reached Scotland via the Irish sea (*SP Scot.* I, 117, and *SP Dom.* I, 61). In addition in the same year a number of galleys led by Peter Strozzi crushed the rebellion in St Andrews Castle and then departed.

[133] *SP Scot.* I, 247, PRO SP50/IV/33 (*SP Scot.* I, 251).

[134] *Ham.* II, 453 and 459, and *SP Scot.* I, 265.

[135] PRO SP10/I/23, *APC* II, p. 44, *SP Scot.* I, 30, and Selve, 247.

[136] *SP Scot.* I, 114 and 342 (misdated), PRO SP10/IV/4 and PRO SP50/IV/2 (*SP Scot* I, 219).

[137] PRO SP10/IV/9, *SP Scot.* I, 258, and *Ham.* II, 451.

[138] See *SP Scot.* I, 313, and *Scottish Correspondence*, clxxx.   [139] *SP Dom.* I, 44.

[140] Somerset required the forces of the three marches to scourge the Scots, particularly 'to base and cool the pride and encouragement which the enemy have taken of their small succours out of France' (PRO SP50/III/23 (*SP Scot.* I, 140)).

camp in Lothian, was designed principally to prepare for French intervention.[141] As Somerset explained to the imperial ambassador, the intention of the garrisoning programme was not only to subject the Scots but also to withstand the French.[142] The news that the French were coming certainly affected the character of the garrisons. The original concept of a garrison was a fort held by a few hundred men. Initially Somerset had hoped to man the garrisons with no more than 1,000 troops, at least for the first winter, and to recruit these troops simply by reducing the size of the old border garrisons.[143] The rumour of French preparations, however, introduced the idea of garrisons as army camps. Early in 1548 the government planned to house as many as 1,000 troops in Kirkcudbright alone.[144] In February Lord Grey was troubled by the fact that, in spite of the garrisons already set up, 'at this time we have no place of sure strength for a multitude.'[145] In March and April, moved by the prospect of a French army arriving, the government committed itself to the establishment of a large fortified army camp at Haddington. Haddington was but one of a number of large garrisons which the government considered in response to the French, but the other plans, which involved Kirkcudbright, Lauder and a garrison in Fife, failed to materialize.[146] While the rumour of French assistance led to the Haddington garrison, their actual arrival made its defence a priority since it became the focus of French aggression. From then on the English government sent armies into Scotland to relieve and provision it—in August 1548, and in January and July 1549—thus defeating the intention of using garrisons in order to dispense with armies. Moreover, new garrisons were planned in Lothian to make the victualling of Haddington easier, another clear response to the French, and also in Fife in the hope of diluting the concentration upon Haddington by providing other targets, as well as in order to stem the supplies coming from Fifeside.[147] In all these ways the French presence had a profound influence upon Somerset's Scottish policy.

The English could not have predicted the generosity which the French showed towards the Scots, nor the durability of the Franco-Scottish alliance. Consequently their policy was shaped by the expectation that the French would soon exhaust themselves or lose patience with the Scots and retire. At times it seemed the English were pursuing the correct course, particularly when the French were driven out of St Andrews by its prior and out of Edinburgh by its citizens.[148] In view of the news that 'the governor waxeth weary of the French',[149] there seemed good reason to believe that the passing of time would solve England's problem.

[141] Lord Grey hinted at the consideration when he claimed that the fort at Lauder would soon be impregnable 'though a right mighty power of any foreign prince laid siege to the same' (PRO SP50/IV/4 (*SP Scot.* I, 221)).

[142] *SP Span.* 1547-9, p. 250.

[143] PRO SP15/I/38, PRO SP50/II/32 (*SP Scot.* I, 80) and SP15/I/55.

[144] *SP Dom.* II, 7 and 8.   [145] PRO SP50/III/58 (*SP Scot.* I, 175).

[146] Kirkcudbright, see n. 144; Lauder, see *Ham.* II, 444; and Fife, see *Scottish Correspondence.* clxxx.

[147] *Ibid.*, cxciv, and PRO SP10/IV/9.

[148] BM MS Cotton Caligula B VII, ff. 471 and 478; *ibid.*, f. 332b.

[149] *Ibid.*, f. 478b.

Yet time disproved John Brend's prediction: 'the French . . . will get the hatred of the people and cause the Scots to revolt', and demonstrated the correctness of his diagnosis: 'the enemies be full of variance and suspicion among themselves and yet always agreeing against us.'[150] Faced by the French in Scotland, and under-estimating their perseverance, the Somerset regime's only positive response was to enlarge the network of garrisons and to make alterations in the language of its policy.

Somerset's Scottish policy needed to respond not only to the French presence in Scotland but also their success in annexing Mary Stuart. Her abduction to France in August 1548 deprived English policy of its original *raison d'être* which centred on her marriage to Edward VI. Nevertheless, this event was probably less in-fluential than the military intervention of the French in determining England's course of action. In the absence of the Scottish queen, the English continued to urge the union of England and Scotland by marriage and to use the Scottish repudiation of the treaty of Greenwich as the justification for their military action.[151] Furthermore, although the abduction left the possession of Scotland as the only alternative, Somerset took no positive action to realize this inevitability. In mid-1548 the language of policy changed when the English came to lay less emphasis upon the union by marriage and more on the king's right of superiority over the kingdom of Scotland. This change, for example, was clearly evident in the contrast between the *Epistle* issued in February and the *Epitome* composed in late 1548.[152] Nevertheless, while urging the marriage, the *Epistle* had also asserted the rightful claim of superiority as a possible reason for its actions, whereas the *Epitome*, although stressing the king's rightful ownership of Scotland, did not for-sake to promote the union by marriage.[153] The difference lay in the frequency with which the 'godly purpose' and the ancient claim were cited, and the fre-quency with which the Scots were termed rebels, rather than enemies. However, if a turning point for this change is identifiable, it seemed a response to the news of the French arrival rather than of the queen's departure. Generally, in the matter of declared aims, as with the actual methods, a remarkable continuity is evident in spite of the successful intervention of the French.

The character of the Scottish policy was finally determined by the failure of the garrisons to perform their intended function. The pacific role of the garrisons was clearly demonstrated by the government's attempts to make and maintain friends. No taxes were imposed upon the Scots, no rents exacted of them. The govern-ment scrupulously insisted on paying for the victuals and supplies which it requisitioned;[154] and even awarded compensation to assured Scots whose

---

150 *SP Scot.* I, 299; PRO SP50/IV/119 (*SP Scot.* I, 337).

151 *SP Scot.* I, 345 and 346, BM MS Cotton Caligula B VII, ff. 443 and 462, and BM MS Harley 523, f. 28b.

152 Both printed in EETS, extra ser., 17.

153 *Ibid.*, pp. 242 *f* and p. 253.

154 E.g., *SP Scot.* I, 143. This failed at times, but only under extreme stress, see the unpublished D.Phil. thesis of C. S. L. Davies, 'Supply Services of English Armed Forces, 1509-50' (Oxford, 1963), p. 260.

property was accidentally pillaged.[155] Somerset's belief in the need to win the friendship of the Scots could cause him to advise a gentle approach, as he did with the garrison at Broughty Craig soon after its establishment.[156] But significantly in this respect, Broughty Craig was a dismal failure. Its strength could never convince the locality of its ability to provide a sure defence against the reprisals of hostile Scots. In October 1547 Andrew Dudley, its captain, reported that the only Scots to make assurance so far 'be as yet very few but poor fishermen'. Protestant

Table 2.1 **The main garrisons: manning and cost***

Garrison	Cost of fortification (£)	Serving troops		Diets and wages (£)
Eyemouth	1,908	399	(September 1548 to August 1550)	3,598
Roxburgh	1,899	441	(September 1548 to August 1550	5,303
Hume	734	67	(July to December 1548)	253
Haddington	1,423	4,529	(September 1548 to November 1549)	31,641
Broughty Craig	2,245	240	(September 1547 to May 1548)	16,708
Fast Castle	—	13	(February to November 1549)	170
Dunglass	2,301	586	(October 1548 to August 1550)	5,954
Castlemilk	—	143	(October 1548 to February 1549)	1,370
Jedburgh	—	149	(October 1548 to January 1549)	487
Lauder	1,583	671	(September 1548 to August 1550)	6,646

* See PRO AO I/283/1067, PRO E351/213, and BM MS Harley 353, ff. 94b*f*.

gentlemen, moreover, in the region informed him of their lack of courage to embrace the English cause even with the garrison.[157] Instead of a haven for anglophiles, an important role which it was expected to play, it functioned mainly as a base for acts of coercion and reprisal, a bleak home for foreign mercenaries in English pay engaged in plundering Fife, and an unsatisfactory harbour for a fleet intent on burning and requisitioning in the regions of the Forth and the Tay. Broughty Craig was typical of most of the other garrisons. Protection was a function none of them could perform convincingly. Economy, manning and victualling problems dictated the size of the garrisons, keeping them small.[158]

[155] E.g. Sandy Rotherford, an assured Scot, was given £6 13s. 4d. in recompense 'of spoils done to him by soldiers' (PRO AO I/283/1067).
[156] PRO SP50/II/5 (*SP Scot.* I, 56).
[157] *Ibid.*
[158] For their size, see table 2.1.

Their size determined their function, since the garrisons for the most part could not match an enemy force. They could hold it at bay, but neither defeat it nor drive it off. Consequently, the appearance of a Scottish or French force could easily persuade the assured Scots to switch their allegiance. As Lord Grey of Wilton expressed it, the country will 'bend always to the master of the field',[159] in spite of the presence of English garrisons. This was shown at Broughty Craig in January 1548. With the arrival of a Scottish army, Andrew Dudley noted: 'all the gentlemen of the country are clean gone from us and we must trust to ourselves.'[160] It was also demonstrated in the southwest when, following his defeat by the earl of Angus, Thomas Wharton had to admit: 'the Annandalers for the most part are turned to them.'[161] Only Haddington had the resources to provide protection against the Scots but, enclosed by the French, it could not make use of them. Hence, the acquired character of the garrisons determined policy. The garrisons, if they did anything, functioned essentially to take violent reprisal against the Scots. For this reason, no matter what the aims and claims of the government, coercion took the place of a wooing.

There is no reason to believe that this distressed Somerset, since it cannot be said that he preferred protection to reprisal, or even regarded the failure to provide it as the certain road to ruin. Faced by the constant disobedience of the Scots, he could see no alternative to a policy of 'fire and sword'. He was prepared to offer terms of peace and to stress the need for concord between the two kingdoms, but he was also a consistent advocate of force. It would be quite wrong to think that his policy towards Scotland became harsh and repressive only by accident. It became repressive because the Scots refused to submit to his will. Somerset's exhortations to Lord Grey in 1547 and early 1548 to burn Lothian and his criticism of Grey for his tenderness with the Scots declared Somerset's faith in repression. During this time Wyndham was raiding in the Tay and the Forth and Wharton was similarly engaged, deep in the Scottish West March. As a result, the Scots, particularly of the latter region, were pouring in to assure.[162] Grey's relative slowness to act produced directives to him from the government which clearly revealed its belief in a policy of devastation. In October 1547 Somerset recommended the wasting of parts of Lothian 'whereby they shall be driven either to seek our favour or else be the less able to do us hurt.'[163] Rains and frost held Grey back until January when he burnt the town of Buccleuch.[164] This did not satisfy the government and on 7 February he was strongly reproved for spending so much and doing so little, while Wharton 'who had scoured and brought into the compass of forty miles' was held up as the shining light. At this time both Somerset and Warwick bragged about their devastation of the Scots 'by incessant enterprises' when they were wardens. Somerset opined that if Grey had really exerted himself, he might have burned and pillaged beyond Edinburgh in the

[159] *SP Scot.* I, 179.
[160] PRO SP50/III/27(1) (*SP Scot.* I, 144).
[161] PRO SP15/II/27.
[162] E.g., *SP Scot.* I, 127, and *SP Dom.* I, 31.
[163] PRO SP50/II/12 (*SP Scot.* I, 62).
[164] *SP Scot.* I, 129.

winter season with less than 200 men.[165] In late May the government dispatched Grey into Scotland with further instructions to destroy, a consequence of Somerset's order in early March 'to burn as much corn and houses beyond Musselburgh water as ye can during the fortification'. Compliantly, Grey in early June burnt the countryside in a radius of two miles of Edinburgh.[166] He burnt Musselburgh and its environs, reporting that he had acted 'to the utter ruin and destruction of that country', and completed his work by burning Dunbar.[167] This was not enough for Somerset who, upon Grey's return, criticized him for destroying so little.[168] Destructive reprisals were an essential element in Somerset's method of persuasion. In January and July 1549 his government ordered further expeditions into Scotland to commit specific acts of devastation against lapsed Scots.[169]

Somerset's acceptance of the garrisons as scourges is evident in the justifications offered by officials and the government for the establishment of garrisons, and also in his lack of complaint when the garrisons resorted to rapine. Thus Grey justified placing troops at Jedburgh and Kelso by stressing their ability 'to correct the enemies' as well as 'to strengthen the friends'.[170] He reported that if the Billie Tower garrison met with uncooperative Scots it could 'so whip them as may be both for the terror of the rest and your grace's contentment'.[171] He wrote of Haddington: 'In these parts it will be the daunter of Scotland.'[172] In the southwest, the government called upon Thomas Wharton to establish garrisons which could 'daunt the country and subject the people'.[173] Thomas Holcroft wrote of Dunglass Castle in September 1548: 'this piece once put in strength . . . the king's majesty shall be answered of the revengeance of all betwixt this and Berwick and from Lauder to Dryburgh and part of land unto Dunbar.'[174] In addition, the destructive actions of the garrisons produced no complaint or misgivings from Somerset. In the Tay his instruction to act gently was soon overlooked: in December the fleet proceeded from Broughty Craig to burn a nunnery near Perth and brought away the nuns and also the gentlewomen schooling there. In October the Broughty Craig garrison bombarded Dundee into submission.[175] In January and February 1548 Roxburgh Castle realized its role as a base for raiding parties in the Merse and Teviotdale, and again in January 1549 when, as a reprisal for the loss of Hume Castle, the garrison men of Roxburgh Castle, Jedburgh and Kelso burnt the town of Hume and the surrounding villages.[176] In late 1547 the garrisons of the southwest conducted a terrible devastation, burning as far as the Clyde.[177] In late 1548 the new Dunglass garrison proved its worth by burning down the town of Dunbar.[178] All these activities squared with the government's

[165] PRO SP50/III/32 (*SP Scot.* I, 149).
[166] PRO SP50/III/87 (*SP Scot.* I, 214) and BM MS Harley 289, f. 33.
[167] PRO SP50/IV/22 (*SP Scot.* I, 240) and *SP Scot.* I, 242.
[168] *Ibid.*, 248.
[169] *SP Dom.* III, 23, and BM MS Cotton Caligula B VII, ff. 384f.
[170] SP50/III/12 (*SP Scot.* I, 129).   [171] SP50/III/26 (*SP Scot.* I, 143).
[172] SP50/IV/11 (*SP Scot.* I, 228).   [173] *SP Dom.* I, 44.
[174] BM MS Cotton Caligula B VII, f. 473.   [175] *SP Scot.* I, 119; *ibid.*, 74.
[176] *SP Scot.* I, 129 and 151, and *Ham.* II, 458.   [177] *SP Dom.* I, 34.
[178] BM MS Cotton Caligula B VII, f. 471b.

intentions. In behaving in this way, the garrisons were carrying out a designated task.

Nevertheless, while the garrisons' inability to fulfil their dual function determined their character, it did not alter the government's attitude towards them. Somerset persisted in wishing to woo the Scots through the garrisons. For this reason he never subscribed to a policy of indiscriminate destruction. Through thick and thin, he retained some faith in the device of assurance. Feeling that success eventually depended upon making friends in Scotland, he could not share the sentiments of Thomas Wharton who, riled by his recent defeat wrote in March 1548: 'the natural inclination of that realm has ever been against this realm with falsehood and cruelty since the realms had their names of England and Scotland, and ever so will persevere I think, so that to be won of them must be with fire and sword.'[179] Nor could he conform with Thomas Wyndham who wrote from the Tay: 'these assurances doeth us much hurt for if they had been put to sword and fire since my coming, they would have been in more fear, for we do trust too much to their false words and they doeth seek assurance to serve their turn.'[180] Somerset persisted in believing that a means of securing and maintaining Scottish obedience to the English cause was to make friends through the garrisons, while overlooking the fact that, if the friends were to work constantly for the English cause, they would have to receive proper protection. This the garrisons did not provide, and with no alternative protection offered, the policy had to fail.

The Scottish policy, then, ceased to be simply a composition of aim and method and was moulded by the force of Somerset's personality, the failure to realize the originally conceived garrisoning system, the intrusion of the French and the inability of the garrisons to fulfil their intended function. Of minimal importance among the formative influences was the contrary opinion of Somerset's colleagues and officers. Somerset was undoubtedly in command. This was evident in the establishment and maintenance of Haddington which at his trial was alleged to have been his sole idea;[181] and also in the mass of instructions Somerset personally issued to the officials engaged in the war whom he advised on every conceivable military matter.[182] There is no reason to think that the Scottish policy was the product of conciliation, the outcome of opposed views. Somerset proved capable of overriding the criticism made of the policy. More important,

---

[179] PRO SP15/II/27.

[180] PRO SP50/V/1 (*SP Scot.* I, 342, misdated).

[181] *APC* II, p. 330.

[182] The surviving letters which can be safely attributed to Somerset alone are few and far between: two survive for October 1547 (*SP Scot.* I, 62, and *SP Dom.* I, 37); one for January 1548 (*Scottish Correspondence*, clii); two for September 1548 (*SP Scot.* I, 325 and 328); and one for December 1548 (*ibid.*, 338). Nevertheless, the existence and part of the contents of many of his letters which have not survived are recorded in the surviving replies to them: see *SP Dom.* I, 28 and 29; *SP Scot.* I, 73; PRO SP15/I/55 and 61; *SP Scot.* I, 120, 130 and 132; *SP Dom.* II, 2, 5, 7, 8 and 11; SP15/II/15; *SP Scot.* I, 140, 165, 196 and 231; *SP Dom.* II, 20, 23 and 27; SP15/II/32; *SP Dom.* II, 42, 47 and 47 (1); *SP Scot.* I, 242, 248, 251, 259; *SP Dom.* III, 6; *Ham.* II, 447 and 449; SP15/III/11; *Ham.* II, 448, 450 and 456; *SP Scot.* I, 290, 312, 332 and 342; and BM MS Cotton Caligula B VII, ff. 471 and 478.

conciliation was unnecessary because, in spite of differences over details,[183] the general policy of the war and the establishment of the garrisons seemed to command general support. In August 1549 Paget had doubts about the Scottish war, but in addressing them not to Somerset but to Somerset and the council, he seemed to imply that in the council was general agreement over the Scottish war.[184] This agreement was confirmed by the attempt to maintain the war upon Somerset's fall. In waging war against the Scots Somerset was following his own ambitions, but in doing so he did not appear to be acting counter to the beliefs of his colleagues. He seemed to have a free hand in the general direction of the war because of their consent and approval. In this respect, the Scottish war was not, it appears, influenced by a division of opinion among Englishmen.

Failure

In the first instance the establishment of the garrisons produced spectacular results: the Scots of Lothian, the Merse, Teviotdale and the southwest poured in to assure. On 12 November 1547 Thomas Wharton claimed to have 6,000 Scots under his protection.[185] In view of this response Somerset must have felt in those early days that the Scottish problem was solved, and that the dream he had described on the battlements at Berwick was no more than a comment on the past. Nevertheless, within a year success turned to failure. By late 1548 the Scots were retracting their support; observing their willingness to victual the French and their failure to warn the Haddington garrison of a surprise attack in October 1548, Thomas Fisher expressed doubts about the allegiance of the assured Lowland Scots.[186] In November 1548 the ambivalence of the assured Scots in Fife caused John Luttrell to explode: 'From henceforward there is no hope of any practice for friendship to be ministered but rather an extreme plague with fire and sword which shall reduce them to poverty and submission or otherwise your grace can never prevail here.'[187] The presence of the French and the inability of the English to offer effective protection to the Scots were undoubtedly the cause of the failure. In these circumstances the garrisons ceased to work. They also ceased to be a genuine alternative for armies royal since armies were needed to relieve and victual the garrisons, particularly Haddington and Lauder. Pressed by the French and the re-inspired Scots, the garrisons by late 1548 became incapable of doing anything, other than to engage enemy forces, and to call for and to consume supplies. However, it would be wrong to attribute the failure of the garrisons wholly to the French. Some of the provisioning, manning and financing problems, which helped to render them useless, were evident before the French arrived. In view of the limited resources of the English monarchy, the failure of the garrisons was probably due not just to misfortune but to something inherent in the idea.

---

[183] See below, p. 37.

[184] PLB, Paget to Somerset and the council, 28 August 1549.

[185] SP *Scot.* I, 168, and *SP Dom.* I, 50.

[186] BM MS Cotton Caligula B VII, ff. 332*ff.*   [187] *Scottish Correspondence*, cxci.

Somerset had valued garrisons because of the costliness as well as the ineffectiveness of armies royal. The maintenance, protection and manning of the garrisons, however, proved prohibitively expensive and well beyond the financial means of even a government which could resort for revenue to the debasement of the coinage and the sale of church and chantry lands. The compulsion to establish larger garrisons than originally planned, the price of victuals in the Lowlands unnaturally inflated by an initial policy of devastation, the need to raise forces to revictual Haddington and Lauder, but not the cost of fortification which was remarkably low:[188] all this presented the government with a bill for a Scottish war of two years' duration which almost doubled the massive cost of Henry VIII's five years of war against Scotland in the 1540s.[189] Moreover, nothing was gained by garrisoning as opposed to invasion since, in addition to the sum spent in wages and diets in the garrisons, Somerset spent £351,521 16s. od., against Henry VIII's

Table 2.2 **The relative cost of the Eight Years' War***

	Coat and conduct (£)	Diets and wages (£)	Freightage (£)	Rewards (£)	Munitions and ordnance (£)	Fortifications (£)
Henry VIII	38,952	235,383	10,060	19,824	5,984	27,458
Edward VI	29,720	423,653	22,963	42,322	22,080	39,655

* BM MS Harley 353 ff. 94b*f*.

£235,383 8s. 3d., for troops to man the border garrisons and to serve in the field. The only saving made by Somerset's system was in coat and conduct money.[190] Garrisoning was so expensive that an annual invasion would have worked out cheaper. Somerset's steadfast refusal to exact tribute and to seize supplies from the Scots intensified the financial problem. As Somerset had justified the garrisoning of Scotland in terms of economy, the enormous expense of his policy marked the failure of his schemes.

From the start Somerset was aware of the spiralling costs. In his management of the war he constantly tried to economize: that is, within the framework of his obsessive attempts to produce the perfect network of garrisons, he either reduced the numbers of troops involved, or delayed the payment of wages or imposed fierce restraints upon official fees. In late 1547 Lord Grey's request for the wages of the garrison troops received the stony response: 'the garrison troops were accustomed to forbear for three or four months.'[191] In August 1548 Somerset sought to reduce the force engaged to relieve Haddington.[192] He frequently tried to con-

[188] See table 2.1, p. 28.
[189] See BM MS Harley 353, f. 96.
[191] PRO SP50/II/24 (*SP Scot*. I, 72).
[190] See table 2.2.
[192] *SP Scot*. I, 312.

tain the cost of office. He objected to the promotion of Oswald Wylstropp when Grey placed him in charge of Jedburgh and Kelso because it would 'increase the [king's] superfluous charges'.[193] He also opposed the raising of Grey's salary, and Robert Bowes was denied any increase in pay when made to serve simultaneously in both wardenries of the March.[194] Throughout, Somerset continually admonished his lieutenant, Lord Grey, 'for the good husbanding of his highness' treasure'.[195] Partly responsible for the constant complaints made by the garrison troops was the tightfistedness of a government ruled by a mean man. According to the imperial ambassador Somerset's meanness particularly in the Scottish war was a source of criticism among leading government officials early in 1548.[196] Somerset's measures of economy were not simply an expression of his personality, but also the result of deliberate policy. In March 1549 he remarked to the imperial ambassador: 'You see how careful I am to avoid any expense for the king my master, if it is possible to do so.'[197] Nevertheless, conflicting with his financial stringency, which largely fell upon those serving in the wars, was a feverish need for military action in Scotland, which considerations of economy never managed to cool. Needless to say, his attempts at economy had no substantial effect in curtailing the cost of the Scottish war, and mainly succeeded in alienating or discouraging the officials and troops engaged in it.

Closely connected was another outstanding problem, also well beyond the government's competence to solve. It lacked adequate manpower. The miserable conditions in the garrisons[198] made men unwilling to serve in them from the start; they ran away from Eyemouth and later from Haddington, rebelled at Hume Castle, refused to go to Lochwood Castle and proved so obstreperous at Yester Castle that Grey reported in April 1548 that the budding Haddington garrison 'already . . . seemeth to have subdued all this country, saving the house of Yester [an English fort] kept mostly by the Spaniards'.[199] The troops in the garrisons tended to be demoralized or antagonized by the lack of pay and the living conditions, and also weakened by the prevalence of the ague, dysentery and the plague. In late 1548 Thomas Holcroft, writing from Dunglass Castle, reported that large numbers had fallen sick and that he was 'lying in my bed more ready with great pain to go unto the stool than unto a fair woman'.[200] At Haddington, the plague struck so decisively in November 1548 that only 1,000 troops, less than half the garrison, were able to man the walls.[201] At Broughty, in late 1547 the troops had

[193] PRO SP50/III/26 (*SP Scot.* I, 143).

[194] PRO SP50/IV/16 (*SP Scot.* I, 233) and *SP Scot.* I, 222.

[195] PRO SP50/III/9 (*SP Scot.* I, 126).

[196] *SP Span.* 1547–9, p. 245.

[197] *Ibid.*, pp. 351*f.*

[198] See, for example, Holcroft's description of Dunglass (BM MS Cotton Caligula B VII, f. 481), Luttrell's description of Broughty Craig (*Scottish Correspondence*, cxci) and Rutland's general comments on the garrisons (*HMC* Rutland IV, pp. 193*f*).

[199] *SP Scot.* I, 245 and 267; *ibid.*, 155; *SP Dom.* II, 32; PRO SP50/IV/11 (*SP Scot.* I, 228). For the problem of absconding troops, also see *HMC* Rutland I, pp. 35*f* and 50*f*, *ibid.*, IV, p. 193 and *SP Scot.* I, 204.

[200] BM MS Cotton Caligula B VII, ff. 481*f.*   [201] *SP Scot.* I, 329.

to 'lie together like swine as wet as though they lie abroad in the field', and contracted the ague. This created such tension in the garrison that its captain, Andrew Dudley, claimed to be 'in as much danger of my soldiers and mariners as I do of the Scots'.[202] Lack of pay, moreover, aroused such discontent and non-cooperation that, before the French could make much impact, John Uvedale, treasurer of the Scottish war, reported he 'never saw nor heard such a universal disease among soldiers for lack of money'.[203]

An additional difficulty was to find sufficient troops to man the garrisons, a repercussion of England's military system with its primitive dependence upon the private armies of subjects, the shire levy, border service and a small, fully occupied standing force consisting of the king's bodyguard and the troops belonging to the traditional continental and northern border garrisons. The unreliability of the borderers, the poor quality of the bishopric men[204] and the government's inability to call upon the militia or private retinues for regular service, left it with the choice of employing either Scotsmen or foreign mercenaries in its Scottish garrisons. It was not keen to employ Scotsmen. In May 1548 it instructed: 'No Scot be in wages in any fortress except by special letter from the council.'[205] The only garrison to employ them in any number was Castlemilk.[206] When Scotsmen received wages from the English, it was mainly as retainers of loyal Scottish lords who for purposes of protection received the means to employ a number of troops.[207] The government's only alternative was therefore to rely upon expensive and wilful mercenaries from abroad. During the war as many as 7,434 Italians, Spaniards, Almains, Hungarians, Albanians and Irishmen served in English pay on the northern border and in the Scottish garrisons.[208] Yester Castle, Hume Castle, Dunglass Castle, Jedburgh, Kelso, Broughty, Haddington and Lauder were all held by large contingents of foreigners. Those at Yester Castle seemed unmanageable. Those at Hume Castle planned to change sides early in 1548 and were only thwarted by swift military action.[209] Those at Haddington refused to sleep in the open.[210] Then, as conditions worsened in 1549, particularly with the onset of the plague and the lack of funds and provisions, the mercenaries refused to serve in Scotland[211] and the English cause was virtually lost. Eventually the problems of manning were decisive in bringing the garrisons to an end.

Finally, the problem of providing the garrisons with victuals and other supplies was also evident from the start. It derived from the roughness of the terrain, high

---

202 PRO SP50/II/26 (*SP Scot.* I, 74).

203 *Ham* II, 447.

204 For complaints against borderers: *Ham.* II, 454 and 459, and *SP Scot.* I, 240, 251, 258, 259 and 297. For complaints against the bishopric men: *SP Scot.* I, 118 and 265.

205 PRO SP50/IV/16 (*SP Scot.* I, 233). Also see *APC II*, p. 520.

206 Of the 143 troops, 120 were Scotsmen in English pay (PRO AO I/283/1067).

207 Ormiston, for example, was allowed 150 men in wages, as was Brunstane (*SP Scot.* I, 220); Patrick lord Gray was allowed 300 horse in wages (*SP Scot.* I, 188); Bothwell was allowed 100 light horse in wages (*CPR* 1549–51, p. 110).

208 Out of a total of 17,315 (PRO AO I/283/1067).

209 *SP Scot.* I, 155 and 228.   210 *SP Scot.* I, 332.

211 See *HMC* Rutland, IV, pp. 193 and 199, and *ibid.*, I, pp. 51 f.

seas and inadequate land transport.[212] Later the presence of the French introduced another serious impediment. But before this happened the garrison at Inchcolm had to be dismantled because of its logistic difficulties.[213] At Broughty the lack of supplies seriously restricted the garrison's activities. In early 1548 munitions were in such short supply that the citizens of Dundee were paid, with some effect, to return the cannonballs fired at the town by the English.[214] Supplying the garrisons became a major concern and headache for the government. It was clear that the original plan had failed since forces had to be put into the field to supply the garrisons in August 1548, January 1549 and in the following July. The arrival of the French, however, only intensified a problem present before their arrival. Lord Grey put his finger on the essential difficulty. When Somerset chided him for doing less at greater charge than he himself had accomplished as lord warden in the early 1540s, Grey retorted: 'I trust your grace will consider, it is not now to lie there with such small charges as it was at that time, for accounting then the inhabitants for enemies, the soldiers might well for his relief, aid and succour take where he would corn, victuals and other things without paying one penny. . . . And now being won and sworn to the king's majesty's godly purpose, we can have nothing of that country without ready payment . . . else would it soon cause them already come into revolt and the others to keep out.'[215] The need to win and maintain friends in Scotland compelled the English to pay for the victuals which they requisitioned. For this reason the problem of finance was closely related to the provisioning problem. The ravaging of the Lowlands by the English intensi-fied the victualling problem, making victuals scarce and expensive before the arrival of the French.[216] After their arrival victuals remained scarce because the Scots were keener to supply their French allies. The victualling problem finally defeated the government particularly when it proved incapable of supplying the garrisons at Lauder and Haddington without the assistance of an army.

The failure of the government's garrisoning programme resulted mainly from the inadequacy of its schemes. It cannot be attributed to the 'decay' of England, to a decline in England's traditional military resources. It is true that Edward I had employed garrisons to much greater effect in imposing himself on Scotland,[217] but as the respective garrisoning of Scotland by the two governments was different in character little can be concluded from the comparison.[218] In the first place Edward VI did not seek to occupy Scotland, and therefore lost all the advantages of the direct rule upon which his forerunner had insisted. Secondly un-like the Somerset regime, Edward I did not regard the garrisons as an alternative

[212] For some of the problems see C. S. L. Davies, 'Provisioning for Armies, 1509–50', *Econ HR* 2nd ser., 17 (1964), pp. 236 and 239.

[213] *SP Scot.* I, 93, and Selve, 310.   [214] PRO E351/213.

[215] PRO SP50/III/26 (*SP Scot.* I, 143).   [216] *SP Dom.* II, 32 and 59.

[217] M. Prestwich in *War Politics and Finance under Edward I* (London, 1972), p. 136, makes a compari-son of military operations as a whole. This is difficult to accept as valid because Henry VIII was involved with war against France at the same time as his war against Scotland, and Somerset was seeking de-liberately to dispense with invading forces.

[218] For Edward I's garrisoning system, see *ibid.*, p. 36 and pp. 111*f.*

to invasions by armies royal. For this reason his use of armies royal cannot be regarded as a mark of failure, as it clearly can be in Edward VI's case. Thirdly the nature and function of the garrisons of Edward I were vastly different from those of Edward VI. Edward I's garrisons were strongholds manned by handfuls of men. Essentially they aimed to maintain presence during the process of conquest by invading armies.[219] In contrast, Edward VI's garrisons were less of the nature of fortresses. The failure to take Dunbar Castle and Edinburgh Castle, and the possession, at the most, of only two formidable fortresses—Hume Castle and the Hermitage—the latter, if ever held, acquired late and the other lost early, meant that Somerset's garrisons were a collection of camps with improvised ramparts, although often positioned on the sites of old castles. Consequently, the Somerset garrisons were manned by much larger numbers of troops, and this feature of the garrisons rather than their existence presented Somerset with his major difficulties. Finally, Edward I in Scotland only had to deal with the Scots, not with the French as well. The failure of the garrisons during the protectorate indicated the presence of a much more formidable task.

The defectiveness of the garrisons brought them to an end. Upon Somerset's overthrow, the new government seemed prepared to maintain them. It had disagreed with Somerset over the running of the garrisons and over enterprises which he had planned on the West March 'besides many other unprofitable devices', but it had not disputed the need for garrisons, with the possible exception of Haddington. Such was its faith in them that it established two commissions to see to their refortification and revictualling.[220] Moreover, in treating with the French in 1550, the government's original intention was to cede some of the garrisons in return for the recognition of its marriage claim to Mary Stuart, but not all.[221] The English finally abandoned the garrisoning policy, not because its chief advocate fell from power, but because the taking of Broughty and the siege of Lauder early in 1550 underlined the unrewarding and insoluble difficulties of maintaining the garrisons and convinced the government of their impracticability.[222]

As the principal director of the policy Somerset is the man to blame for its failure. But it cannot be said that the failure derived from his complete unwillingness to let others influence the policy, from his inability to delegate or to listen to advice, as Jordan seems to suggest.[223] The error of his military leadership was probably to delegate his authority as captain-general of the king's forces in the north to a lieutenant and the captains of the garrisons, instead of personally leading into Scotland a second army to evict the French. He appeared unable to do this because of its inconsistency with the garrisoning programme. Moreover, the officials to whom he delegated the conduct of the war could influence policy by acts of personal initiative and by Somerset's toleration of their disobedience. Lord

---

[219] For the difference in the size of garrisons, compare the system of Edward I in which Edinburgh Castle was the largest garrison with 325 men (*ibid.*, pp. 111*f*), and the system of Edward VI in which 4,529 men served in Haddington in the space of one year (see table 2.1).

[220] *HMC* Rutland IV, pp. 192*f*, and *APC* II, p. 345; *SP Dom.* III, 55, and *HMC* Rutland IV, p. 200.

[221] Jordan II, p. 120.

[222] *Ibid.*, pp. 147*f*.   [223] See Jordan I, p. 284.

Grey early in 1548 was criticized for requiring constant direction.[224] Several instances survive of officials effectively ignoring instructions. Thomas Wyndham remained abroad in Scottish waters with his fleet early in 1548 although commanded home at the close of 1547; Lord Clinton ignored Somerset's order to proceed to the Tay in August 1548 and kept the fleet in the Forth; and Shrewsbury and Grey in the same month refused to obey Somerset's order for the dismissal of troops in their charge.[225] Officials at times acted in a way which assumed some licence of private initiative by Somerset. Thus, in June 1548 Lord Grey informed Somerset how he had dispatched troops to Haddington which 'varies somewhat from your order'; and in September 1548 Thomas Holcroft without much apology could admit to Somerset that he had dispensed with his instructions.[226]

In addition, Somerset in his Scottish policy was prepared to accept advice from his fellow councillors. While not complying with all Paget had to suggest, he heeded much of what he had to say, consoling Grey for the English defeat in July 1548, permitting the eventual abandonment of Haddington, and employing the earl of Warwick in 1549 to sort out the Scottish problem.[227] Furthermore, he did not entirely exclude the rest of the council from either the formulation or the application of the Scottish policy. Several directives exist from the council on Scottish affairs covering a wide range of matters, and letters addressed to Somerset could be answered by the privy council.[228] The Scottish policy was the product of an obsession, but not the unshared belief, of one man. The failure of the policy indicated miscalculation as well as misfortune, but a miscalculation for which a group of men was responsible.

Somerset's policy and its failure sprang not from an ideal but an *idée fixe*, an obsession with a military technique for forcibly keeping the Scots in order.[229] This obsession derived partly from his frustrating experiences in Henry VIII's reign, but also from his inability to make a system work properly when he had the chance to apply it. In the circumstances, he could argue that the system was failing not because it was impracticable or rendered redundant by the French presence, but because the scheme formulated in 1544 and 1545 had not been satisfactorily applied. This shored up his faith in garrisons and allowed him to persist with them although, after the halcyon days of early 1548, they achieved very little at enormous cost. Adaptability was principally needed which, caught in the web of his own policy, Somerset could not provide. This was the essence of his

224 *SP Scot.* I, 149.
225 *SP Scot.* I, 114–15, and PRO SP10/IV/4 for Wyndham's eventual return in March; *SP Scot.* I, 313; *ibid.*, 312.
226 PRO SP50/IV/24 (*SP Scot.* I, 242) and BM MS Cotton Caligula B VII, f. 473.
227 PLB, Paget to Somerset, Candlemas, 1547 (1548); BM MS Cotton Titus F III, f. 276, and *SP Scot.* I, 303; PLB, Paget to Somerset and the council, 28 August 1549.
228 Of the 127 letters and instructions known to have been issued by the Somerset government in connection with the war, 75 came directly from Somerset and the rest from Somerset and the council. For evidence of the council replying to letters addressed to Somerset on Scottish matters, see *APC* II, p. 543, and *SP Scot.* I, 148; and *APC* II, p. 546, and *SP Scot.* I, 170.
229 For a view of Somerset as an idealist, see R. B. Wernham, *op. cit.*, p. 167.

personal failure. Perhaps, as Jordan suggests, he should have had the sense to wait for the reformation in Scotland to tip the scales in England's favour, but this was a lot to expect of a soldier whose battlefield had been Scotland.[230]

Somerset's Scottish policy failed dismally. At great expense nothing positive was achieved. Nevertheless, the garrisons succeeded in fulfilling one function for which they had been designed. They managed to defend the English border. In spite of the hostility of the Scots, a French army in Scotland, a domestic problem of peasant rebellion and an involvement with Boulogne, England in this time was never subjected to the threat of invasion from the north. Thanks to the garrisons in Scotland, the massive resources which the French and the Scots employed against the English were dissipated in seeking to exclude the English from Scotland. In this respect, the arguments presented by Somerset in the previous reign in favour of garrisons as a means of self-defence, were justified by the course of events.[231]

[230] Jordan I, p. 300.
[231] See *LP* XX (2), 96.

3

Social Policy 1: The Programme of Social Reform

Measures and Concerns

Somerset's applied programme of social reform rested upon four main issues: inflation, depopulation, injustice and the inadequacy of university education. His government believed that inflation could provoke insurrections and render military operations prohibitively expensive, and that depopulation reduced the manpower available to the Crown for waging wars to defend the realm and to acquit the king's honour. Remedy was therefore urgently required to prevent the dishonouring of the king and the destruction of the kingdom either by revolution or foreign conquest. Impartial justice was insisted upon both because it was the traditional hallmark of a government's virtue, and because of the emphasis which protestantism attached to the connection between charity and godliness. Finally, the government's interest in university education was politically motivated; changes were required so that universities provided for the professional service not only of the church but also of the state. What appeared to have no appreciable effect upon the government's social policy was any consideration of society or the economy as subjects in their own right, rather than as off-shoots of political or religious concerns. The government like its predecessors was unable to appreciate poverty for its own sake, or to prefer the interests of the lower orders before those of the aristocracy in the cause of social justice. Essentially, it regarded society from a political standpoint. It treated society to solve political problems. Similarly, it could not conceive the economy in autonomous terms. It acted neither to ensure economic growth nor a regulated economy, but to maintain the security and stability of the realm. In this respect, the government acted conventionally.[1]

The programme was characterized by its emphasis on practical, political matters. Significantly, it did not include the impractical, moral issue of usury, which the government's financial needs compelled it not to question. Another prominent feature was the government's insistence upon effectiveness, and its keen desire to avoid a policy of fiscalism. Rather than being content merely to raise money by the enforcement of agrarian laws the government appeared bent on curing the ills of society. It social policy only became a fund-raising exercise

[1] For the standard view, see Pollard, ch 8, and Jordan I, ch. 14. Both Pollard and Jordan asserted that Somerset was conservative in his social policy (Pollard, p. 221; Jordan I, p. 427), and then implied that he had unusual and radical social aims (Pollard, p. 317; Jordan I, pp. 416, 427 and 435, and II, p. 210).

because certain measures of the second parliamentary session were designed as concessions to society and aimed to make the government's fiscal demands acceptable.[2] The programme's most prominent characteristic, and one long recognized though wrongly explained, was its concentration on the agrarian problem of declining arable and flourishing pastoral farming. This concentration was not due to an inability to think beyond the agrarian problem, nor to a pre-occupation with enclosure.[3] To deal with inflation, for example, the government employed a wide range of remedies which included the restriction of exports, price-fixing, the abolition of compulsory purveyance and the preservation of fast days.[4] But the agrarian measures were particularly important since they dealt with two of the government's major concerns. The protection of tillage was regarded as an answer both to dearth and to depopulation. However, the agrarian matter acquired its actual prominence in the government's programme because of incidental factors rather than deliberate choice. In the first place a policy of curtailing sheep-farming did not interfere with the government's main interest, the Scottish war. Although clearly responsible for inflation, because it encouraged debasement, and for the exhaustion of the country's military resources, the war was continually overlooked as the culprit. This was not because of economic ignorance or a lack of political awareness: influential contemporaries such as Hugh Latimer, Thomas Smith and William Thomas stated that debasement caused inflation, the first in his Lenten sermon to the Court in 1549; and William Paget and John Hales perceived the prolonged war's contribution to the present military inadequacy of the realm.[5] The failure to blame war simply expressed the government's unwillingness to make peace. A dependence upon war meant particularly a dependence upon debasement.[6] It was therefore impossible to remedy inflation by proceeding against debasement until the termination of war in 1550. Before this, to exculpate itself and to show its concern, the government attributed the damage inflicted by war to sheep-farming. It made sheep the scapegoat for the economic problems of the time.

In the second place the government's concentration upon the agrarian problem derived from an economic fact—the prevalence of good harvests in 1547 and 1548. Like the government's interest in war, this influenced its choice of the current theories on the causes of inflation, and hence its remedial measures. Besides the debasement theory three were commonly held: the first attributed inflation to marketing, the second to production, and the third blamed rents.[7]

[2] See below, pp. 50 and 142 *f*

[3] An implication of the standard interpretation.

[4] 2/3 Edward VI, cc. 3, 19, 26 and 37; and Hughes and Larkin, 285, 295, 304, 310, 315, 336 and 345.

[5] A. B. Ferguson, *The Articulate Citizen and the English Renaissance* (Duke University, 1965), pp. 295 and 296 n. 40; PLB, Paget to Somerset and the council, 28 August 1549; Lamond, p. lv.

[6] See C. E. Challis, 'The Debasement of the Coinage, 1542–1551', *Econ. HR*, 2nd ser. 20 (1967,) p. 454.

[7] The first two theories are present in Hales's memorandum on dearth and in his parliamentary drafts for the second parliamentary session (Lamond, pp. xlii–lii, and PRO SP10/II/21). An example of the production theory is in the proclamation announcing the 1548 enclosure commission (Hughes and Larkin, 309), and in Thomas Smith's *A Discourse of the Commonwealth of this Realm of England*

The government's difficulty in adopting the 'rents' theory as a basis for action was the lack of certainty as to whether the raising of rents was the cause or the effect of inflation.[8] In addition it was not easy to act upon such a theory in a society dominated by a rentier aristocracy. The problem in adopting the 'marketing' theory was the difficulty of appreciating it at a time when corn prices were very low. The peculiar discrepancy between the high price of victuals and the cheapness of corn, an economic fact for much of the protectorate, made men look beyond marketing for the causes of inflation. The government produced certain market regulations to control prices; exports were restricted or prohibited in a traditional manner, the government also distinguished itself by abolishing compulsory purveyance which was thought to affect market prices, and, in the restricted matter of wool, where there seemed to be no problem of production but, nevertheless, a problem of inflation, measures were passed to curb malpractices in buying and selling.[9] Furthermore, Hales produced an internal marketing measure to prevent forestalling and regrating in the second session, and an act was passed to prevent victuallers and handicraft men from contriving prices by private agreement.[10] But much of this belonged to 1549. Only with the termination of the period of good harvests was internal marketing seriously attended to as a cause of inflation, and Somerset fell before a substantial body of regulations could be enacted or issued. Also working against the employment of market controls to restrict inflation was a loss of faith in the effectiveness of taxing prices, an experiment of the 1530s which was almost played out by Somerset's time. He resorted to it only once, in desperation in 1549.[11] Thus, as economic conditions and the government's material needs and previous experience closed off the options, the government became heavily inclined to blame inflation upon a loss of production, and to seek, by enforcing the agrarian laws, the promotion of tillage which it regarded as a more fruitful source of cheap victuals than pastoral farming.[12]

The final reason for the government's concentration upon agrarian reform was its lack of success with such a policy. The failure of the 1548 commission against enclosures led to further commissions in 1549, and the attempted agrarian legislation of the second session. As with the garrisoning of Scotland, failure produced persistence not flexibility.

Besides steering the government away from accepting debasement as responsible for inflation, war helped to determine the character of the government's social programme by thwarting some of its original aspirations. The government's interest appeared to embrace much more than the problems of inflation,

---

(Lamond, pp. 20 and 60). An example of the rents theory, with evidence that it was currently discussed at Court, is in 'Copy of a Letter' (F. Rose-Troup, *The Western Rebellion* (London, 1913), App. K, p. 491).

[8] This is strongly suggested by 'Copy of a Letter' (*ibid.*).

[9] Hughes and Larkin, 331 and 345.

[10] See below, p. 51, and 2/3 Edward VI, c. 15.

[11] Hughes and Larkin, 336, and see below, pp. 151-3

[12] See Hughes and Larkin, 309, and Strype II (2), P.

shortage of manpower, injustice and university education, since it considered using the wealth of the confiscated chantries, gilds and colleges not just to preserve their educational and charitable services, but also to extend them.[13] War, however, intruded and snatched the funds away. Under the protectorate only the status quo was maintained. The considerable wealth realized by the confiscation was spent in engaging the Scots and the French in war. Only with the termination of the war was there an extension of state-subsidized social services, and that was unspectacular and owed much to the pressure of private initiative.[14] How seriously the government held these thwarted aims remains unknown. What is certain is the Somerset regime's preference for war. In these circumstances social aspirations which required government money were bound to be neglected, and measures like the restriction of sheep-farming which required no capital outlay, preferred.

The government was remarkably slow in producing its social reforms. Until the commission against enclosures of June 1548 substantiated by the legislative attempts of the second session, it did not appear to have a positive programme. There is, for example, a sharp distinction between the second parliamentary session beginning in November 1548, with an urgent and extensive programme of reform, and the first session of November and December 1547 which did no more than to consider momentarily the decay of tillage, enact a vicious poor law and make promises about putting chantry lands to good use.[15] In fact not until May 1548 did the actual policy which distinguished the regime seem to have any real existence. In that month the government decided to dispark the chase at Hampton Court.[16]

[13] The act of confiscation, 1 Edward VI, c. 14, mentioned putting the wealth 'to good and godly uses as in the erection of grammar schools to the education of youth in virtue and godliness, the further augmenting of the universities and better provision for the poor and needy. . . .'

[14] Early in 1548 the government appointed two commissions, one to supervise the sale of chantry, gild and college lands for the purposes of war (*CPR* 1548-9, pp. 57*f*, and *A.P.C.* II, pp. 184-6), the other to preserve the secular function of the chantries, gilds and colleges (*CPR* 1547-8, pp. 417*f*). This was the extent of its achievement. Through the sales, the Somerset regime acquired over £200,000 for the war-effort (W. C. Richardson, *History of the Court of Augmentations, 1536-1554* (Baton Rouge, 1961), p. 177 n. 35), which represented half the available capital value of the confiscated wealth (Jordan II, p. 200). Jordan calculates that before the confiscation, 11·26 per cent of the capital value of the total wealth of the chantries, gilds and colleges was devoted to social purposes, and after the confiscation in the reign of Edward VI, 11·67 per cent. The evidence seems to indicate that this slight increase in social expenditure occurred after the fall of Somerset, followed the termination of the war, and related particularly to the foundation of grammar schools and London hospitals (Jordan II, p. 197 and pp. 216-18, and Joan Simon, *Education and Society in Tudor England* (Cambridge, 1966), p. 231). I plan to substantiate these points in a separate paper. Some guidance of the minimal role played by Somerset in the foundation of grammar schools in the north is provided by P. J. Wallis and W. E. Tate, 'A Register of Old Yorkshire Grammar Schools', *University of Leeds Institute of Education Researches and Studies*, 13, and P. J. Wallis, 'A Preliminary Report of Old Schools in Lancashire and Cheshire', *Transactions of the Historic Society of Lancashire and Cheshire*, 120 (1968), tables 2 and 3, pp. 10-21.

[15] *Journals of the House of Lords*, 8, 12 and 14 November; C. S. L. Davies, 'Slavery and Protector Somerset: the Vagrancy Act of 1547', *Econ. HR*, 2nd ser., 19 (1966), pp. 533 *ff*; see n. 13.

[16] *APC* II, pp. 190-92.

It justified the decision partly in practical terms: Edward had no need of it since, unlike his aged father for whom the chase had been made, he could easily hunt in Windsor Forest; and occupied by men rather than deer the land would realize more profit to the Crown. But this was not its full explanation. It claimed also to be moved by the complaints 'of many poor men of the area'. Responding to the allegation that 'very many households of the same parish be let fall down, the families decayed and the king's liege people much diminished', the government claimed to act not simply for reasons of self-interest, but also for 'the conservation of his people'.

The primary consideration of the 1548 commission against enclosures was one expressed frequently by contemporary commentators: laws were made but lacked effect.[17] The commission's role was to give teeth to a number of statutes.[18] Like these statutes,[19] its terms of reference comprehended much more than the somewhat dated issue of enclosure. The title of the commission is therefore a misnomer. John Hales, the principal commissioner, could describe its purpose without even mentioning enclosing. To the juries of presentment, oppointed for the execution of the commission, he declared: 'it extendeth to five principal points, that is, for the decay of towns, villages, houses of husbandry, converting arable ground into pasture, the multitude of sheep, the heaping together of farms, the not keeping hospitality and household on the sites of the monasteries and religious houses that were dissolved by statute . . . and occupying of tillage on the demesnes of the same monasteries.'[20] Moreover, even when Hales used the term enclosure, he clearly did not mean simple enclosing. As he informed the earl of Warwick: 'I mean not here hedging lands but decaying tillage and husbandry.'[21] To the jurors of presentment he explained: 'it is not taken where a man doth enclose and hedge in his own proper ground where no man hath commons, for such enclosure is very beneficial to the commonwealth; it is a cause of great increase of wood; but it is meant thereby when any man hath taken away and enclosed any other men's commons, or hath pulled down houses of husbandry and converted the lands from tillage to pasture.'[22] The term was a form of shorthand, used for convenience, and not meant to be taken literally.

Principally, the commission was preoccupied with the decay of tillage, not with enclosures. The latter were only regarded as offensive when they caused the former.[23] The commission considered the decline of tillage an urgent problem because it was thought to endanger the internal security and military capacity of the state. As the accompanying proclamation indicated, the realm 'must be

[17] W. R. D. Jones, *The Tudor Commonwealth, 1529–1559* (London, 1970), pp. 204–6.
[18] Hughes and Larkin, 309 and 327.
[19] 4 Henry VII, c. 19; 6 Henry VIII, c. 5; 7 Henry VIII, c. 1; 25 Henry VIII, c. 13; and 27 Henry VIII, c. 22.
[20] Strype II (2), p. 356.
[21] BM MS Lansdowne 238, f. 322b.
[22] Strype II (2), pp. 361 *f.*
[23] The aims of the commission are stated in a proclamation (Hughes and Larkin, 309); in the wording of the commission itself (Strype II (2), P) and in the instructions with which Hales charged the presentment juries (*ibid.*, Q).

defended with force of men and the multitude of true subjects, not with flocks of sheep'. It felt that the neglect of tillage had reduced 'the force of men' through causing depopulation, and was depriving the realm of 'the multitude of true subjects' through causing the inflation which, in the words of the commission's patent, left the people 'in extreme misery and poverty'. The commission's basic concern was that, if unrestrained, pastoral farming would lead to 'the subversion, utter undoing and decay of the realm'. The commission revealed a concern for poverty, but poverty was appreciated as a threat to the order and independence of the realm, and as an offence to God if it did not inspire charity.[24] The commission was not stirred by any basic objection to the existence of poverty.

The commission of June 1548 was not meant to hear and determine. Like Wolsey's commission, it ostensibly aimed to conduct an enquiry so that informations could be laid in Chancery.[25] But this was not its sole, and perhaps not even its main, purpose. According to John Hales, the commission 'was chiefly sent forth to the intent my lord protector's grace and the council might know by part the whole state of the realm, and so proceed to redress of all', presumably, not simply by the prosecution of offenders but also by the enactment of new laws.[26] Hales expected the commission to provide information for the next parliamentary session. In July 1548 he urged Somerset to call all the planned commissions into operation so that 'the thing being done before the parliament, all our world then might be informed what hurt hath grown, and what is like to follow to the realm if it be not in time resisted.'[27] No matter what its purpose, the 1548 commission undoubtedly failed. As only one commission went into operation (for the Midland counties of Oxfordshire, Berkshire, Warwickshire, Leicestershire, Bedfordshire, Buckinghamshire and Northamptonshire),[28] the exercise did not produce a general survey of the agrarian situation. Moreover, the only commission in operation failed to start proceedings against anyone. Juries were empanelled and some evidence reached the commissioners, but no presentments were taken because it was felt, with due respect for the law, that the accused should have the chance of self-acquittal before being formally charged. For that year, Hales and his fellow commissioners therefore called it a day.[29] The government's only gains from the commission's activities were an awareness of the inadequacy of existing agrarian legislation which could place innocent men in danger of the law, an

[24] For Hales's keenness to assert the commission's role as 'the fruit of the gospel, that is charity to our poor neighbours' see his letters to Warwick and Somerset (BM MS Lansdowne 238, ff. 319b *ff* and 321b *ff*, and Tytler I, pp. 113 *ff*).

[25] For the procedure, see E. Kerridge, 'The Returns of the Inquisitions of Depopulation', *Engl. HR* 70 (1955), pp. 214 *f*.

[26] See Lamond, p. lxi.

[27] Tytler I, p. 116.

[28] Others were intended. See the letters patent for the Midlands commission which authorized that 'like commissions with the instructions shall be directed to such persons as the protector and the rest of the council shall name in all other shires' to make their returns by next Michaelmas (*CPR* 1547–8, p. 419).

[29] Lamond, p. lxi. In 1607 the judges declared a commission of enquiry illegal because the accused had no redress against their informers. Such a ruling could not possibly have invalidated the commission of June 1548 (Kerridge, *op. cit.*, p. 222).

intimation of the worthlessness of an enquiry commission because of its limited powers and because of the impediments local gentlemen could place in its way,[30] and the chance to exercise clemency. In an unusual pardon, former agrarian offenders were forgiven on a strict condition of their future reform.[31]

This pardon cannot be interpreted as an act of gentle idealism. Although without precedent, it was not unique since the Northumberland regime employed the same device.[32] Essentially it declared the government's intention to secure remedy not revenue.[33] It also prepared the way for future action. As in Scotland, Somerset resorted to gentleness as a preliminary move, not a final solution, and used it to render himself blameless when he reached for tougher measures. The pardon laid down a 'deadline' for private remedy. When this ran out the work of the commission was resumed.[34]

Somerset revealed his keen support for an enclosure commission, especially one which provided remedy rather than made money, when in 1548 he told Hales: 'maugre the Devil, private profit, self-love, money and such like the Devil's instruments, it shall go forward.'[35] He revealed his support again when on his own authority he revived the commission in 1549. In April, within a month of the pardon, a proclamation, for which Somerset was later held solely responsible, announced the prosecution of offenders against the agrarian laws 'without pardon or remission' because they had shown contempt for the king's mercy.[36] In June the government girded its loins with a commission to 'disforest, dischase and dispark' the forfeited estates of the duke of Norfolk and Thomas Seymour. It also intervened to save the town of Godmanchester by ordering a distribution of ex-gild lands to the inhabitants and an increase in the number of available residences.[37] Then, early in July, during a temporary lull in the peasant risings, Hales with a different panel of commissioners from the previous year, received instructions to resume work in the Midlands and by September he was again at work.[38] Commissioners were appointed for other parts of the realm. A pro-

---

[30] Hales made these points in September 1549 (Lamond, pp. lix and lxi).

[31] See *ibid.*, Hughes and Larkin, 327; and 2/3 Edward VI, c. 39 (xvi).

[32] Northumberland's terms were identical, with the natural difference of the date (3/4 Edward VI, c. 24 (vi)). Normally general pardons excepted offences against the agrarian laws from the pardon.

[33] In the government's mind was probably the commission of 1517 which remedied little but raised revenue. Hales claimed that some subjects 'were persuaded that the end of the commission should be but a money matter, as it had been in times past' (Lamond, p. lix).

[34] A May proclamation (Hughes and Larkin, 333) claimed that a 'deadline' had been proclaimed, but there is no surviving proclamation. The 'deadline' was before 11 April when a proclamation announced an execution of the agrarian laws (Hughes and Larkin, 327), and was probably the last of March, the date mentioned in the statutory pardon (2/3 Edward VI, c. 39 (xvi)).

[35] Tytler I, pp. 115 f.

[36] Hughes and Larkin, 327. For Somerset's sole responsibility, see n. 183, p. 76.

[37] *CPR* 1548–9, p. 304, and *APC* II, pp. 294–6.

[38] The commission's activities have survived in a number of presentments, *The Domesday of Inclosures, 1517–18*, ed. I. S. Leadam (London, 1892), II, pp. 656 ff). The commission which received these presentments is to be distinguished from the 1548 commission which did not take presentments and which, except for Hales and Sir Fulke Greville had a different membership (Strype II (2), p. 348). For the instructions of the 1549 commission see PRO SP10/VIII/10, printed mistakenly as a proclamation by Hughes and Larkin (338). Hales seemed to write his 'Defence' while serving on the commission in September 1549 (Lamond, pp. lxii f).

clamation implying their existence for every county was probably an exaggeration,[39] but one was certainly planned for the West Country, and others operated in Cambridgeshire, Kent and Sussex.[40] In contrast to the 1548 commission, in 1549 the emphasis was upon direct action. No longer was the commission regarded as an enquiry, but as an instrument of 'redress and reform'.[41] In 1549 it may even have proceeded to try cases. At his trial Somerset was charged with establishing a commission to hear and determine.[42] This could not possibly have applied to the Midlands commission of 1548, but might well have related to the commissions of 1549. There was a tang of illegality about the commissions of 1549 which contrasted sharply with the strict adherence to legality shown in 1548. The instructions originally appended to the commission of 1548, for example, as well as the membership, were altered radically without further authentication by the seals. The amended instructions clarified clauses, included new instructions and, at the end, inserted: 'that then the same shall be reformed by the said commissioners'.[43] This final instruction caused problems for some of the commissioners. Because of it, those for Kent and Sussex certainly regarded their charge as one of redress, but found that the commission, which presumably was the one patented in June 1548, did not authorize it. They therefore called for letters of authority from Somerset and the council, but may have received, if anything, no more than a letter of exhortation from Somerset to reform themselves and another of instruction to proceed with a quorum of at least four commissioners.[44] Somerset's letters failed to state that the commissioners were to adjudicate, although both stressed the commission's function as one of redress, and Hales in September seemed to have no difficulties with his instructions. But this does not mean that Hales was merely conducting an enquiry, and that the commissioners of Kent and Sussex had fallen into a misunderstanding. Hales in September wrote a letter of self-defence to a friend at Court which contains an apparent contradiction: at one point he declared the commission useless, at another appreciated its outstanding value. These contrary statements are only reconcilable if Hales was discussing two distinct commissions—the commission of enquiry of 1548 about which he remarked: 'and yet if we had done the uttermost that it

[39] See Hughes and Larkin, 341.

[40] See Pocock, p. 17; F. W. Russell, *Kett's Rebellion in Norfolk* (London, 1859), App. K, and C. H. Cooper, *Annals of Cambridge* (Cambridge, 1842–1908), II, pp. 38–40; a further commission functioned which was led by Thomas Darcy and John Gates (see PRO SP10/VIII/24), which suggests that it encompassed the counties of Kent and Sussex.

[41] Compare the proclamation of June 1548 (Hughes and Larkin, 309) and the accompanying correspondence (BM MS Lansdowne 238, ff. 318b*ff*, and Tytler I, pp. 113 ff) with the enclosure proclamations of 1549 (Hughes and Larkin, 327, 334 and 341) and the attendant correspondence (PRO SP10/VIII/11 and 25).

[42] Foxe VI, p. 291 (xi).

[43] See PRO SP10/VIII/10 for the 1549 instructions and *CPR* 1547–8, pp. 419 *f* for the 1548 instructions.

[44] SP10/VIII/24. Somerset composed two letters in July for the further instruction of the enclosure commissioners (SP10/VIII/11 and 25). Each was signed by Somerset alone and survive in multiple copies, all signed by Somerset (4 for SP10/VIII/25 and 8 for the other letter). There is no evidence to suggest that either letter was dispatched.

required, we could have done little good, for it extended only to enquire and not to hear and determine', and a further commission, presumably functioning in 1549, which did possess these powers.[45] In 1548 Hales in a letter to Somerset had questioned the value of returning presentments to the central courts.[46] In 1549 it seemed that, backed by the protector who by July was keen 'on present reformation' rather than the future remedy he had promised in 1548, Hales sought to overcome the defects of the normal enclosure commission by infringing the law.[47]

The commissions of 1549 reflected badly both upon the government of the protectorate and upon the rule of the protector. While the government's plans were clearly the fruit of practical considerations, in seeking to implement its practical concerns, it showed itself grossly impracticable and inept and totally ignorant of what was possible. In the face of setbacks and towering difficulties, Somerset persisted stubbornly with inadequate measures essentially to satisfy the need for action and to justify earlier decisions. The affinity between his enclosure commission and his garrisons in Scotland is remarkably close.

In the interval between the enclosure commissions of 1548 and 1549, the government sought to further its social programme in parliament. Some of its attempted legislation was undoubtedly a response to the failure and revelations of the first commission, just as the revival of the commission in 1549 was a desperate consequence of the legislative failures of the second session.[48] But it would be wrong to regard the government's social policy in the second session as a simple and singleminded concentration on the agrarian problem. The planned reforms also included measures to preserve the quality of manufactured goods, anti-inflationary restrictions on foreign and domestic trade and a number of concessions to society which related to the taxes of the session. As with the enclosure commissions, the government acted because of the need to cope with inflation, but also to mollify society, and to make it accept the taxes granted in the same session. Rather than representing the basic substance of the government's social programme, the significance of its attempts at agrarian legislation lies in their failure. They formed that part of the government's programme which parliament found indigestible and spat out.

Four bills regulating the manufacture of goods were passed with no difficulty— two related to leather, one to malt and one to the false substitution of iron for steel.[49] Another concerning cloth collapsed.[50] Although the question of official

---

[45] See Lamond, pp. lii *ff*, especially pp. lvi and lxi.   [46] Tytler I, pp. 116*f*.

[47] Compare the insistence on immediate action in Somerset's letter to the enclosure commissioners in 1549 (PRO SP10/VIII/11) with his instruction to Hales in 1548 that he should inform the people that the government 'mind the due reformation of things amiss as time and occasion shall best serve to purpose' (BM MS Lansdowne 238, f. 319).

[48] For the connection between the 1548 commission and the second session, see Lamond, p. lxii. For the connection between the failure of the second session and the 1549 commissions, see Hales's remark in September that reform 'as yet in this realm cannot otherwise be done but by the execution of this commission' (Lamond, p. lvi).   [49] 2/3 Edward VI, cc. 9, 10, 11, 27.

[50] The bill for the false-making of cloth received no more than a first reading in the Commons (*Commons Journals*, 3 January), and was enacted in the following session (3/4 Edward VI, c. 2).

or private initiative remains unanswerable,[51] it seems that this body of measures received government support. The only measure which was clearly the fruit of private initiative, the failed cloth-manufacture bill, was adopted by the government which, as an interim arrangement, issued the regulations by proclamation.[52] Of the four acts, only the malt measure was a petition. The remainder appear to be official: they were framed as resolutions, and one was introduced in the Lords, and the other two were concluded hastily at the close of the session when Paget was accusing Somerset of extending the life of the session unnecessarily.[53] While the acts had a variety of purposes, they all seemed to be addressed to the problem of inflation as all of them sought to maintain value for money by preserving quality, and were attempts to maintain confidence and order as demonstrations of the government's concern for the plight of its subjects. A variety of official measures more directly related to inflation were also enacted; price-rigging by the private agreement of victuallers and of handicraft men was restrained, the export of bell metal and white ashes was forbidden, fast days were preserved so that 'much flesh shall be saved and increased' and for the sake of cheaper fish, those fishing in Iceland, Newfoundland and Ireland were freed of the exactions of the admiralty.[54] None of them were petitions, and there is no reason to doubt that they were government sponsored, while it is likely, as they were first introduced in the Lords, that the acts relating to fishing, Lent and the export of white ashes, began with the government. In addition, also to combat and relieve dearth, the government introduced a number of connected bills for the abolition of compulsory purveyance, the respite of homage, allowances to sheriffs and the commutation of town fee-farms for poor relief and local public works.[55] They were all part of one official scheme. Their interconnection is clearly evident in a memorandum of John Hales, composed before or early in the session, which mentioned all of the bills, related them to a tax on sheep and cloth and justified the tax as enabling the Crown to dispense with the funds sacrificed by the other bills.[56] The group of bills was probably first put to parliament in a portmanteau bill entitled 'bill for the commonwealth', since their introduction followed the disappearance of this bill.[57] In the closing days of the session all of the bills, but

---

[51] In identifying the official and private nature of the acts of the second session, I have used the guide-lines laid down in G. R. Elton's *Reform and Renewal* (Cambridge, 1973), ch. 4, particularly pp. 86 f.

[52] See Hales's 'Defence' in Lamond, pp. lxv f and Hughes and Larkin, 328.

[53] In a letter of 12 March (PLB) Paget called upon Somerset 'to end the parliament which both the houses say stays only upon your grace's pleasure'. The bills for the currying and the tanning of leather were both concluded on 13 March, and in great haste since both were only receiving their second reading in the Commons on 9 March, and came before the Lords for their first reading on 11 and 12 March (see *Journals of the House of Lords* and *Commons Journals*).

[54] 2/3 Edward VI, cc. 15, 26, 37, 19 and 6.

[55] *Ibid.*, cc. 3, 4 and 5. A bill for the respite of homage received two readings and disappeared (*Commons Journals* for 27 February and 8 March).

[56] See Lamond, pp. xlii *ff*.

[57] The bill received its only reading on 25 February (*Commons Journals*); the separate bills appeared in the following week: fee-farms (1 March), purveyance (26 February), respite of homage (27 February) and sheriffs (25 February), all in the Commons.

for the one relating to the respite of homage, were rushed into the statute book.[58] Although petitions, there can be no doubt that the bills were part of the government's programme. They were accepted by the government long before they were introduced,[59] and presumably provided another reason for Somerset's delay in closing the session. What is not so certain is the government's motive for supporting this package. Hales proposed the measures as remedies for society; in February Paget referred to them as concessions made to society to preserve its sympathy,[60] as did the government's instructions to the commissions involved in collecting the Relief.[61] As measures of reform the bills were clearly peripheral, while as concessions they appeared to serve a real purpose.

The failed agrarian programme rested on two bills devised by John Hales, one to promote the breeding of dairy cattle, the other to prevent the engrossing of farms. Although the government's connection is not explicit, it would be difficult to accept either as simply the public concern of a private member. Their basic issues, dearth and depopulation, to which Somerset had shown his attachment in the enclosure commission, and Hales's admission that, having failed with the commission, he resorted to statutory remedy, make it safe to assume that Somerset at least was one of the wise men whom Hales claimed to have made privy to his measures, and that, in this way, the bills received some government support and came to form part of its legislative programme.[62] In the case of the milch-kine bill there can be no doubt of official involvement. Its form, that of an official bill professing the king's intentions, and its persistence in parliament, in spite of a rough passage in the Commons, strongly imply government backing.[63] The official nature of the other bill is not so evident; its form, a petition to the king, and its parliamentary life which was so brief that it received no mention in parliamentary records, weigh against the fact that it was first introduced in the Lords 'and was the work of an associate of the government. What is known is that Hales devised it in the course of the session. It therefore constituted no specific part of a pre-planned programme. This, however, does not necessarily exclude it from the government's general policy. The bill suffered a quick death. When put to the Lords it seems to have raised such an outcry that it was immediately dropped.[64] The milch-kine bill had a much longer life, but never left the lower house. After amendment and redrafting it was finally rejected three months after its first reading.[65] Two further bills, one for disparking and the other for

---

[58] The fee-farms bill received its second reading in the Lords on 12 March, and, after being committed, was concluded on 14 March; the purveyance bill passed the Lords on 8 and 9 March; the sheriff's bill was concluded on 11 March (see *Journals of the House of Lords*).

[59] The government had accepted the scheme by 2 February, see Paget's letter of that date to Somerset (PLB).   [60] *Ibid.*

[61] R. C. Anderson, *Letters of the Fifteenth and Sixteenth Centuries* (Southampton Record Society, 1921), pp. 62–4.   [62] PRO SP10/II/21 and Lamond, pp. xlv *ff*; *ibid.*, p. lxii.

[63] Introduced on 26 November, it was committed twice, redrafted on 25 January and, after four readings, was dismissed on 23 February (see *Commons Journals*).

[64] The bill mentions petitions in the parliament to prevent the depopulation of towns (Lamond, p. xlvi). This might refer to the bill which received one reading on 18 January 'for inhabiting of cities and towns' (*Commons Journals*); Lamond, p. lxii.   [65] See n. 63

limiting the ownership of rabbit warrens, may also have been the work of the government.[66] Both related to the agrarian complaints of the time, and the former fell within the enclosure commission's range of concern.[67] Both were first put to the Lords and sailed through, a strong suggestion of government support. Then the first sank and the second stuck in the Commons. By the end of the session the rabbit warrens' bill had received only two readings in the lower house, and the imparking bill was rejected shortly before its close.[68] In spite of the number and variety of the agrarian bills placed before parliament, the only success, a small compensation, was an official act which safeguarded leasees and copyholders against the escheators on estates entering the king's hands as a result of wardship and forfeiture.[69]

Not only the government's agrarian reforms failed in this session. Noticeably, measures to prevent regrating and forestalling also come to grief, the chief of which was another bill devised by Hales.[70] This bill can be attributed to the government. It seemed part of an official plan to implant important measures of reform in the opening stages of the session. While two days after the opening, the milch-kine bill was introduced in the Commons, a few days later Hales's regrating bill was put to the Lords.[71] If these were tactics, they failed to work. The regrating bill succeeded in receiving the assent of the Lords, but it was then mauled by the lower house and at the close of the session still awaited its second and third reading.[72] In view of these failures, at the end of the session Somerset and his advisers must have felt unfulfilled and frustrated, particularly as valuable time had been wasted which might have been employed in preparing for the Scottish war.[73]

---

[66] Neither bill survives, but an idea of the content can be gleaned from the titles used in the *Commons Journals* and the *Journals of the House of Lords*. The parks bill is referred to as 'bill for the appointing of parks' (21 January, Lords), 'bill for putting down parks' (5 February, Commons), 'bill for having number of parks' (9 March, Commons), and clearly aimed to restrict the individual ownership of game parks. The rabbit bill likewise sought to restrict the possession of rabbit warrens, in this case to one per person. At various times it was entitled the bill 'touching the taking of warrens to farm' (6 February, Lords), the bill 'that no person shall take to farm any more warrens of game of coneys than one' (18 February, Lords) and 'the bill for having no more warrens of coneys but one' (7 March, Commons).

[67] It was a matter of concern for the enclosure commissions of 1548 and 1549 and gave rise to additional instructions in 1549 calling upon the commissioners to discover the number of ploughs and houses which had decayed because of new parks (see *CPR 1547–8*, p. 419, and Hughes and Larkin, 338). The measure was also in keeping with the government's disparking of Hampton Court Chase.

[68] See *Commons Journals* for 20 February and for 7 and 11 March.

[69] 2/3 Edward VI, c. 8. This appeared to be another part of the package of official bills which included the purveyance, sheriffs and fee-farms bills. Initiated in the Commons at roughly the same time, all proceeded through parliament together. For the escheators bill, see *Commons Journals*, 26 February, 6 and 7 March, and *Journals of the House of Lords*, 8, 9 and 11 March.

[70] The bill does not survive. For Hales's description of it, see n. 189, p. 77.

[71] See *Commons Journals* for 26 November and *Journals of the House of Lords* for 1 December.

[72] See *Journals of the House of Lords* for 24 January. The bill was committed in the Commons on 26 January, gave way to a new bill on 20 February (*Commons Journals*), the new bill was committed on 1 March, and it received its first reading in the Commons on 12 March. For its handling by the Commons, see Lamond, p. lxiii.

[73] The time wasted was reiterated by Paget in his correspondence with Somerset during the course

The failure of the government's agrarian policy in the second session is neither contradicted nor even qualified by the enactment in the same session of a tax on sheep and cloth. Although generally held to be a tax with a specific agrarian purpose,[74] the memorandum of John Hales and the preamble and terms of the statute itself give no indication that the act was regarded at the time as a device for restricting the number of sheep.[75] The assessment was noticeably geared to the weight of the fleece, whereas, if the tax had been intended as an agrarian measure, one would have expected either a flat rate on all sheep or the assessment to relate to the size of the flocks.[76] Moreover, Hales's primary interest in the tax was not because of the growth of sheep-farming but because of the financial needs of the government and the decline in government revenue from the sheep industry. In 1547 a proposal for a tax on sheep and other grazing stock had noted, by comparing the times of Edward III with those of Henry VIII, the gigantic decline in government revenue from sheep and cloth.[77] Hales pinpointed this in his memorandum: 'it appeareth by the records of the exchequer that Edward III had more revenue yearly by the custom of the staple than the king that dead is had by all the customs of the staple and cloths by £32,202 8s. 4d. at the least.'[78] In view of this historical information and the current boom in sheep-farming and cloth manufacture, a tax on sheep and cloth was the obvious answer for a government in search of new revenue. Only one contemporary has left evidence that the tax was regarded as a device to reduce sheep-farming. But the idea was proposed after the act had come into being, and rested on the assumption that the act did not perform this function.[79] Thomas Smith's *Discourse of the Commonweal* certainly mentioned the tax but presented it only as a design to discourage clothiers from following their trade; it said nothing of the tax's purpose in relation to sheep-farming. Moreover, the tone of the passage suggests that in discussing the tax Smith was indulging in heavy irony rather than seeking to state the truth about its real purpose.[80]

Nevertheless, the tax cannot be dismissed as a purely fiscal measure. In his memorandum Hales linked it with a recommendation for the abolition of purveyance and the commutation of the fee-farms of towns. He argued that purveyance was a major cause 'of the universal dearth of victuals in this realm'

---

of the parliamentary session (PLB, his letters to Somerset of 25 December 1548 and 25 January and 12 March 1549). Somerset's dissatisfaction with parliament was expressed not only by his revival of the commission, but also, if it were true, by the charge brought against him at his first trial that 'you said that the lords of the parliament were loth to incline themselves to reformation of enclosures and other things' (Foxe, VI, p. 291 (xvi)).

[74] See M. W. Beresford, 'The Poll Tax and Census of Sheep, 1549', *Agricultural History Review*, I (1953), pp. 10–12.

[75] Lamond, pp. xlii *ff*, and 2/3 Edward VI, c. 36.

[76] The act made a differentiation in assessment only between flocks of ten or less, twenty or less, or more than twenty (*ibid.* (vi)). But this was merely a concession to the poor.

[77] PRO SP10/II/13.

[78] Lamond, p. xliii. For the correct sum of money, see PRO SP10/V/20.

[79] See the anonymous tract *Policies to Reduce* which proposed a heavier levy on flocks over 200 (*TED* III, p. 327).

[80] Lamond, p. 91.

which the Crown could only afford to surrender if it found alternative revenue. In serving this purpose, the tax on sheep and cloth became more than simply a fiscal measure. It was also thought to provide the means for allowing the Crown to devote the fee-farms of towns for the benefit of the poor and the upkeep of roads and bridges, and was equally a social measure for this reason. Furthermore, as the tax insisted upon a survey of the sheep population, it provided a means of enforcing the Cromwellian statute for limiting the size of flocks, although there is no evidence of a contemporary appreciation of this fact.[81] The tax therefore did no more than to allow for the existence or possible enforcement of other social legislation. This was the nature and the extent of its non-fiscal function. The tax itself was clearly no consolation for the failure either of the first commission against enclosures or of the agrarian legislation of the second session.

The government's activities in the second session show that the programme of social reform was not a matter of top priority, and that it did not aim especially to favour the lower orders. In the early stages of the session, the government's priority seemed to be religious reform;[82] in the latter stages its priority seemed to be the grant of supplies and the concessions which the government felt it needed to sugar its fiscal demands. When the religious reforms had been enacted, the request for supplies began. When the supplies had been granted and the concessions made, the session was brought to an end. The measures of the government had no class preference, only a preference for the traditional order. It was not bent on serving the communalty at the expense of the chivalry, nor even the poor at the expense of the rich. The concessions and the subsidy were meant to appeal to aristocrat as well as peasant, to offer something to the rich as well as the poor, to the urban as well as the rural subject. The government was as much concerned about the oppressed aristocrat as the oppressed peasant.[83] Essentially the government's measures opposed the excesses which were destroying the traditional society and undermining the state. Its basic aim was not to redistribute wealth nor to encourage economic growth, but to preserve social harmony and political security. In particular, its main aim was to sustain the war-effort. The grant of supplies with its attendant reform acts was a matter of top priority because of the government's military ambitions. In addition the act against substituting iron for steel referred to the efficacy of weapons as well as tools, while the acts prohibiting the export of metal and of white ashes had guns and saltpetre in mind. Likewise, the agrarian programme justified itself in terms of military needs. Throughout the session, the government was deeply conscious of the fact that it was at war.[84]

[81] Lamond, pp. xlii *ff*, 2/3 Edward VI, c. 36 (xxxiii), and 25 Henry VIII, c. 13. This statute was included in the terms of reference of the enclosure commission.

[82] PLB, Paget to Somerset, letters of 25 December 1548 and 12 March 1549.

[83] The subsidy on goods rather than lands, the failed bill for respite of homage and the act for sheriffs' allowances were all concessions to the aristocracy (see below, p. 142 (n. 76) and above (pp. 49*f*). The enclosure commission's concern was for gentlemen whose capacity for hospitality had been reduced by inflation (Strype II (2), p. 363), and the milch-kine bill was moved by a similar concern (PRO SP10/II/21).

[34] See below, p. 142; 2/3 Edward VI, cc. 26, 27 and 37; see above, pp. 44*f*.

The government's final measures of social reform, those concerning the universities, again rested upon political considerations. In spite of the educational plans proposed at the time of the dissolution of the chantries, gilds and colleges, the government had been mainly content to preserve what already existed. Only in the universities did it take action to change the educational system.[85] The government's instrument of university reform were the two visitations of early 1549; its source of advice and inspiration, in all probability, was Thomas Smith.[86] Besides testing the religious conformity of the universities, the visitors had two main tasks: to reform the curriculum in order to provide a non-vocational humanist education which was designed to impart wisdom to the ruling class; and to promote a vocational side of university studies which had languished with the recent abolition of canon law as a university subject, in order that the universities should provide a training for other services than the church. Somerset, the patron of Thomas Smith and chancellor of Cambridge University, appeared involved in both matters. In each case the end in mind seemed political. His appreciation of a humanist university education, particularly for the aristocracy, is evident in his response to a suit for college lands: 'if learning decay, which of wild men maketh civil, of blockish and rash persons wise and godly counsellors, of obstinate rebels obedient subjects, and of evil men good and godly christians, what shall we look for else but barbarism and tumult.'[87] His inactivity in extending the system of secondary education and his support for a curriculum reform which threw out grammar and firmly established a schooling in classical and scriptural exegesis, indicated his eagerness to apply the humanist canon in the universities. More explicit was his interest in universities as a source of professional training, particularly through the study of civil law. At Cambridge it was planned, by merging Clare Hall with Trinity Hall, to produce an institution wholly devoted to civil law called King Edward's College. At Oxford it was hoped to establish a base for the subject in All Souls College by converting the fellowships in divinity to fellowships in civil law. The government's interest in vocational training was not confined to the civil law since it planned to found two colleges of medicine as well, but civil law seemed its major concern. By means of the study of civil law Somerset's aim was that the universities should continue to make the contribution to a trained bureaucracy which they had previously provided through the abolished study of the canon law. He acted in the belief that men trained in the civil law were vital to the state both as ambassadors and as civil servants.[88] If applied, this plan could have transformed the professional function

---

[85] For an account of the reforms, see J. Simon, *Education and Society in Tudor England*, pp. 252 *ff* Jordan I, pp. 326–38, M. H. Curtis, *Oxford and Cambridge in Transition, 1558–1642* (Oxford, 1959), chs. 1 and 6, and H. F. Kearney, *Scholars and Gentlemen* (London, 1970), pp. 22–4 and 34 *f*.

[86] The reformed curriculum as well as the idea of a college of civil law seemed closely related to Smith's academic interests (see M. Dewar, *Sir Thomas Smith, a Tudor Intellectual in Office* (London, 1964), ch. 2, and the views on education expressed in *A Discourse of the Commonweal*, Lamond, pp. 22–30).

[87] See W. Harrison, *Description of Britain*, ed. G. Edelen (New York, 1968), p. 81.

[88] His views on the matter were stated in a letter to Gardiner written before 25 March 1548: 'if many be incorporate to that study . . . among the more peradventure some shall rise well learned and

of the universities which had been essentially to train clergymen.[89] But Somerset proved as inept in this matter as in his direction of agrarian reform. After lying in the pipeline for well over a year,[90] the scheme finally collapsed in June 1549 when, faced by Ridley's objections, Somerset recalled him from the visitation and expected the remaining visitors to proceed in his absence. This they refused to do.[91] In the crisis of foreign war and insurrection the scheme sank, and, as a university subject, civil law, which had shown little life since the establishment of the regius professorships in the subject in 1540, withered away.

This was the substance of Somerset's public acts, but not the sum of his social programme which was also expressed by his own private deeds, chiefly a private act in the second session for granting greater security of tenure to some of his tenants, and his involvement in a private capacity with the supplications addressed to him by subjects. Neither adds much to the agrarian aspect of his policy. Essentially they represent a token effort on his part to live up to his exhortation that reformers should not forget the reformation of themselves.[92] Such private deeds reveal a man who was as acquisitive of virtue as he was of riches. They illustrate a further strand in his social policy which was the traditional aristocratic and regal desire to earn virtue by dispensing charity and justice.

His private act of parliament stated that he was acting 'of his charitable mind and accustomed goodness'.[93] In the absence of evidence for a profit motive, it would be uncharitable to deny this claim. What can be safely said is that the act was not unique,[94] and that it did not improve the security of tenure of all Somerset's customary tenants, since it affected only the minority of tenants who held demesne land by copy of court roll. As they were neither customary tenants nor lease-holders by indenture, these tenants lacked a means of action against their landlord in any court beyond a claim for the safety of their crops. Furthermore, as tenants at will, they could be evicted without reason or delay. Greater protection to these vulnerable tenants could be offered in two ways—by converting each individual tenancy into a leasehold by indenture, or by using a parliamentary statute to convert demesne copyholds *en bloc* into customary copyholds. In either way, the tenant received the additional protection of manorial custom, a means of personal action at common law and final redress in equity.[95] Tenure, it

---

fit for the commonwealth; whereas now . . . it is hard to find one . . . indeed there is none, whom for excellency we can have commended unto us.' In the same letter he mentioned a plan to establish a house of civil lawyers in London, equipped with the cream of the civil lawyers provided by Oxford and Cambridge 'to be ready . . . to show their advice . . . and so to practise in the Admiralty Court, or others, as they may' (Muller, App. 3). On 10 June 1549 he elaborated upon his design in a letter to Ridley: 'necessity compelleth us also to maintain the science [of civil law as opposed to divinity] and we are sure ye are not ignorant how necessary a study that study of civil law is to all treaties with foreign princes and strangers' (Burnet II (2), 60 (p. 331)).

[89] See Kearney, *op. cit.*, pp. 23 f.   [90] See n. 88

[91] PRO SP10/VII/34.

[92] Made, for example, to the enclosure commissioners in 1549 (PRO SP10/VIII/11).

[93] 2/3 Edward VI, c. 12.

[94] I. S. Leadam, 'The Security of Copyholders in Fifteenth and Sixteenth Century England', *Engl. HR* 8 (1893), p. 689.

[95] E. Kerridge, *Agrarian Problems in the Sixteenth Century and After* (London, 1969), pp. 86–9.

E

is true, remained vulnerable.[96] Even after the act, these tenants as customary copyholders could not regain possession through the common law, only money damages, not having a means of real action. Moreover, the tenant was obviously at a disadvantage in the manorial court when the defendant was the lord of the manor. Finally, remedy in equity was subject to the feeble enforceability of the prerogative courts. Nevertheless, the conversion of the demesne copyholder into a normal customary tenant imparted some security and protection.

Few could have gained all that much from Somerset's action. In contrast to the historians of the twentieth century, the contemporary social and political commentators, who were ready to applaud virtue as well as to condemn vice, made no comment. The evidence suggests a minor act, in keeping with the paternalism of the time and also with the government's agrarian concern since it made the conversion of the demesne into a simple sheep run more difficult. It was certainly not a challenge to contemporary values and practices, nor even an act of original and outstanding magnanimity, but essentially a bid for virtue at minimal cost.

In October 1549 Somerset was charged with holding 'against the law in your own house a court of requests'.[97] No other evidence indicates that this was so. Somerset certainly employed a master of requests, but his duty was administration not adjudication, particularly of the bills of complaint which were addressed to Somerset instead of to the king. The work involved placing the bills with their proper court, or establishing a private commission to hear and examine them. Of the surviving bills addressed to Somerset, the bulk were filed in the proceedings of the court of requests, clearly suggesting that while Somerset had no private court of requests, he was quite deeply and extensively involved in the work of the official court of requests. This involvement must be accepted as part of his social policy. But there is no reason to regard it as an important component of his agrarian programme, since it was not concerned too much with the interests of the down-trodden peasant.

Of the surviving suits, which passed through the hands of his master of requests, those involving rack-renting, enclosure, loss of common rights and deliberate depopulation are at a minimum. In fact, of the ninety surviving bills addressed to Somerset during the protectorate only two dealt with the agrarian problem as the commentary, statutes, commissions and proclamations of the time defined it. The nature of Somerset's concern is revealed in his reaction to all these bills. Without a doubt, his involvement was with the court of requests rather than with the courts of star chamber or chancery. But he seemed to appreciate Requests because of the degree of personal participation it allowed him, not because he regarded it as the poor man's court. The bills directed to Requests suggest that he saw the court essentially as a source of justice for the unfortunate.

Occasionally he used a private letter to refer a complaint either to Nicholas

[96] E. Kerridge, *Agrarian Problems in the Sixteenth Century and After*, pp. 70 *f* and 73 *f*.

[97] This matter is dealt with at length in my article 'Protector Somerset and Requests', *Historical Journal* 17 (1974), pp. 451 *ff*.

Hare, one of the official masters of requests, or to local commissioners. Of the twenty-six surviving letters, most lack social or sentimental comment and merely call for equity to be dispensed; but in eight instances they expressed an element of favour. This was not in support of a victim of landlord exploitation or of poverty. In five of the instances, the plaintiffs were women, in four, widows, with no clear indication of impoverishment. Somerset meant it when in one of his letters of commission he asserted: 'We consider it no small part of our charge to defend the widows and such as lack defence and succour.' Furthermore, there is no discernible correlation between his degree of participation and the plaintiff's poverty. One finds him supporting the suit of a gentleman with a letter of commission and also the suit of one of the king's bodyguard, while the two bills involving enclosure of the common were dispatched to Requests without any personal involvement.

Somerset was undoubtedly prepared to respond conscientiously to the bills of complaint addressed to him, but not because of an idealistic preference for the lower orders, nor because of a need for a further instrument to remedy the agrarian problem or to protect the poor. He acted because of a conventional concern for the prosecution of justice. He summed up his interest himself when in December 1547 he justified his interference in a Requests matter with the words: 'We, minding that justice shall not decay for lack of prosecution.' Essentially he sought to acquire the traditional badge of a virtuous ruler, a concern for impartial justice.

Somerset's social concern was basically political and personal. In this respect his consideration for poverty cannot be described as a genuine concern for the plight of the poor. Poverty was appreciated as a cause of military insufficiency and peasant insurrection, and as a means of earning virtue by remedial acts of justice and charity. The scale of his attack on poverty and its justification allows no other conclusion. Somerset had some concern for the lower orders but because he subscribed to common aristocratic feelings, not because of an unusual compassion. As a ruler he acted conventionally for the preservation of the state; as a person he sought for a virtuous reputation. His measures were less ordinary than his motives. An enclosure commission to hear and determine and a tax which allowed traditional resources to be used for social purposes were original, but neither imaginative, practical nor penetrating. The measures tended to be minor and superficial, and, in the case of the second enclosure commission, even illicit, and generally prone to failure. The outstanding feature of the programme was its lack of success. This failure did not stem from the fall of the government and the victory of reaction. It derived from the inadequacy of Somerset's chosen means. In comparison with Somerset's enclosure commissions, those of Wolsey were a dazzling success. In comparison with his legislative achievements, no other government could be said to have failed. He even failed in the relatively simple task of uniting Clare Hall and Trinity Hall to found a college of civil law. Somerset succeeded only to the extent of acquiring a reputation for goodness in spite of his activities as a builder of sumptuous houses, as a sheep-master, as an encloser and a rack-renter;[98] but by the time of his fall even his reputation was not what he would have wished, having become tangled with a reputation for radicalism, largely because of his behaviour towards peasant rebels.[99]

Conditions and Comment

The social policy of the Somerset regime with its characteristic emphasis upon agrarian problems cannot be dismissed as an anachronistic attempt to solve problems which belonged to the past.[100] Although heavily reliant on old devices and old laws, basically it was a response to the present, in particular the exceptional pressures bearing upon English society in the 1540s largely as a result of the prolonged wars with Scotland and France.

The outstanding pressure was inflation. The late 1540s were rivalled only by the 1590s in the sixteenth century, and the sixteenth century only by the twentieth century for the rate at which prices rose. The inflation of these years was extreme and unprecedented, and by the 1550s agricultural prices exceeded those of the 1530s by 95 per cent.[101] While the debate on its character and cause continues, one fact seems established—its specific connection with war. The government's feverish search for cash to pay for its wars resulted first in heavy taxation, land sales and loans, which acted together to discourage private saving; and secondly in the debasement of the coinage which affected the exchanges, the supply of money and, because of its effect on the bimetallic flow, the stock of precious metals. The outcome was a spectacular eruption in prices, already rising in response to the gradual growth of the population and the recovery of the economy after the stagnation and decline of the late middle ages.[102] In this situation, three abundant harvests in 1546–8 provided relief, as well as masking the rate of inflation of consumables in the general statistics of the price rise.[103] At the same time, the glaring disparity between grain prices and the prices of other victuals helped to focus contemporary attention on the latter,[104] persuading the government to blame production rather than marketing, sheep-farming rather than regrating for the dearth.[105] In this decade of inflation, the run of good harvests probably

---

[98] See n. 124, p. 63. These private activities will be the subject of a further study.*

[99] See below, pp. 98 f.   [100] Jordan I, p. 412.

[101] R. B. Outhwaite, *Inflation in Tudor and Early Stuart England* (London, 1969), pp. 13 and 43. While questioning the concept of a 'price revolution', J. D. Gould accepts a spectacular rise in the 1540s which was 'comparable with 20th century experience', see 'The Price Revolution Reconsidered' in *The Price Revolution in Sixteenth Century England*, ed. P. H. Ramsey (London, 1971), p. 94.

[102] Outhwaite, *op. cit.*, pp. 43–55.

[103] W. G. Hoskins, 'Harvest Fluctuations and English Economic History, 1480–1619', *Agricultural History Review* 12 (1964), pp. 28 and 32. In 1547 the price of wheat was lower than it had been for twenty years (P. Bowden, 'Agricultural Prices, Farm Profits and Rents', in the *Agrarian History of England and Wales*, ed. J. Thirsk (Cambridge, 1967), IV, p. 596). Also see J. D. Gould, *The Great Debasement* (Oxford, 1970), p. 83.

[104] See for example, *Sermons of Hugh Latimer*, ed. G. E. Corrie (Parker Society, 1844), pp. 98 f, and Lamond, pp. 37 and 52.

[105] See above, pp. 41 f.

helped to promote grazing at the expense of tillage through increasing surplus purchasing power, thus creating a buoyant demand for wool, and through reducing the incentive to concentrate upon farming corn by lowering its price. Similar runs of good harvests in the late fifteenth century, in the second decade of the sixteenth century and in the 1530s had had the same effect.[106] For this reason sheep-farming, which benefited from a booming cloth trade with Antwerp, most likely received an additional stimulus, and thus, in an age of land shortage and rising food prices, was able, at least, to hold its own and to remain with some justification the villain of the piece.[107]

The good harvests ended in 1548 and three wretched harvests followed.[108] The harvest failure of 1549, however, cannot be held responsible for Somerset's social programme which was well under way before April 1549,[109] the earliest possible date for predicting the harvest, although it may have influenced the employment of enclosure commissions in that year. Poor harvests were much more responsible for the social programme of the succeeding regime. Somerset's government provided agrarian measures during a glut of corn. This behaviour was certainly abnormal by the standards of the late sixteenth century when agrarian measures normally accompanied harvest failure, but not by the standards of the early sixteenth century when, with the exception of the early 1530s, the opposite happened, presumably because of the effect of good harvests on the development of sheep-farming.[110] It is clear then that Somerset acted typically in critical circumstances when the persistence of good harvests seemed the only barrier against a terrible dearth which contemporaries felt could weaken the military might of the realm, cause insurrection and lead to political disaster.[111] As cheap corn could not be relied upon to last for ever, a responsible government had no choice but to act.

The second outstanding pressure was the demands of war. Having lasted so long, the wars by the late 1540s were placing an impossible strain upon both the state's finances and its military capacity. Traditionally commentators had moaned that the English were losing the ability to fend for themselves. This was spotlighted in the 1540s when the lack of troops and their poor quality was a source of constant worry and complaint, solved only by employing foreign mercenaries, even

---

[106] Bowden, *op. cit.*, pp. 629 *f* and 634–8.

[107] I. Blanchard in his 'Population Change, Enclosure and the Early Tudor Economy' (*Econ. HR* 2nd ser., 23 (1970), pp. 427 *ff*) questions the extension of sheep grazing as a source of social pressure in the sixteenth century in view of the failure of pasture rents to rise noticeably, and because of the relative unprofitability of sheep-farming as shown by his calculations (*op. cit.*, p. 443, App. A). These calculations lack conviction because they omit from consideration the crucial decade of the 1540s. Moreover, if sheep-farming was extended by means of common and demesne pastures and more intensive use of the existing pastoral acreage (see Gould, *op. cit.*, p. 152), this would not necessarily have led to a dramatic rise in the rent of pasture lands, but could still have caused hardship.

[108] Hoskins, *op. cit.*, p. 28.

[109] As Hoskins suggests, *ibid.*, p. 28.

[110] The generalizations of L. A. Clarkson (*The Pre-Industrial Economy in England 1500–1750* (London, 1971), p. 164) and M. W. Beresford (*The Lost Villages of England* (London, 1954), p. 133) which present a simple connection between bad harvests and government intervention, need to be modified.

[111] E.g., Lamond, pp. 52 *f*.

for the defence of the realm and the maintenance of order within it.[112] At the root of the problem was not so much the process of depopulation, but the exhaustion of the country's traditional military resources by the very size, ambitiousness and duration of the government's military commitments. Nevertheless, although the diagnosis was incorrect, the complaint of the enclosure commission that 'the force and puissance of this our realm which was wont to be greatly feared of all foreign powers, is very much decayed', had a precise contemporary relevance.[113] The diagnosis, moreover, was something thrust upon the government by its inability to grasp the obvious remedy and bring the war to an end.

There is no reason to believe that the government regarded the realm's military incapacity as a recent development. It knew that by a process of depopulation the major damage had occurred between the reigns of Edward I and Henry VII.[114] Nor did it believe that the military problem was a result of population decline. As it regarded depopulation in a military context, it used the term to express a decline in the quality of the population. In its view prosperous homesteads engaged in husbandry provided the best soldiers. When it mentioned depopulation and its effect upon the military resources of the state it meant the reduction in prosperous homesteads, particularly of family farms, not a reduction in the population.[115] The government could therefore talk of depopulation in a period of population growth without being unrealistic. Nor was the government rendered unrealistic for exaggerating the rate at which tillage was converting to pasture. Even if the pace of conversion was no longer rapid, [116] grazing remained a reasonable culprit for the political difficulties of the realm since its prevalence and flourishing state prevented any recovery of military strength, except by a major change in the military system itself. Aware of a long-standing decline, the government with modest realism did not act to provide a complete remedy. Its measures were meant to prevent the rot from extending further.[117] It can therefore be accused of conservatively retaining the traditional military system which social changes had debilitated, but not of parroting former complaints about depopulation which had no relevance to the needs and conditions of the present, nor of seeking to prevent developments from occurring which had already happened. The government was responding to present needs while being aware of the long-term developments which had made these needs so difficult to meet. Sustaining the government's social programme was the knowledge that once upon a time England had been more capable than at present of indulging in prolonged wars.[118] In this respect the decay of the commonwealth was an obvious fact, and its recovery, in the circumstances, an urgent requirement. As this knowledge was brought home not only by an awareness of the achievements of Edward I but also by the difficulties of

---

[112] See my article 'The Problem of the Far North: a study of the crisis of 1537 and its consequences, *Northern History*, 6 (1971), pp. 61f, and above, p. 35, and below, pp. 92 and 95.

[113] Strype II (2), p. 349.

[114] See Lamond, p. lxiii. Paget believed that enclosures were at least sixty years old (Strype II (2), p. 432).

[115] See *ibid.*, P and Q.

[116] See Blanchard, *op. cit.*, pp. 438f.

[117] See Hales's 'Defence' in Lamond, p. lxiii.

[118] See Strype II (2), Q.

waging war in the late 1540s, the programme of the government can be said to have related closely to its basic needs which Somerset as a soldier and advocate of war must have fully appreciated.

Other factors such as the problem of the released church and chantry lands, the demands of a growing population and the social conscience of protestantism played some part in the programme's evolution but they were supplementary to the condition of war which gave the decade its economic and political character. The close connection between the war and the social programme lies in the fact that the latter's beginning coincided not with Somerset's acquisition of the protectorship but with the resumption of war. The programme's character, moreover, relied upon the government's war requirements which prevented it from dealing with the evil of debasement and silenced its comments on usury. Its essential purpose was to meet the military needs of a state at war: to maintain stability at home so that the government could concentrate on foreign affairs, and to find the finances, victuals and manpower for continuing the war abroad.

While conditions provided the necessity for action, impassioned comment also summoned the government to act. The atmosphere of crisis in which the programme emerged was charged not only by economic circumstances and government interest, but also by the public concern of a number of social and political commentators. In inciting the government to act and in proposing remedies they had a role to play in the social programme.

Although often described as a group or a party, these commentators on the commonwealth did not share an organization or speak with one voice.[119] They neither worked together nor participated in any way to formulate a common programme. They were a party only because, while divided by a variety of beliefs, they shared many assumptions and a small number, as individuals, were allowed to advise the government. Without exception they subscribed to the traditional ideal of the state as a body politic in which every social group had its place, function and desert. They assumed that, while before God all men were equal in the last resort, on earth social inequality represented by degree and recognized by adherence to vocation was essential for the maintenance of good governance. They execrated covetousness and idleness as the twin evils besetting society, and, as a means of reforming society, tended to exhort man to reform himself. In addition, none of them looked kindly on sheep-farming while revering tillage, and all were deeply concerned about the price rise and its effects. In these matters they pleaded with rulers to reform society, and proposed various means, but not by changing its structure. Their thinking was paternalistic and conservative. Although they censured the nobility, it was for malpractices, not for being the ruling class. Their ideal was a benevolent aristocracy, maintaining harmony by acts of hospitality and charity. They all showed concern for the poor, but accepted

[119] This impression is based on W. R. D. Jones, *The Tudor Commonwealth, 1529–1559*; A. B. Ferguson, *The Articulate Citizen and the English Renaissance*; J. W. Allen, *A History of Political Thought in the Sixteenth Century* (London, 1928); R. B. Outhwaite, *Inflation in Tudor and Stuart England*; and my own study of the surviving tracts and sermons of social commentary.

the need for poverty. None questioned the necessary existence of the rich and the poor. As a spur to the charitable impulse, a punishment for sin and an exercise for virtue, the poor were appreciated as invaluable. At the same time all of them condemned the oppression of the poor, not necessarily because of a genuine concern for the personal plight of the victims, but because of a practical political concern for the security of the state, and a christian concern, intensified by protestantism, for the godliness which rested on charity. What moved them basically was not the prospect of people starving to death, but the wrath of God and the fear of oppressed peasants failing to provide the state with its military needs or rising to destroy the nobility, the linchpin of order and the bulwark against foreign conquest.

The remarkable flood of published comment in these years sprang from a number of sources. Humanism made a contribution with its emphasis on civic virtue and state regulation; and so did protestantism with its insistence on organized charity, its need to match the corruption of the Roman church with the worthiness of the reformed regime, and its revaluation of the role of good works. Rebellion in 1549, moreover, produced defences against the ancient charge that heresy was socially disruptive, arguing that they were not the work of the commentators, but of conspiring massmongers and covetous sheep-masters, and reiterations of the necessity for obedience. Finally, the minority of Edward VI occasioned the publication of advice to a ruler while inflation provided evidence with which covetousness could be condemned, as well as reasons for proposing forms of state interference and regulation. Above all, the flood of comment stemmed from the crisis of the time and the permission granted by a monarchical and aristocratic system which it sought to uphold. The commentary was encouraged because it possessed a general appeal. Just as there is no reason to believe in an exclusive relationship between the commonwealth commentators of the 1530s and Thomas Cromwell, there is no evidence to suggest an exclusive relationship between the protector and the commentators of the late 1540s. Somerset spoke their language, but it was the *lingua franca* and the popular literary conceit of the time.[120] Somerset undoubtedly responded to the climate of opinion which commentary generated as well as reflected, but so, it seems, did most politicians, particularly the advanced protestants.

While it would be misleading to regard Somerset alone as being moved by contemporary commonwealth comment, it would also be wrong to regard the whole corpus of its concerns as acceptable to him. Because of the government's dependence upon debasement, the commentators who explained the price rise in terms of it had to be ignored in preference to those who attributed it to less inconvenient causes such as sheep-farming and covetousness. For Somerset the

---

[120] For Somerset's use of 'commonwealth' language, see n. 35 and n. 202, pp. 6 and 79, and his declared wish to Ridley that 'flesh and blood and country might not more weigh with some men than godliness and reason' in Cooper, *Annals of Cambridge*, II, p. 34. The use of the language in government circles, not only under Somerset but also after his fall, is evident in royal proclamations, e.g., Hughes and Larkin, 373 and 377.

choice lay between the views represented by Sir Thomas Smith which connected inflation with debasement, and those of John Hales which connected it with large-scale sheep-farming, purveyance and the regrating of victuals.[121] Somerset's preoccupation with Scotland determined his choice. Hales was backed up to the hilt, and Smith eventually fell into disfavour. Smith's influence was only paramount in the field of university education, to the exclusion of the ideas of the clerical commonwealthmen who tended to insist on preserving the universities primarily as a training ground for the clergy.[122] The priority of war also caused Somerset to resist the strong feeling of commonwealth comment that the confiscated wealth of the church and chantries should be used to improve society,[123] and not be dissipated simply as revenue.

The material needs of the state determined the government's selection of the current ideas and proposals of reform. The same cannot be said of Somerset's personal material needs. His own activities as a sheep-master and imparker did not deter him from applying a public policy which realized the public criticism of such practices.[124] Somerset was capable of operating a double standard. He possessed the versatility to practise what in others he found virtue in condemning. For this reason he enjoyed the best of both worlds and was able to accept into his service and to receive sympathetically commentators who by implication condemned him with their criticism.

Two commentators contributed directly to the programme of social reform. Thomas Smith's educational concerns dominated the instructions issued to the university visitors of 1549.[125] On the other hand, John Hales was the intellect behind the economic measures. He was undoubtedly the master-planner of the enclosure commissions. Warwick accused him of originally suing for the commission, a responsibility Hales denied.[126] Nevertheless, he was the chief commissioner of the only commission which operated in 1548—evident in his correspondence with Somerset while serving on it—and his concern for the enterprise as a whole was expressed in his request that the other commissions be set afoot.[127] He reappeared on the Midlands commission in 1549, the only member of the

[121] For Smith's economic and social views, his authorship of *A Discourse of the Commonweal* and his relationship with Somerset, see Mary Dewar, *op. cit.*, pp. 49–54; for Hales's economic and social views, see Strype II (2), Q, Lamond, pp. xlii–lxvii and PRO SP10/II/21.

[122] The opposing clerical view was put by Ridley and by Latimer (Cooper, *op. cit.*, II, pp. 33–5 and 26).

[123] In this respect, Lever's sermon preached before the king in 1550 contained an attack on the actions of the Somerset regime (Thomas Lever, *Sermons, 1550*, ed. E. Arber, English Reprints, 25 (London, 1870), pp. 32*f*, 37 and 81).

[124] At his death he owned 2,000 sheep (BM MS Egerton 2815); earlier in the reign he received a licence to impark (*CPR* 1547–8, pp. 123*f*), and during the time of the protectorate he was engaged in enlarging Savernake park (Kerridge, *op. cit.*, p. 101), an act which, although accompanied by compensation, suggested that Somerset's private and public life existed in separate chambers. For the family's rent-raising activities see Kerridge, *Victoria County History*, Wiltshire, IV, pp. 60–62. For an intimation of Somerset's contribution, see his 'exploitation' of the Lisle estate once it was in his hands (Thesis, pp. 249*f*).

[125] See n. 85 and n. 86, p. 54.   [126] BM MS Lansdowne 328, f. 322.

[127] Tytler I, pp. 113*ff*, and BM MS Lansdowne 238, ff. 319b*ff*.

1548 commission to do so except for Sir Fulke Greville, and also featured on the commission for examining the forfeited estates of Thomas Seymour and the duke of Norfolk for unnecessary enclosure.[128] He was certainly responsible for the pardon which paved the way for the commissions of 1549,[129] and his express dissatisfaction with a commission of enquiry may well have produced the commissions to hear and determine of 1549.[130] The declared purpose of the commissions, moreover, complied closely with his economic thinking.[131] In addition, the measures of the second session were also inextricably connected with him. He formulated the scheme which produced the acts for the abolition of compulsory purveyance, the commutation of fee-farms and the relief on sheep and cloth, as well as devising three bills which appeared to have government sanction.[132] If ever an intellectual who was not a member of the government but merely a consultant can be said to have directed policy in this period, it was Hales.

He certainly lacked the brilliance and originality of Thomas Smith, but possessed more commonsense in his thinking,[133] if not in his actions which were prone to extreme indiscretions. Part of the trouble with the first enclosure commission was the fiery exhortations he delivered to the assembled Midlanders, and the farms bill presumably sank so abruptly in the Lords because of the denunciation of the nobility in its preamble.[134] His commentary resembled Latimer's in both manner and inspiration. It possessed only a smattering of humanism. Basically it was moved by protestantism. To avoid the wrath of God and the fate of Sodom, he urged the need to follow the teaching of the gospel and to care for the poor. In spite of his proposals for remedy by the state, reform, as he saw it, lay for the most part with the private individual. Covetousness could only be overthrown and the realm revived by following Christ's example. His letters to Warwick and Somerset, the speeches he delivered in June 1548 and the letter he wrote in self-defence in September 1549 all indicate a man who saw the traditional wrongs of society in an extremely vivid light because of the fervour of his protestantism.[135] He differed from Latimer in having proposals for the constructive reform of society by state action. He was not content merely to bully the English with the threat of Judgement Day.

[128] See n. 38, p. 46, and *CPR* 1548–9, p. 304.
[129] Lamond, p. lxi.   [130] See above, pp. 47 f.
[131] See above, and p. 44 f n. 121.   [132] See above, pp. 49–51.

[133] The character and quality of their minds is evident in a comparison of the 'Defence' and the *Discourse*. Lacking in the 'Defence' is the ingenuity of the *Discourse*, but also absent is the *Discourse*'s tendency to sweep away difficulties: for example, in response to the view that the device of prohibiting imports might affect the country's foreign affairs, all the Doctor can say is that the good of the commonweal should come before foreign leagues (pp. 67–9), and the objection that foreigners might exclude English exports in retaliation for the exclusion by the English of their products is dismissed on the grounds that this would not happen because foreigners had more need of English goods than the English had of theirs (*ibid.*); a further objection that the recommended free export of corn might cause continual dearth at home is dismissed with the opinion that this would only happen in the short term (pp. 53–5). While Smith's diagnosis of the causes of inflation seems more convincing than Hales's explanation, Hales's remedies have a practicality which Smith's devices appear to lack.

[134] See below, p. 78.
[135] BM MS Lansdowne 238, ff. 319b *ff* and 321b *ff*, Strype II (2), Q, and Lamond, pp. lii *ff*.

His protestantism may have helped in establishing the rapport he enjoyed with Somerset. Nevertheless any explanation of his influence as a government consultant cannot overlook an outstanding and unusual feature of his work, its preoccupation with war. His first known tract had commended Henry VIII for maintaining peace, but, ironically, its presentation was soon overtaken by war.[136] By the late 1540s Hales had changed his tune and matched Somerset as a fervent supporter of the Scottish war. Not only did he enthuse over it; he also justified the necessity for reform in terms of waging the war more effectively. He argued that the government needed to implement reforms now rather than wait for a more suitable moment for three reasons. Two of them related to foreign war, the third, to peasant insurrection. He partly upheld the need to fight for Boulogne, a matter without appeal to Somerset, but he also declared the necessity of immediate social remedy because of 'Scotland, parcel of the kingdom of England, which I believe we shall never obtain but by force, as long as the world doth stand.' Hales was unique among contemporary commentators in conceiving the problem of dwindling military resources specifically in terms of war abroad as opposed to home defence. He presented a direct connection between the Scottish war and the enclosure commission by holding:

> In the mean season great loss is of our men, as it is not possible but to be as long as wars do continue. And therefore methinketh that as the wise husbandman maketh and maintaineth his nursery of young trees to plant in the stead of the old, when he seeth them begin to fail because he will be sure at all times of fruit, so should political governors (as the King's Majesty and his council mind) provide for the increase and maintenance of people so that at no time they may lack to serve his highness and the commonwealth, which thing as yet in this realm cannot otherwise be done but by execution of this commission.[137]

In making this point, Hales was holding a view which directly opposed Smith's belief that while a problem, the decay of tillage would only seriously affect the realm's military capacity if it continued over the next twenty years at the rate of the last twenty.[138] The immediate problem, according to Smith, was inflation and the basic remedy was to end debasement and reform the coinage.[139] Hales was also concerned with inflation; but he was the most systematic exponent of the idea, a cornerstone of Somerset's social programme, that inflation was not the result of debasement but other factors such as sheep-farming, cattle-grazing, the decay of tillage and marketing abuses such as regrating and purveyance.[140] Faced by this choice of remedy, Somerset's predilection for Hales seemed inevitable. How could he resist what so exactly met his needs? As a governor intent on an active foreign policy, as a military leader long engaged with the

---

[136] *LP* XVII, App. 1.
[137] Lamond, pp. lv f.
[138] Lamond, p. 48.
[139] *Ibid.*, p. 69.
[140] For its most direct statement, see his memorandum on dearth (Lamond, pp. xlii *ff*).

problems of finding adequate troops and cheap victuals, as a ruler committed to the debasement of the coinage for his financial resources, Somerset must have inclined naturally towards Hales's measures and proposals which concentrated on improving the country's military power while managing not to blame, even by implication, Somerset's aggressive and sustained warfare for the plight of the realm.

The connection between the programme and other commentators is not so clear-cut and conclusive. The likelihood is that Latimer carried some weight, especially as he was allowed to preach the Lenten sermons to the Court in 1548 and 1549; and, probably, so did William Turner, Thomas Becon and John Hooper whom Somerset admitted either to his service or to his hospitality during the protectorate. Other influences which can be taken into account are William Forrest's *Pleasant Poesie of Princely Practice* and the two tracts, one by Robert Crowley, the other anonymous, published at the time of the second session. On the other hand, a certain amount of commentary which has been associated with the social measures can be excluded from consideration simply because it post-dated them—particularly, the sermons of Thomas Lever which belong to 1550 and 1551, and both *Policies to Reduce* and Smith's *A Discourse of the Commonweal* which appeared late in 1549.[141]

The problem is not only to demarcate the area of likely influence but to pin-point the impact of these sources of influence upon the social programme. The evidence of Latimer's surviving sermons, those of 1548, 1549 and 1550, reveal little concern with agrarian matters. In January 1548 Latimer delivered his suggestive 'Sermon on the Ploughers', but its subject had nothing to do with sheep-farming and tillage. The plough was merely a metaphor for the function of the clergy.[142] His Lenten sermons of 1549 began relevantly by charging 'you landlords, you rent-raisers, I may say you step-lords, you unnatural lords' with oppressing the poor and debilitating the realm, and in this first sermon Latimer was presumably bewailing the failure of the second session, and perhaps also the feebleness of the 1548 enclosure commission, since he declared: 'We have good statutes made for commonwealth as touching commoners and enclosers, many meetings and sessions, but in the end of the matter there cometh nothing forth.'[143] However, the agrarian problem was not the main secular subject of this group of sermons. It took second place to his plea for impartial justice and proper official conduct. The covetousness he largely attacked was that of judges and government officials, and the sympathy he expressed for the poor related to their legal rights. The same can be said of his 1550 Lenten sermons which have also survived. After initially dwelling upon the causes of poverty and the evils of enclosure, essentially to exonerate himself of the responsibility for the risings of 1549, he confined himself

---

[141] For the dating of the *Discourse*, see Mary Dewar, 'The Authorship of the Discourse of the Commonweal', *Econ. HR* 2nd ser., 19 (1966), p. 389. The *Policies to Reduce* postdated the price-fixing proclamation of 2 July (*TED* III, pp. 340*f*).

[142] *Sermons of Hugh Latimer*, pp. 59 *ff*.

[143] *Ibid.*, pp. 98*f* and 101.

to a discussion of official corruption and injustice.[144] All that is known of the missing 1548 Lenten sermons is their subject—restitution.[145] As the sermons inspired certain officials to hand back ill-gotten gains the subject was clearly the familiar one of official corruption.[146] Whether landlords were also called upon to make restitution remains unknown but, in the light of Latimer's tendency to dwell discursively and repetitiously upon a few themes, it is a distinct possibility that, as with his later sermons, those delivered to the Court in 1548 mainly called upon officials to reform themselves by performing their duties properly.

It cannot be ruled out that Latimer had some effect on the agrarian programme. Strikingly, the interval between the pardon offered to offenders against the agrarian laws and the proclamation in which Somerset, apparently on his own initiative, declared its revocation was filled by five of Latimer's Lenten sermons. But their responsibility for the revival of the commission is rendered doubtful for the reason that the pardon came after Latimer's plea for remedy, and the pardon's revocation was in rough agreement with the terms of the statutory pardon which proposed a 'deadline' for the end of March. However, as the rest of the council seemed against the revival of the commission, Latimer's sermons might have exerted influence in encouraging Somerset to proceed alone.[147]

While some doubt must surround Latimer's direct responsibility for the enclosure commissions of 1548 and 1549, what is undeniable is his contribution, not in defining problems and suggesting remedy, but in generating and maintaining the charged atmosphere of the time which centred on an urgent feeling that things were out of joint and immediate remedial action should be taken. Furthermore, Somerset's programme included not only economic measures but also good intentions to safeguard justice and, in a minor way, to counter corruption.[148] Although he was fulfilling by such actions a duty which, with the defence of the realm, was traditionally expected of the virtuous ruler, it is possible that his keenness to conform with tradition owed something to Latimer's hot breath.

Some time in 1550 Thomas Smith sought to defend himself in a letter to Somerset's wife, mainly against the charge of being corrupt and neutral in religion. In doing so he condemned 'these hotlings' who shrank away when danger was present and now when it was past 'they can come to kneel upon your grace's carpets and to devise commonwealths as they like, and are angry that other men be not so hasty to run straight as their brains crow.'[149] The danger to which he referred was the persecution of Henry VIII's closing years; the men accused of shrinking away were those who had gone into hiding or exile. There can be

---

[144] E.g. *ibid.*, pp. 126–8, 139–40, 142, 145–6, 152, 155–60, 171, 178–82, 185–8 and 191; *ibid.*, pp. 247 *ff* and 255 *ff*.

[145] At Lent 1550 Latimer stated: 'I have now preached three Lents. The first time I preached restitution' (*ibid.*, p. 262).

[146] A. G. Chester, *Hugh Latimer, Apostle to the English* (University of Pennsylvania Press, 1954), pp. 165 *f*.

[147] See n. 34, p. 46, and below, p. 76.

[148] See above, p. 57, and the official statute for the protection of pensioners, 2/3 Edward VI, c. 7.

[149] BM MS Harley 6989, f. 146.

little doubt that the target of the criticism was the ex-refugees William Turner, Thomas Becon and John Hooper, authors of works which condemned covetous landlords, avaricious rulers who failed to dispense justice, and irresponsible noblemen who failed to care for their tenantry and the poor. Nevertheless, at the time of the protectorate, as far as it is possible to tell, only Thomas Becon had elaborated such complaints on paper. Hooper in June 1549 informed Bullinger: 'the people are sorely oppressed by the marvellous tyranny of the nobility' yet he seemed to be echoing current sentiments.[150] His earlier writings had failed to stray beyond the realm of theology, and his *Declaration of the Ten Commandments*, finally published in November 1549, failed to mention sheep, although managing to label the present nobility as 'degenerate'. It seemed estranged from English conditions which was not surprising as Hooper wrote it in Zurich after spending several years in exile.[151] Not until May 1549 did he reach England and take up residence in Somerset's house, long after the government's policy had been formulated and substantially applied. However, while a greater awareness of the problem and proposals for remedy could not be said to have stemmed from him, it is possible that, like Latimer, his passion, his sense of urgency, his ability to present a commonplace as a cross, compelled Somerset's actions, particularly his issue of the enclosure commissions in July 1549. Struggling against the cool reason of humanists, who in the Paget and Smith manner called for moderation and the right moment, was the dramatic pull of men like Hooper and Latimer calling for immediate action. Their fervour matched the crisis of the time. It is possible that without them Somerset may have been less distracted from his main passion, the Scottish war.

A similar influence was probably exerted by William Turner who returned from exile in 1547 and came into personal contact with Somerset as his physician and daily waiter. As with Hooper, his early writings failed to focus on social and economic matters. Only his *A New Book of Spiritual Physic*, published in 1554 and written after Somerset's fall, dealt directly with them. Until then, his discussion of social responsibility had proceeded no further than to insist that poverty should occasion charity 'and then do ye honour Christ as ye should do'.[152] Turner was most likely moved by his social concerns long before he wrote about them, but if his book reflected truly these concerns, it suggests that Turner was impressive in spotlighting the need for action, but not in providing adequate solutions. In a long tradition to which Latimer and Hooper belonged, he was

150 *Original Letters*, ed. H. Robinson (Parker Society, 1846) I, p. 66.

151 See *A Declaration of Christ and his Office* (Zurich, 1547), *Answer to My Bishop of Winchester's Book* (Zurich, 1547) and *Declaration of the Ten Holy Commandments of Almighty God* (Zurich, 1548), printed in *Early Writings of John Hooper*, ed. S. Carr (Parker Society, 1843) *passim*. For details of his earlier life, see below, p. 104 and pp. 108 f.

152 For his early life and connection with Somerset, see below, pp. 104 and 108. Excluding translations and works on natural history, his published works were *The Hunting and Finding of the Romish Fox* (Basle, 1543), *The Rescuing of the Romish Fox* (Zurich, 1545), *A New Dialogue wherein is contained The Examination of the Mass* . . . (London, 1548), *A Preservative or Triacle against the Poison of Pelagius* (London, 1551), *The Hunting of the Romish Wolf* (Zurich, 1554), and *A New Book of Spiritual Physic* . . . (Basle, 1555). The quote appears in *A New Dialogue*, unpaginated.

strong on moral exhortation and feeble on remedy. For him remedy lay with the aristocracy. He called upon them 'to give the one half of all thy goods to the poor, if thou hast taken away from any man unjustly' and to invite to their feasts the poor instead of their friends. Otherwise, all he could propose was proclamations announcing the government's willingness to receive complaints against certain named subjects, and for parliament to license nobles and gentry to apprehend upstarts when found parading in silks, velvet and gold chains. If the upstarts were worth less than £20 p.a. in lands, the licensed aristocracy would have the right to cut their clothes to pieces publicly in the next market town and to distribute half the value of their gold chains to the poor.[153] Turner's remedies compounded plain silliness with a deep ignorance of the governmental system. They were quite beyond application or serious consideration. His one constructive and sensible solution, the distribution of the chantry lands for the benefit of the church, education, the poor and public works fell predictably upon deaf ears. He recorded having discussed the scheme with a great man, presumably Somerset as he was attending him 'when he was sick', and was merely told to 'be good unto the king'.[154]

In contrast the character of the policy, as opposed to the simple decision to act, may have owed something to the third 'hotling', Thomas Becon. Unlike Turner and Hooper, he has left evidence of being attuned to the English agrarian situation both before and during the protectorate. When the new reign opened he had already condemned gentlemen for engrossing tenements and raising rents in his *The Policy of War*.[155] In the course of 1547 and 1548 he composed his *Jewel of Joy* which opened with a passage expressing the concerns of the enclosure commission.[156] In part, it attacked everything that Somerset stood for, casting a withering eye on sumptuous houses and extravagant clothes, the former being held as 'a great token of the day of Judgement being at hand'. He also relegated the nobility with the rhetorical question: 'Are not the carcasses of all personages meat for worms alike?'[157] Like Latimer's sermons, the work was exhortatory and apocalyptic. Also like Latimer, Becon offered little constructive guidance on the righting of social wrongs. Yet the work did fix upon depopulation and dearth. It railed against the engrossing of farms and the evils of sheep-rearing, explaining them as acts of covetousness and regarding them as a menace not only to the poor but also to the defences of the realm.[158] There is no certainty that any member of the government saw this work before its publication in 1550. Its importance lies in revealing the preoccupations of one of Protector Somerset's chaplains.[159] Becon probably not only raised the temperature of concern, but also pointed a

[153] *A New Book of Spiritual Physic for Divers Diseases of the Nobility and Gentlemen of England*, ff. 61b, 68, 85 and 86.   [154] *The Hunting of the Romish Wolf*, unpaginated.
[155] *The Early Works of Thomas Becon*, ed. J. Ayre (Parker Society, 1843), p. 253.
[156] D. S. Bailey, *Thomas Becon and the Reformation of the Church in England* (Edinburgh, 1952), p. 142 (23).
[157] *The Catechism of Thomas Becon*, ed. J. Ayre (Parker Society, 1844), pp. 430 and 436.
[158] *Ibid.*, pp. 432–5.
[159] For the connection, see D. S. Bailey, *op. cit.*, pp. 54 *f*, and below, p. 108.

finger at the problem which the government's social programme sought to remedy. In this respect, Becon may have been responsible for persuading Somerset both to act, and to act in a certain way.

The 'hotlings' seem closely connected with Hales and Latimer, particularly since all were preoccupied with christian conduct. As protestants who had rejected good works as a means of grace, their thinking represented an urgent attempt to revalue the role of good works and to assert their necessity.[160] All insisted upon the social responsibility of dispensing charity to the poor. Also for the benefit of the poor, Becon and Hooper, like Latimer, were insistent that rulers should maintain the indifferent prosecution of justice. Somerset, in this respect, seemed caught in a vortex of protestant feeling which strove to rescue works from neglect. The cumulative effect of this preoccupation upon the government is indefinable, but its existence and connection with Somerset's circle of advice suggests that the compulsive, intellectual force behind the government's reform programme was the reformation.

Three tracts remain for consideration as likely sources of influence, one a poem by William Forrest and dedicated to Somerset, the others, advice to parliament at the time of the second session. Forrest's poem, 'Pleasant Poesie of Princely Practice', is an oddity: an illuminated manuscript, the work of a priest and a conservative in religion who in 1553 became one of Mary's chaplains. Internal evidence suggests that it was presented after the Pinkie campaign and before the June commission.[161] For the most part, it rehashes the thirteenth-century treatise *De Regimine Principum*, itself an adaptation of the *Secreta Secretorum*, the letter of advice supposedly composed by Aristotle for Alexander the Great. In this section it confined itself to the platitudes and generalities of a long tradition of political commentary.[162] Yet in the last part, it suddenly concentrated on the England of 1548 and its economic and social problems. Forrest attributed inflation to rackrenting. He regretted depopulation, bewailed the danger to the defence of the realm, censured noblemen with wide acres and without ploughs and blamed deserted villages upon sheep.[163] Moreover, Forrest was not content merely to make a moral exhortation against the sinfulness of man. He also proposed constructive remedy. He urged the government to cure the body politic by limiting the export of raw wool, a device which featured in the *A Discourse of the Commonweal*. Forrest also called upon the government: 'Grounds and farms to peruse and survey,/Rents to reform that be out of the way', a suggestion of the enclosure commission of June 1548.[164] Forrest could not be classed a policy-maker on such

160 For the 'hotlings'' concern with conduct, see below, pp. 106f.

161 *DNB*, see under William Forrest. The work is part printed in EETS extra ser., 32 (1878), App. The printed extract omits the dedication which provides some indication of when it was presented to Somerset. The victory of Pinkie is commended but no mention is made of the government's agrarian programme which began in mid-1548. In view of Forrest's agrarian concerns and his desire that the government should act, the likelihood is that the presentation preceded the government's actions (BM MS Royal 17 D 3, f. 3).

162 A. B. Ferguson, *op cit.*, pp. 24 f and 145.

163 EETS, *op. cit.*, pp. lxxxvii *ff.*

164 Lamond, p. 54; EETS, *op. cit.*, p. xcvii.

flimsy evidence. It is not even certain that Somerset appreciated the contents of his poem. But because of the chance that he did so, Forrest needs to be linked with Becon as a commentator who may have contributed to the government's social policy not only by urging prompt action but also by heightening its awareness of the situation and by defining the crux of the problem.

Finally, two tracts were addressed to Somerset, not individually but as a member of the second session of the first parliament. In view of the concurrence of concern, the likelihood is that he read or learned of their contents. Both were the work of fervent protestants, imbued with the familiar sense of urgency. Robert Crowley's *An Information and Petition against the Oppression of the Poor Commons* was an exhortation to repent. It threatened uncooperative landowners and members of parliament with the wrath of the Lord in the manner of Latimer and Becon. According to Crowley, wealth was a badge of social obligation. Those who ignored this fact and enjoyed their riches simply by consuming them 'shall at the day of their account, be bound hand and foot and cast into utter darkness'. It was a disturbing document, delivered with the confidence of a prophet.[165] As well as reflecting the atmosphere of crisis which attended the second session, the work must also have added to it. The second tract, *Piers Ploughman's Exhortation unto the Lords, Knights and Burgesses of the Parliament House*,[166] was a sophisticated work of economic reasoning which employed statistics to present the problem, and called upon devices rather than exhortation to provide the remedy. Nevertheless, it again brought home the direct connection between the spirit of protestantism and the passion for social reform, concluding with the question: 'and for a common practice among us one man to encroach so much ground into his hands that he shall thereby expel four or five hundred persons from their livings: how doth this trade of living agree with the gospel . . . for these injuries that we do unto the poor members of Christ we do unto him, saith he?' The subject of the work was idleness, not the vice but the product of economic conditions, particularly population growth and a society in which 'a few men . . . shall . . . keep . . . so many whole towns and fields.' The concern of the work was the fear that unable to cope with the excess of poverty resulting from unemployment and depressed wages, the realm 'shall come to utter ruin and decay'. The distinction of the work is its conception of a problem of overpopulation rather than depopulation, and its remedy of state action rather than self-reform. The charity of the rich, a revered remedy, was dismissed as totally inadequate. The only solution lay with parliament. Three statutes were proposed, one for the conversion of waste into pasture or arable, another for the encouragement of tillage by allowing the free export of corn, and a third for the promotion of home manufactures by means of heavy import duties on foreign manufactures. Unencumbered by apocalyptic warnings and exposing a real problem for which it elaborated a constructive and feasible remedy, the work was in a higher category than most of the comment. However, although it neither criticized the war nor blamed

[165] R. Crowley, *Select Works*, ed. J. M. Cowper (EETS extra ser., 15 (1872), pp. 150 *ff.*
[166] BM unpaginated.

F

debasement, its proposals did not carry effect. Again, the contribution was probably to emphasize the illness of the body politic and to assert the need for immediate reform.

A connection undoubtedly existed between contemporary commentary and the government's social policy. It cannot be precisely defined or fully substantiated because of the nature of the evidence, but Somerset's excessive concern for dispensing impartial justice, his agrarian remedies, his university reforms all relate to the preoccupations of commentators with whom he had contact. The danger is to exaggerate the role and extent of this connection. As far as it is possible to judge, the government's agrarian reform programme appeared to have but one planner outside of the government. Some commentators may have contributed by insisting on the urgency of the problem, but the solutions adopted sprang from Hales. Moreover, it is likely that the policy would have been applied in some form without their exhortations. The social concerns of the government have been thought to stem not from basic material needs but from a group of intellectuals who managed to capture the ear of an idealist.[167] But the protectorate was a time of economic and political crisis, and the government's programme was a direct response to pressing needs and problems. Intellectuals were not required to open the eyes of the government to the difficulties which faced it.

The economic crisis, moreover, released an upsurge of complaint from the realm. The government acquired knowledge of the state of the country from sermons and tracts, but also from petitions and informations filed by ordinary subjects. To assess properly the role of the commentators, they need to be viewed in a framework of crisis which led the realm itself to urge remedy upon the government, and the government to respond. When disclaiming authorship of the enclosure commission Hales declared that it 'proceeded at the suit partly of poor men', an opinion reflected in the proclamation announcing the commission of June 1548 which presented the commission as a response to 'divers supplications and pitiful complaints of his majesty's poor subjects'.[168] Both Tawney and Pollard believed references was being made to a commons complaint printed in the 1550s with the title: *The Decay of England only by the Great Multitude of Sheep*.[169] But this is by no means certain. The complaint was addressed to the king's council and 'the lords of the parliament house' by spokesmen for the counties of Oxfordshire, Buckinghamshire and Northamptonshire. It contained an agrarian and political problem which coincided remarkably with what the commission aimed to rectify. The complaint reasoned that the extension of sheep-farming was harmful because the accompanying depopulation increased the price of victuals through diminishing their production and weakened the country's military resources because 'we reckon that shepherds make but ill-archers.' But this coincidence was, in all likelihood, consequential rather than causal, since the complaint was probably

---

[167] See Jordan I, pp. 386, 388 f, 411 f and 421.

[168] Lamond, p. liv, and Hughes and Larkin, 309.

[169] Pollard, p. 210, and R. H. Tawney, *The Agrarian Problem in the Sixteenth Century* (London, 1912), p. 365.

not exhibited during the period of the protectorate. The failure to mention the protector in its address arouses scepticism, and its remarks about the scarcity of corn strongly suggests that, as a response to contemporary conditions, it belonged not to the period of abundant harvests, that is from 1546–8, but to the lean years of 1549–51.[170]

If there was one single petition responsible for the commission, the evidence for it is lost. Nevertheless, during the protectorate other complaints of a similar nature were made. One persuaded the government to dispark Hampton Court Chase. Others survive in the files of Star Chamber, Requests and Chancery. In addition, private informations relating to the agrarian laws were laid in the court of exchequer. The complaints chiefly concerned the enclosure of commonland, occasionally rack-renting. No complaint related to the wholesale eviction of a community. Their subject was the crippling hardship caused by the denial of common rights and the raising of entry fines. Three of the complaints eventually filed in the equity courts were addressed to Somerset and passed through the hands of his staff. The complaints, like the informations, did not amount to a flood, but were sufficient in number to convince a government that in choosing to operate through an enclosure commission it had selected an apposite device for the ills of the realm, and also that in proceeding against enclosures it was dealing not with a corpse but a living issue.[171]

What is required is a more complicated explanation of the genesis of the government's programme. A role was played by intellectual consultants, but a contribution was also made by critical economic conditions which necessitated government action. Taking prime place in the programme's formulation was clearly the government's war needs and the paradox of cheap corn and galloping inflation, which between them compelled the government to search for measures of reform, and helped to determine its policy by closing off certain obvious avenues of remedy.

Individuality

In the context of the Tudor age the Somerset regime's programme of social and economic reform had a certain distinction, partly because of what it eschewed.

---

[170] *TED* III, p. 51.

[171] *APC* II, pp. 190–92; ten bills of complaint exhibited by village communities in the time of the protectorate belong to Star Chamber, eight of them predating the first enclosure commission, PRO St. Ch. 3/III(50), St. Ch. 2/XX(125), St. Ch. 3/III(80), St. Ch. 3/IV(80), St. Ch. 3/III(22), St. Ch. 3/VI(80), St. Ch. 3/III(7), St. Ch. 3/VIII(1). For the two bills which followed the issuing of the commission, St. Ch. 3/VI(13) and (47). In addition there are two undated bills which possibly belong to the protectorate, St. Ch. 3/VI(107) and St. Ch. 3/II(33). In Requests are six dateable complaints addressed by communities during the protectorate, PRO Req. 2/14/33 and 41, Req. 2/17/6 and 73, Req. 2/18/114, Req. 2/19/29. Only two predate the first enclosure commission: Req. 2/14/33 and Req. 2/17/73. In Chancery five cases survive for the period 1547–51, but cannot be dated with any precision, PRO C1/1281/60, C1/1272/88–90, C1/1214/14, C1/1217/25–6, C1/1208/25 and C1/1188/28–33. For the informations laid in the court of exchequer see M. W. Beresford, 'The Poll Tax and Census of Sheep, 1549', *Agricultural History Review* 2 (1954), pp. 21 f.

Compelled by prevailing conditions and for its own convenience, it did nothing about usury or debasement, imposed next to no regulations on internal marketing and did not interfere with the currency exchange.[172] In addition, its urgent desire for reform was impressive, and, if a prime reason for Tudor reform was revenue,[173] its determination to place considerations of reform before those of profit, adds to its distinction. Some of its measures were original, particularly the commission against enclosures with the power to hear and determine, and the subsidy on sheep and cloth. Furthermore, as the later enclosure commissions of the Tudors were specifically authorized by statute, and as the fiscal device of indirect taxation was hardly developed in sixteenth-century England, the same measures were remarkably unusual.[174] But the programme did not express a new outlook. It was not driven by exceptional or novel ideas. Protestantism only imparted an intensity of feeling. The programme's concern with the state's security and its military resources, impartial justice and the protection of tillage and law enforcement, were all in accordance with a pattern of behaviour typical of the Tudor state, while the educational programme was essentially a continuation of Henrician developments and schemes. Since Somerset's social policy upheld conventional concerns, it inevitably received substantial support from his colleagues. It is wrong to conceive the policy as the exclusive vision of one member of the government and a group of dedicated intellectuals, or its applications as a declaration of war on the aristocracy or the rich.[175] The revolutionary character it acquired was due to the interpretation placed upon it as a result of Somerset's behaviour towards peasant rebels which was emphasized by his opponents to justify his overthrow.[176] It was not inherent in the programme's original aims. The better society Somerset and his advisers envisaged was only the existing one without its abuses. Members of the government opposed parts of the policy—the enclosure commissions, Somerset's intervention in poor men's suits, and some of the measures of the second session—but because they were inopportune or unconstitutional, not because they outraged any other principle.

In the first instance most of the government appeared to support the enclosure commission.[177] Hales remarked in September 1549 that the 1548 commission 'proceeded at the suit partly of poor men as the proclamation declareth, and partly of some of those that be now most against it . . . and chiefly for that the king's majesty, my lord protector's grace and many of the council saw what hurt had grown and what was like to ensue to this realm if the greediness of graziers and sheepmasters were not in time resisted'. By mid-August 1548 the earl of Warwick

---

[172] Accounts of the social policies of Tudor governments are provided by G. R. Elton, *Reform and Renewal*, ch. 5, J. Thirsk 'Enclosing and Engrossing' in *The Agrarian History of England and Wales*, ch. 4, and L. A. Clarkson, *The Pre-Industrial Economy in England 1500–1750*, ch. 6.

[173] Clarkson, *op. cit.*, p. 193.

[174] See 5/6 Edward VI, c. 5 (ii), 2/3 Philip and Mary, c. 2 (iii), and 5 Elizabeth, c. 2 (xiii). Only the Marian act authorized a commission to hear and determine.

[175] Jordan I, p. 427.

[176] See below, pp. 98 f.

[177] Jordan's impression of hostility rests upon confusing the commissions of 1548 and 1549 (Jordan I, pp. 428–31).

was strongly opposed, basically because he objected to an enclosure commission 'in this troublesome time'.[178] Rumours of popular rioting in the areas visited by the commissioners had turned him against it, and so had reports that Hales was stirring the commons against the nobles and the gentry. At the empanelling of each jury, contrary to the wishes of some who, according to Hales, 'would have had that nothing should have been said to the people, but only the commission and instructions barely read', Hales delivered lengthy speeches both as a prelude and in conclusion to the reading of the commission and the relevant proclamation. In these speeches he dwelt not only on the illnesses of the body politic but also on the political importance of the people. Although he warned the people against taking matters into their own hands, and assumed a society based upon hierarchy and degree, the inflammatory character of his speeches was hard to deny.[179] Nevertheless, Warwick's alienation was temporary and, according to Hales, it had disappeared before the end of August. By this time Hales had written to Warwick reporting and justifying his own proceedings, and he had also met him to discuss the matter. Hales informed Somerset after the meeting: 'I found him very reasonable and left him in that mind that he both thought it necessary that the matter should go forward and will gladly further the same, as a thing for God's glory, the king's honour and the commonwealth of the realm, albeit he was somewhat instructed in the adversaries arguments.'[180] It seems that Warwick, a major opponent of this first commission, had no qualms about it if it did not provoke popular disorder. Somerset undoubtedly shared this consideration. Full of concern, on 21 August Somerset relayed to Hales the current news that the people of the Midlands, 'in a marvellous trade of boldness', were claiming that 'if other remedy be not presently had by the king's majesty's authority for the reducing of farms and copyholds to the wonted state, there shall not fail among themselves by a common assent the reformation thereof to be attempted'. He also reported the allegation that the commissioners had encouraged this unruly behaviour, a reference to Hales' address to the presentment juries. Somerset concluded his letter by emphatically condemning popular rioting as an intolerable form of redress. To safeguard against it, he ordered the commissioners 'in your return homewards' to announce in all the places where they had formerly sat that the government would proceed in time to remedy the wrongs uncovered, and that in the meantime subjects were not, under pain of punishment, to take the matter into their own hands.[181]

The outbreaks of disorder exposed the commission as a dangerous instrument, as well as destroying one of its objects which was to maintain order. Presumably on these grounds the government abandoned its original intention and failed to issue commissions for other areas in that year. So far, Somerset had been in agreement with his colleagues. If a proclamation is to be trusted, the next step, the pardon

---

[178] Lamond, p. liv; and see Hales's letter to Warwick of 12 August 1548 (BM MS Lansdowne 238, ff. 321b *ff*).

[179] Lamond, p. lviii; Strype II (2), Q.

[180] BM MS Lansdowne 238, f. 321b.   [181] *Ibid.*, ff. 318b *ff*.

and the 'deadline', also received general consent.[182] He only came to differ with them by persisting with further commissions in circumstances which seemed hazardous and in a manner which offended the law. By deciding to resume action in 1549, and then with commissions of redress rather than enquiry, Somerset acted arbitrarily, and directly counter to the wishes of the rest of the government. The first breach came in April when Somerset issued a royal proclamation declaring the king's intention to punish offenders against the agrarian laws 'without pardon or remission'. According to the charges brought against him in October 1549, this proclamation 'went forth against the will of the whole council'.[183] In July commissions were issued which appeared to rest on the sole authority of the protector. These commissions of 1549, not the commission of 1548, aroused the opposition Hales mentioned in September 1549, and were a source of objection at his trial.[184] However, the differences over the 1549 commissions did not mean that Somerset and the other councillors were now advocating differing social policies. Social disorder remained a common consideration of prime importance. That Somerset was as moved by this threat as in the previous year is clearly revealed in the delay between the proclamation declaring intention in April and the commissions issued in July. In May a proclamation declared the king's resolution, in view of the disorders, to remedy agrarian ills only 'when his highness sees time convenient', and the commissions were issued at a moment when insurrection seemed to be on the wane.[185] In their attitude towards the enclosure commission, Somerset and his colleagues were moved by a similar concern for the decay of tillage and peasant uprisings. They differed because of Somerset's insistence upon action after the failures of the first commission and the second parliamentary session, and because of the other councillors' preference to respect the commotions of 1549 by holding fire until a more suitable time.

   Likewise, the legislation of the second session cannot be regarded as the brainchild of a commonwealth clique of which Somerset was the chief and from which the other councillors were excluded. During the session William Paget in a number of letters criticized Somerset's actions in this parliament, but the burden of his criticism was that the time was not ripe because of the urgent need to prepare for war.[186] In his opinion the session had to be regarded exclusively as a means of raising supplies, and was to be prorogued once they were granted. This made him criticial of the religious as well as the social measures. Faced by widespread peasant risings he later found further objections to the social programme. But, while questioning the need for immediate action, criticizing Somerset's lust

182 Hughes and Larkin, 333.

183 Foxe VI, p. 291 (x). The actual proclamation was not specified, but was presumably the one issued on 11 April (Hughes and Larkin, 327), in view of the lack of contention over the enclosure commission of the previous year.

184 Lamond, p. liv; charge xi (Foxe VI, p. 291) accused Somerset of issuing on his own initiative a commission to hear and determine, clearly a reference to the 1549 commission, not that of 1548 which was merely to enquire.

185 Hughes and Larkin, 333. The proclamation of April and the risings of May seem to explain why in late May Warwick came 'very lustily on to the court' (*HMC* Rutland I, p. 36).

186 PLB, Paget to Somerset, 25 December 1548, 2 February 1549 and 12 March 1549.

for popularity and believing the social problem to be exaggerated, he did not appear to object to the policy itself either on the grounds that he thought it revolutionary or completely unnecessary. His view was that, with peasant re-bellion, foreign war and reformation on its hands, the government needed to postpone the remedy of society's ills. This view was undoubtedly shared by the opposition which successfully conspired against Somerset in October 1549, and was explicitly stated in Lord Riche's speech to the mayor and aldermen of London at the time of the *coup* when he accused Somerset of creating disorder 'under pretence of [reform of] such matters as all men desired might be redressed more gladly than he [Somerset], but in a more quiet and settled time'.[187]

In addition parliament proved critical by axeing some of the government's major measures, yet, if the Hales bills are any guide, not because they were unpalatably idealistic or radical. In dealing with dearth and depopulation, Hales's bills concerned problems which by common consent were important, pressing and worthy of redress. The bills themselves were not out on a limb, and conformed with earlier and later legislation. The milch-kine bill became a statute in 1555, although enforced by informer action in the manner of the Cromwellian sheep act, rather than by a survey of the cattle population as Hales had proposed.[188] The regrating bill was probably enacted by the Northumberland government.[189] The farms bill was in keeping with draft legislation of the Wolsey era, the legis-lation of the early 1530s and the parliamentary business of the Northumberland regime.[190] It aimed to stop the commonly condemned practice of engrossing leaseholds, a cause of depopulation which the tillage acts had failed to prevent.[191] Its proposals for the restriction of farms were certainly less rigorous than those of Cromwell's farms bill, since they placed no specific limit on the number of farms that individuals with a landed income of 100 marks or more could hold, and sought only to limit the purpose of such farms by insisting that they served the needs of the household and were used for the keeping of horses.[192] Like the Cromwellian bill it included other proposals as well, one of which merely extended a clause of the act, 27 Henry VIII, c. 28, so that tillage was maintained on

---

[187] Strype, II (2), HH; John Hayward, *The Life and Reign of King Edward the Sixth* (London, 1636), p. 215.

[188] 2/3 Philip and Mary, c. 3, 25 Henry VIII, c. 13, and PRO SP10/II/21.

[189] Hales described the missing bill as 'for regrating of victual and other things wherein I remember one principal point, that graziers nor no man should buy any cattle and sell the same again within a certain time' (Lamond, p. lxii). This seemed closely related in content to 3/4 Edward VI, c. 19. A second act of the session sought to deal with the regrating of cheese and butter (3/4 Edward VI, c. 21). For the official nature of these acts, see n. 216, p. 82.

[190] See Thirsk, *op. cit.*, p. 215; Elton, *op. cit.*, pp. 106 n. 17 and n. 19 and 101–6; Beresford, *op. cit.*, *Agricultural History Review*, 2 (1954), p. 21.

[191] See Elton, *op. cit.*, p. 101. At the end of Hales's bill farms were carefully defined as a lease of a demesne worth £5 or more p.a., a lease of a parsonage worth 20 marks a year, and every lease 'of freeland and not copyhold' where, in accordance with the law, there should be a house, two plough-lands and feeding for one bull and twelve kine (Lamond, p. lii).

[192] Elton, *op. cit.*, p. 103; Lamond, p. xlvii. The restriction on the number of farms applied only to subjects with a landed income of less than 100 marks p.a. who could have no more than one farm (*ibid.*, p. xlviii).

ex-chantry demesne lands as well as on ex-monastic demesne lands. The bill also regulated the grazing of sheep, allowing each subject to use only lands to the value of £100 p.a. or less for this purpose, and on lands in farm requiring subjects to graze 200 of every 1,000 sheep for part of the year in common fields.[193] Although a tough, penetrating measure harshly enforceable by stiff fines, the bill could not be presented as a new departure in tillage legislation.

In view of their conventionality, the three Hales bills probably failed at the time for other reasons than their basic concern. The farms bill undoubtedly was poorly received because of its provocative presentation. Its preamble blamed the nobility as a class. It claimed that:

> Divers your grace's subjects called to the degree of nobility . . . have so much neglected their vocations that they be become graziers, sheepmasters and toilers of the earth, having pulled down a great many townships, villages and houses of husbandry and converting the ground which was wont to be occupied in husbandry and tillage into pasture . . . whereby not only the multitude of your grace's subjects in all places of your realm is marvellously abated, your grace's honour greatly diminished and the safety and defence of your royal person and this your realm much weakened, but also the prices of all kind of victuals and other necessaries be so enhanced [that the people are reduced to poverty].[194]

In his account of the bill's reception in parliament, Hales refused to state the reason for its rejection,[195] but the likelihood is that a proposal which in the past had received a rough passage had no chance when coupled with a condemnation of the aristocracy for the ills of the present.[196] Hales provided the reason for the rejection of the milch-kine bill; its system of enforcement, which was based on a survey of the country's cattle, 'bit the mare by the thumb.'[197] Otherwise, it does not seem that the bill was found inherently objectional. The bill for the regrating of victuals has not survived. and Hales did not explain why it blew up a storm in the Commons. It dealt with a vice generally condemned at the time, and it did not threaten the livelihood of the aristocracy. Its easy passage through the Lords implies its conventionality. Again, rejection was probably due not to its basic concern, but the incidental factors of presentation or enforcement. The failure of these three bills may also have stemmed from their connection with John Hales, and parliament's attitude towards them was possibly a personal rather than a principled reaction. Noticeably, two of the bills got into difficulties in the Commons, where Hales was a member.[198] Both with the enclosure commissions and the legislation of the second session, Somerset may have differed from his contemporaries not in his sense of problem or solution, but, to some extent, in his toleration of John Hales as his master-planner.

---

193 Lamond, pp. xlviii–l.
195 *Ibid.*, p. lxii.
197 Lamond, p. lxv.

194 *Ibid.*, pp. xlvi *f.*
196 Elton, *op. cit.*, pp. 103 *f.*
198 See above, pp. 50 *f*, and *DNB*, see under John Hales.

Finally, both the rabbits and parks bills dealt with matters which official legislation frequently accepted as a genuine source of grievance requiring remedy. The tillage act of 1536, for example, introduced a system of licensing deer parks, which Elizabeth's government upheld and developed.[199] Moreover, rabbits had become a serious concern by the late sixteenth century and the Marian government sought to restrict warrens near corn-fields, while Elizabeth's government accepted only ancient warrens and those which received the royal licence.[200] Without a doubt the Somerset acts aimed to proceed further and to destroy some of the existing warrens and parks rather than merely to place restrictions on the creation of new ones.[201] Nevertheless, their easy passage in the Lords, which cannot be simply attributed to government pressure, strongly suggests that the measures were far from outrageous.

The remaining aspects of Somerset's social programme, his keenness to dispense justice to the unfortunate and his educational reforms, also appeared to have the basic approval of his colleagues. After all, justice was conventionally expected of a ruler. When Somerset declared that 'if he were a devil [he] would have him heard', informed Van der Delft, the imperial ambassador, of his desire to secure impartial justice and warned his own brother of his wish to receive the suits of poor men irrespective of the defendant's identity,[202] he was uttering worthy sentiments which were far from alien to the age. His dispensation of justice was criticized at his trial and earlier by Paget. But in both instances the objection was on constitutional grounds. The charges accused him of evading the law by establishing his own private court of requests, and Paget resented his interference with the process of the law by means of private letters in favour of complaints.[203] Neither criticized his intention to uphold justice. The objection was to his methods, not his aims. The educational reforms were also in keeping with the past, the culmination of a process of humanist influence upon the universities, and the idea of a college of civil law had been air-borne for some time.[204] The opposition to the reforms only came from outside the government. It was voiced by clerics who seemed neither worried about a humanist curriculum for the B.A. degree, nor suspicious of civil law, but principally apprehensive of the effect of these changes upon the traditional role of the universities as seminaries.[205] The plans met difficulties in application but not, it seems, in formulation, and appeared to command agreement in government circles.

Somerset was ousted from power by an alliance of men opposing him on personal grounds and of others who opposed the religious settlement. Ideology

[199] 27 Henry VIII, c. 22 (iv), and 5 Elizabeth, c. 2 (viii).
[200] 2/3 Philip and Mary, c. 2 (iii, xii and xxiv), and 5 Elizabeth, c. 2 (viii).
[201] See above, n. 66, p. 51.
[202] Muller, 138 (p. 427); *SP Span.* 1547–9, p. 194; and Tytler, *op. cit.*, pp. 120 f.
[203] Foxe VI, p. 290 (vii); Strype, II (2), p. 437; see my article 'Protector Somerset and Requests' *Historical Journal* 17 (1974), p. 454. Elsewhere Paget urged him to 'Do justice without respect' (PLB, Paget to Somerset, 2 January 1548).
[204] Curtis, *op. cit.*, pp. 67 and 70 f, and Kearney, *op. cit.*, pp. 24 and 34 f.
[205] See above, n. 122, p. 63.

played a part in his overthrow, but related only to the Somerset regime's religious policy.[206] In the charges at his trial, the regime's social measures were used to illustrate his high-handedness and irresponsibility, but not to condemn their original purpose. The new regime was therefore capable of applying a similar social programme—conclusive proof of the basic uniformity in Protector Somerset's and his fellow councillors' social outlook.

The commentators on the commonwealth did not fall with the protector. The new regime allowed them the same licence as the old. Latimer's delivery of his third successive Lenten sermons to the Court in 1550 expressed the continuity of the two governments. In the same year the government again revealed its sympathy for reform when it allowed Thomas Lever to preach in the Shrouds of St Paul's, at St Paul's Cross and before the king at Court.[207] Both regimes were basically concerned with inflation. Their measures for dealing with it, while not identical in method, were closely similar in outlook. In spite of Somerset's fall, depopulation and the protection of tillage remained major interests of the government. In a proclamation of May 1551, the government blamed inflation upon 'farmers, graziers and sheepmasters' for 'unreasonable and fraudulent engrossing of farms, grain, victual', for 'manifest decaying of towns and tillage', and for 'excessive increasing of sheep contrary to divers good laws'.[208] The Northumberland government succeeded where the Somerset regime had failed, passing a tillage act which made it an offence to convert to pasture, land accustomed to tillage for four or more years since 1509, and which authorised a commission of enquiry.[209] Furthermore, if the Northumberland government was responsible for the revival of the statute of Merton, it probably aimed to protect small cottagers seeking to establish new homesteads on waste ground, rather than to protect enclosers generally.[210] In addition the same government may have supported a parliamentary bill to restrict the possession of farms and mansion houses, an echo of the Hales farms bill, which surfaced once in the third session and again in the fourth session when it passed the Commons and reached a third reading in the Lords. It may also have backed the bill for decayed houses which quickly received the Commons' assent, then with modifications was speedily concluded in the Lords, and only came to grief when the Commons found

[206] For the opposition on personal grounds, see Jordan I, ch. 16, and A. J. A. Malkiewicz, 'An Eyewitness's Account of the Coup d'Etat of October 1549', *Engl. HR* 70 (1955), pp. 600 ff. Malkiewicz edits part of a document (BM Add. 48,126), omitting the last section which reveals the importance of the catholic plot (*ibid.*, ff. 15a–16a). For an incorporation of this evidence in an account of the fall, see C. J. Adams, 'Tudor Minister: Sir Thomas Wriothesley' (unpublished Manchester University M.A. thesis (1970)), ch. 5 (3).

[207] Arber's English Reprints, 25, *passim.*

[208] Hughes and Larkin, 373.

[209] 5/6 Edward VI, c. 5. The manner in which its passage failed to lose momentum in spite of three committals, suggests government backing (see the Commons and Lords *Journals* for March), as does the proclamation of 11 May 1551 which expressed the government's anxiety about the decay of tillage (Hughes and Larkin, 373).

[210] Thirsk, *op. cit.*, pp. 224 f. There is no certainty that this act was an official measure; but the speed with which it passed the Commons (late December and late January) and the Lords (late January) suggests government support (see Commons and Lords *Journals*).

difficulty in accepting the Lords' amendment of the original bill.[211] Agrarian problems, traditionally conceived in terms of declining tillage, seemed to be an important concern of both governments.

The new government swept away several of Somerset's measures, but it also secured the enactment of at least one, possibly two, of the official measures which fell upon stony ground in the second session.[212] Moreover, the chief of the repealed measures, the subsidy on sheep and cloth, was abolished because it had proved to be fiscally inadequate and unfair, a fault not only of the original design, but also of modifications imposed during its passage through parliament, which had set the subsidy on sheep and cloth against the normal subsidy and had provided that the former should be exacted only in cases where its assessment exceeded the assessment of the latter. The inadequacy of the act had been accepted in the previous summer by the Somerset government when, in response to complaints from the realm, it had excused flocks of less than 100 sheep from the liability. The small returns of the tax were clearly not worth the resulting public dissension and its administrative problems. For these reasons the Northumberland government's speedy reaction to a petition from the clothiers of Devon for its repeal was not surprising.[213] Had it survived, the Somerset government in all likelihood would have behaved similarly. The new government also disposed of the act releasing fee-farms for the use of the community, but presumably because it had been packaged with the subsidy on sheep and cloth. Originally the loss of revenue which it entailed had been justified because of the gains to be made from a subsidy on sheep. In view of its close connection with the subsidy on sheep and cloth, it was understandable that it should go with the tax's repeal.[214] The repeal of the fee-farms act did not mean a cold-shouldering of the poor: the Northumberland government, in spite of the repeal, allowed the commutation of fee-farms for one year, established a commission to implement this provision, and appeared responsible for the repeal of the harsh vagrancy act of the Somerset regime and for an act of the fourth session which, by providing for the collection of alms, sought to improve upon the act 22 Henry VIII, c. 12 for the relief of the needy.[215] In

[211] The bills do not survive; their possible official nature is suggested by their progress in parliament. After several redraftings, the bill for decayed houses passed the Commons between 22 and 25 January (*Commons Journals*), and the Lords between 28 and 30 January (*Journals of the House of Lords*). The farms bill proceeded less smoothly, but with a persistence which suggests official backing (see *Commons Journals* (4th session) for 9, 12 and 18 February, and *Journal of the House of Lords* (4th session) for 20 February, and 22, 23 and 31 March).

[212] They were Hales's regrating bill (see above, p. 51 and n. 189) and the bill regulating the manufacture of cloth which, although originally a petition, became an official measure when after the failure of the private bill, the government issued the regulation by proclamation (see below, p. 150).

[213] See Beresford, *op. cit.*, *Agricultural History Review* 1 (1953), pp. 9 *ff*, and 2 (1954), pp. 15 *ff*; Pocock, p. 75; 3/4 Edward VI, c. 23 (the preamble).

[214] 3/4 Edward VI, c. 18, and see above, pp. 49 *f*; the passage of the repeal of the fee-farms act was closely connected with the passage of the repeal of the act for the sheep subsidy, following in its footsteps (see *Journals* of the Commons and Lords for January).

[215] *CPR* 1550–53, p. 423, 3/4 Edward VI, c. 16, and 5/6 Edward VI, c. 2. The official nature of the acts is suggested by their introduction in the Lords, their character as resolutions, and their relatively smooth passage.

dispensing with the measures of the previous government, the overriding consideration of the Northumberland regime appeared to be practicability rather than a difference of principle.

The new government had a psychological need to distinguish itself from the one it replaced. But the major differences between the social policies of the two governments seemed the result of changing circumstances, not only the fall of Somerset but also the failure of the harvest in 1549, 1550 and 1551, the termination of war in April 1550, the memory of peasant rebellion following the outbreaks of 1549, and the slump in foreign trade in 1551 and 1552. Without the complication of cheap corn, with the price of victuals generally high, inflation could be more easily attributed to the behaviour of the market. The Northumberland regime distinguished itself by the number of its measures to restrict engrossing, re-grating and forestalling.[216] Furthermore, the peace of 1550 which ended both the Scottish and French wars, also ended the government's dependence upon the debasement of the coinage. It was now possible to blame debasement for the dearth and to seek a remedy with coinage reform.[217] With peace, the military weakness of the realm ceased to be used to justify social measures, leaving inflation as the major reason for remedial action; a more serious attempt could be made to use the remains of the annexed wealth of the church and the chantries for the benefit or society;[218] and having a less pressing need for loans, the government could subscribe to the traditional habit of condemning usury. Permitted by the legislation of 1545 and tolerated by the Somerset regime, the practice of usury was placed under a new prohibition in 1552.[219] As a result of the commotions of 1549, the Northumberland regime was fearfully aware of the need to contain popular action, and therefore possessed a caution which, in acting before the full effect of the risings had been experienced, Somerset had managed to avoid.[220] Its riot legislation was probably a natural consequence of the risings of 1549 rather than of a radical change in government attitude towards the lower orders.[221] Finally, the shrinkage in the exports of short-cloths in 1551 and 1552 introduced preoccupations and remedies which had been unnecessary in the late 1540s when cloth exports were booming. The search for new markets, the attempts to control the exchanges, the hostile attitude to foreign merchants, the restrictions placed on the cloth industry, all features of the Northumberland regime but not of the

---

[216] Hales had brought such a measure before the second session, but this was exceptional and ineffective, and internal marketing measures only became common after the failure of the harvest in 1549. See the circular to JPs (PRO SP10/IX/55) and the proclamations 373 and 377 (Hughes and Larkin), and the statutes 3/4 Edward VI, cc. 19 and 21, 5/6 Edward VI, cc. 14 and 15, and 7 Edward VI, c. 7. There is no reason to doubt the official nature of these statutes in view of the circular and proclamations issued on the same subject, and their smooth passage in the Lords and Commons.

[217] Hughes and Larkin, 372.

[218] See n. 14, p. 43.

[219] Jones, *op. cit.*, pp. 152 f.

[220] A paper by Francis Bacon on enclosures in 1607 made the point that, because remedial action was thought to encourage popular insurrection, 'in Edward VI's his time the remedy was not pursued until two years after the rebellion of Kett' (BM MS Cotton Titus F IV, ff. 322b f).

[221] For the view that the riot act was a reactionary measure, see Pollard, pp. 272 f, and Jordan II, pp. 37 f.

protectorate, are explained by the crisis in foreign trade.[222] Thus, while both regimes shared the same basic social concerns, aims and assumptions, the impression of circumstance gave them different social policies.

Somerset's social programme was in keeping with the age. To be properly explained, it must be linked with the rest of his government policy, particularly his war aims and his reliance upon debasement for supplying funds for the Scottish war, and related to the economic conditions of the time, particularly rampant inflation and the phenomenon of good harvests in 1547 and 1548. The policy acquired its character because of the constraints these factors imposed upon it the choice of remedy. While the policy was for the most part a joint venture rather than the work of one member of the government, its individuality can be said to have stemmed from the personality of Protector Somerset. Somerset impressed himself personally not because of his magnanimity or idealism, but because of his desire for virtue and his obsession in the face of failure with enclosure commissions. The underlying ideas of the policy did not distinguish it. They were conventional and shared by Somerset's contemporaries. The policy was the work neither of a visionary nor an idealist, and it certainly did not express a 'stubborn and highminded devotion to a programme of revolutionary reform'.[223] As far as it is possible to judge, Somerset's basic social aim agreed with the paternalism which Tudor governments generally dispensed. This was designed not to change society but to prevent radical change. Its purpose was to preserve the existing social hierarchy with all its inequalities, and to equip an aristocratic society ruled by a Tudor king with the means of surviving forever.

[222] F. J. Fisher, 'Commercial Trends and Policy in Sixteenth-century England', *Econ. HR* 10 (1940), pp. 103 *ff*.
[223] Pollard, p. 317, and Jordan II, p. 210.

4
Social Policy 2:
The Government and
the Peasant Risings

The Problem

In the spring and summer of 1549 the government was faced with widespread peasant commotions. In May they broke out in Somerset, Wiltshire, Hampshire, Kent, Sussex and Essex;[1] in June the men of Devon and Cornwall rose;[2] in July peasants rebelled in Northamptonshire, Bedfordshire, Buckinghamshire, Oxfordshire, Yorkshire and throughout East Anglia;[3] finally, in August and September disturbances occurred in Leicestershire and Rutland.[4] In extent the risings of 1549 lacked their equal in the sixteenth century, and were probably rivalled only by those of 1381.

Fortunately for the government, the risings possessed a number of features which helped to relieve the pressure brought upon it. Although some risings could inspire similar actions elsewhere, rebels in different parts of the country tended not to cooperate even when their causes coincided.[5] The Devon and Cornwall rebels united, and Ket's rebellion was a coalition of several risings in the East Anglian region. But cooperation seemed only possible within a region. The Yorkshire rebels' plan to connect with the southern risings remained an aspiration; the hope of the men of Sussex and Hampshire to join with the westerners never materialized.[6]

In the second place the proportion of risings explicitly opposed to the government was small. Its religious policy only aroused risings in the west, in Oxford-

---

[1] *HMC Bath IV*, pp. 109 and 111, *HMC Rutland I*, p. 36, R. C. Anderson, *Letters of the Fifteenth and Sixteenth Centuries*, p. 66, BM MS Cotton Titus B V, f. 33, Pocock, p. 24, n. (a), and C. Wriothesley, *A Chronical of England during the Reigns of the Tudors* (Camden Society, new ser., 20), II, p. 13.

[2] See F. Rose-Troup, *The Western Rebellion of 1549*, passim.

[3] *Two London Chronicles*, ed. C. L. Kingsford (Camden Miscell., 3rd ser., 18), p. 18; A. Vere Woodman, 'The Buckinghamshire and Oxfordshire Rising', *Oxoniensia* 22 (1957), pp. 78 ff; A. G. Dickens, 'Some Popular Reactions to the Edwardian Reformation in Yorkshire', *Yorkshire Archæological Journal* 34 (1939), pp. 158 ff; S. T. Bindoff, *Ket's Rebellion* (Historical Association Pamphlet, 1949), passim; W. F. Russell, *Ket's Rebellion in Norfolk* (London, 1859), passim; and J. R. Ravensdale, 'Landbeach in 1549, Ket's Rebellion in Miniature', *East Anglian Studies* (Cambridge, 1968), ed. Lionel M. Munby, pp. 94 ff.

[4] Lodge I, p. 134. Jordan provides a reasonable factual account of most of the commotions, but commits the confusing error of lumping all of them together in one cumulative movement instead of distinguishing between the spring and the summer disturbances (I, ch. 15).

[5] Rumours of anti-enclosure action in Kent and elsewhere led to similar action in Norfolk (BM MS Harley 1576, f. 251) and the Devon and Cornwall rising was initially roused by the spring risings (Rose-Troup, *op. cit.*, p. 489).

[6] Dickens, *op. cit.*, p. 159; PRO SP10/VIII/41.

shire, Buckinghamshire and in Yorkshire;[7] its fiscal policy was militantly opposed only in Cornwall.[8] Ket's followers hated local government officials, particularly escheators and feodaries, and several risings took action against the Crown as a park-owner.[9] But the bulk of the stirs tended to embarrass the government by seeking to implement rather than to resist its policy.[10] The government at no point fought for its life. No rising in 1549 threatened the government physically in the manner of those of 1381, 1450 and 1497 with a sustained march on London. Nor did the rebels plan to release the king from the grip of evil ministers. If anything, the aim was to aid the government against the aristocracy, or to make it change its religious policy.

Also to the government's relief, the 1549 risings stand out for their lack of aristocratic participation and leadership. Only the western rebellion was led by lords;[11] elsewhere, if at all, they participated only in a minor and enforced way. The absence of aristocratic rebels was noticed at the time. In May 1549 John Paston found 'neither gentlemen nor yet a man of any substance' among the Wiltshire rebels.[12] In August Somerset described the risings generally as 'a plague and a fury amongst the vilest and worst sort of men, for except only Devon and Cornwall, and there not past two or three, in all other places not one gentleman or man of reputation was ever amongst them, but against their wills and as prisoners.'[13] This came of social conflict. The inability to cope with the dearth, a feature of all the risings, made the local landlord the target of hostility, even among rebels opposed to the religious settlement.[14] Although many risings were sparked off by specific opposition to a local figure who was not of the long-established gentry but on the make as a landowner—the merchant Dormer in the Buckinghamshire and Oxfordshire rising, Kirby in the Landbeach stir, Smith in the Cambridge rising, White in the Yorkshire commotion and the lawyers Hobart and Flowerdew in Ket's rebellion—once under way they come to possess a bristling hostility and a deep suspicion of the aristocratic order for its irresponsible exploitation, or its failure to stop the exploitation of the people by the raising of rents, enclosing and imparking, and the keeping of too many rabbits, doves,

---

[7] The religious element in the Oxford/Bucks rising is clear in Somerset's remark that it was 'by the instigation of sundry priests . . . for these matters of religion' (Pocock, p. 26) and from the fact that some of the ringleaders were priests (Woodman, *op. cit.*, pp. 82*f*); in contrast the religious element in the Yorkshire rising is only suggested by the rebels' murder of Matthew White, a chantry commissioner and speculator, Foxe's opinion and the circumstantial fact that chantries were particularly numerous in the area of the rising (Dickens, *op. cit.*, pp. 160–62).

[8] PRO SP10/VIII/5 and Pocock, p. 16.

[9] Bindoff, *op. cit.*, pp. 15*f*; Jordan I, pp. 447*f* and *SP Span.* 1547–9, p. 405.

[10] This happened, for example in the Somerset/Wiltshire risings of May (*HMC Bath IV*, p. 109 and Anderson, *op. cit.*, p. 66). The enclosure rioters were responding to the government's proclamation of the previous month (Hughes and Larkin, 327). There had been similar troubles with the anti-enclosure policy of 1548 (see above, pp. 74*f*).

[11] Rose-Troup, *op. cit.*, pp. 98*ff*.

[12] *HMC Rutland I*, p. 36.   [13] Strype II (2), p. 425.

[14] Somerset described the Yorkshire rising as 'for the matter of commons', and featuring 'the pulling down of certain hedges and pales . . .' (BM MS Harley 523, f. 50); for the disparking and deer-killing committed by the Oxford/Bucks rebels, see Jordan I, p. 448.

sheep, bullocks and deer. This did not cause the rebels to question seriously the social structure,[15] but it did render them, in a limited sense, anti-artistocratic. Both the western rebels and Ket's army hounded and looted the gentry indiscriminately,[16] and regarded them with deep suspicion when they came to negotiate. For example Peter Carew's attempts to meet with the western rebels were thwarted by the latter's suspicion 'that the gentlemen were altogether bent to overrun, spoil and destroy them', and in Norfolk the rebels doubted the authenticity of a royal herald who brought the royal pardon, believing him to be 'made by the gentlemen putting on him a piece of an old cope for his coat armour'.[17] In the same atmosphere of crisis, the aristocracy were also moved by a class attitude. They could regard the rebels as revolutionaries without difficulty. In July a gentleman of Devon reported to the Court that some of the rebels 'would have no state of any gentlemen and yet to put all in one bag'.[18] Echoing this sort of evidence, Somerset in August wrote: 'a number would rule another while and direct things as gentlemen have done, and indeed all have conceived a wonderful hatred against gentlemen and taketh them all as their enemies.'[19] Although the rebels produced conservative demands and for the most part refrained from committing murder,[20] the many signs of hostility nourished the aristocracy's traditional fantasy of social revolution. In these circumstances, rapport was difficult between peasant and lord even when non-social grievances, both fiscal and religious, were present. The aristocracy therefore tended not to trouble the government by positively supporting rebellion.

The government's problem arose not from the character of the risings, in spite of their frequency and extensiveness, but because some aristocrats reacted to the threat from below by taking cover or by flight, instead of seeking to restore order. When the local gentry failed to nip a rising in the bud, the onus for restoring order fell upon the government. In the time it took to muster a means of repression, the risings gained the freedom to develop into rebellions. This happened on several occasions in 1549, noticeably in the west and in East Anglia.[21] Where the local authorities acted swiftly and positively, as in the May risings, the Yorkshire rising, in Suffolk, Cambridge and the Midlands, rebellion was contained and the central government went undisturbed.

Since the risings of 1549 occurred in the spring and early summer, there was no question of waiting upon the weather to extinguish them. When let down by the

[15] An exception was possibly the Yorkshire rising which featured a radical prophecy foretelling the eradication of the king and the nobility and that the realm would be ruled in the future by four governors and a parliament of the commons (Dickens, *op. cit.*, pp. 163 *f*).

[16] See Russell, *op. cit.*, pp. 60 *f*, and Rose-Troup, *op. cit.*, pp. 129 and 151.

[17] J. Hooker, *Description of the City of Exeter* (Devon and Cornwall Record Society, 1919), II, p. 61, and BM MS Harley 1576, f. 257b.

[18] Rose-Troup, *op. cit.*, p. 488.   [19] BM MS Harley 523, f. 52b (Strype II (2), EE).

[20] The Yorkshire rebels were the outstanding exception (Dickens, *op. cit.*, pp. 165 *f*). Otherwise, but for those who fell in the streets of Norwich when William Parr's force was repulsed, William Hellyns of Cornwall was the only victim.

[21] For this problem in the west, see Russell's censure of the local gentry (*HMC* MS Exeter, p. 21). For the failure of the Norfolk gentry, see Bindoff, *op. cit.*, pp. 16 *f*.

local gentry, the government therefore had no choice but to intervene. Furthermore, as the royal pardon, the traditional means of bringing the peasantry to order, was on occasions rejected,[22] the government had no choice but to raise troops to deal with subjects. In the absence of a regular army, this meant both a financial burden and the difficulty, not to mention the risk, of raising peasants to deal with their own kind. In dealing with the western rebels, Lord Russell's military problems rested upon his inability, in spite of a commission of array, to raise sufficient troops in Somerset and Dorset to fight against their neighbours in Cornwall and Devon.[23] The only answer was to raise troops in distant counties, but this retarded the confrontation with the rebels. Troops eventually raised in Wiltshire, Gloucestershire and Wales took weeks to reach Russell.[24] The earl of Warwick who also required to cast widely for troops, took a fortnight to mobilize a force to deal with Ket.[25] Somerset in 1549 possessed the advantage of having large numbers of foreign mercenaries in the pay of his government, but he faced the danger of provoking disorder in using them against subjects, and, what is more, he required them principally for the Scottish war.[26]

Persistent peasant risings were a particular problem to Somerset in 1549 because they endangered his top-priority project to plant further garrisons in Scotland. The government could not afford to confront the Scots and peasant rebels with armies simultaneously. It therefore faced a problematical choice of abandoning the garrisoning project and allowing Scottish affairs to degenerate even further, or of risking domestic chaos through delaying military action against the rebels. The war with France which finally broke out on 8 August presented a further problem. At this stage, having postponed the Scottish project in order to deal with the rebels, Somerset now came under pressure to put his house in order to confront the French. The risings acquired a critical importance because they occurred in a time of political crisis when the government was without funds and at war abroad on two fronts.[27]

Because of the state's traditional deficiencies and his present foreign commitments, Somerset had difficulty in taking action against the rebels, but not in deciding to oppose them. He doubtlessly sympathized with their economic grievances.[28] Moreover, since he was pursuing a policy to curb depopulation, he

[22] See below, pp. 89 ff.

[23] Pocock, pp. 32, 40 and 47.

[24] For the various arrangements to provide troops which began on 10 July and which only placed troops at his disposal in early August, see Pocock, pp. 23, 31 f and 35.

[25] His commission authorized him to array the shires of Cambridge, Bedford, Huntingdon, Northants, Norfolk and Suffolk (PRO E351/215 and Tytler I, p. 193). The men of Essex were also summoned (Strype II (1), pp. 272 f). Lord Willoughby joined Warwick with 1,640 men out of Lincolnshire (PRO SP15/III/52).

[26] 1,600 mercenaries were eventually used (PRO E351/43). For popular objections to their employment against subjects, see SP Span. 1547–9, pp. 406 and 424, and Pocock, p. 29.

[27] See below, pp. 91 f.

[28] In view of his social programme. There seems to be some truth in the imperial ambassador's report of 13 June 1549 that 'the protector declared to the council as his opinion that the peasants' demands were fair and just' (SP Span. 1547–9, p. 395) since it reappeared in the charges brought against him at his first trial (Foxe VI, p. 291 (xv)).

was naturally restrained from seeking the mass slaughter of peasant rebels, and as he was keen to blame the risings upon ringleaders, he was prepared to show clemency towards the multitude of misled men. For these reasons he ordered Russell to spare 'the common and mean men' and 'execute the heads and chief-stirrers of the rebellion', and could inform Sir Philip Hoby that 'to spare as much as may be the effusion of blood and namely that of our own nation [is] the thing we most desire'.[29] In dealing with the rebels, he was also keen to apply justice impartially. This meant an insistence that rebels who obtained a pardon should be protected from reprisal and that subjects charged with rebellion should receive a fair trial.[30] In this context Somerset's thirst for virtue could and did lead his contemporaries to misunderstand the nature of his sympathy.[31] Finally, to counter the objections of others that social remedy caused rebellion, he was keen to show that such remedies on the contrary could terminate it. Therefore, in the cause of appeasement and self-justification, he promised the calling down of rents and a modification of the sheep tax; he ordered Russell to seek a remedy for the social causes of dissension in the west; he fixed prices by proclamation, and issued enclosure commissions.[32] But Somerset did not favour rebellion. It was a means of action he abhorred. For him persistent rebellion represented an illness in the body politic which could only be cured by the spilling of blood.[33] His attitude towards rebellion was thoroughly critical and conventional. Rebels were 'lewd, seditious and evil disposed persons'. Reporting upon the final overthrow of Ket, he commented: 'thus are these vile wretches that have now of a long time troubled the realm and as much as in them have gone about to destroy and utterly undo the same come to confusion.' No matter what was said at Somerset's trial, the government's treatment of rebellion in 1549 was not hindered by an unusual sympathy for it, a fact emphatically demonstrated by Somerset's extensive surviving correspondence on the subject.[34]

[29] See Pocock, p. 53, and Strype II (2), p. 424.

[30] *HMC* Bath IV, p. 111, Hughes and Larkin 340, *APC* II, p. 317, Pocock, p. 49, Woodman, *op. cit.*, p. 84, and A. L. Rowse, *Tudor Cornwall* (London, 1941), p. 288.

[31] See PRO SP10/VIII/56 and Foxe VI, pp. 290 f (iii, xiii and xiv).

[32] Russell, *op. cit.*, pp. 58 f, SP10/VIII/5 and Pocock, pp. 61 and 67. His promises should not be taken at their face value. Those promises he made to the Norfolk rebels, for example, were belied by the government report to Russell that the Norfolk rebels 'stand for present reformation, and yet must they tarry a parliament time' (Pocock, p. 32). The price-fixing proclamation emerged from the spring risings and was used to good effect in Kent and Essex (*SP Span.* 1547–9, p. 405). It was thereafter used to appease the Norfolk rebels (Russell, *op. cit.*, p. 58) and the western rebels (Pocock, pp. 17–18). For the use of the enclosure commission as a means of appeasement, see Russell, *op. cit.*, p. 58, and Pocock, p. 17, and see below, p. 90.

[33] Jordan's assertion that Somerset failed to take militant action against the rebels because he was 'wholly unwilling to use troops . . . against his fellow country-men' lacks evidence and conviction (Jordan I, p. 444).

[34] For the year 1549, fourteen letters survive in which Somerset declared his views on rebellion, all belonging to the quarter, June, July, August and September, 1549: to Henry Grey, marquis of Dorset and Francis Hastings, earl of Huntingdon, 11 June (PRO SP10/VII/31); to John Thynne, 15 June (*HMC* Bath IV, p. 111); to George Day, Bishop of Chichester, 25 June (*ibid.*); to Lord Russell, 12 July (Pocock, pp. 25 ff); to the vice-chancellor and mayor of Cambridge, 13 July (Russell, *op. cit.*, App. K); to William Cecil, 16 July (*ibid.*, App. L); to Lord Russell, 27 July (misdated by Pocock) (Pocock, pp. 27 f); to Russell, 8 August (*ibid.*, p. 46); to Russell, 11 August (*ibid.*, pp. 53 ff); to Sir

Government Intervention

The most noticeable feature of the government's treatment of peasant rebellion in 1549 was that with troops available it had no compunction in using them. The rebels of Oxfordshire and Buckinghamshire, for example, rose as Lord Grey with a force of 1,500 men passed on his way to help Lord Russell against the westerners.[35] Without scruple the government directed him against these new rebels. Somerset was clearly involved. He informed Lord Russell on 12 July of his hope that, within six days, Grey 'shall . . . chastise them'. On 18 July he and other councillors reported with some satisfaction how Grey had 'chased the rebels of Buckinghamshire, Oxfordshire and those parties to their houses and taken 200 of them and a dozen of the ringleaders delivered unto him, whereof part at least shall suffer pains of death to the example of all malefactors.'[36] Grey's proximity to the rising was fortuitous. Elsewhere the government was not so well positioned for military action, and with inadequate troops or without troops at all, it intervened with less rigour and more subtlety, but, nevertheless, not with a greater sympathy for militant disobedience than it had shown towards the rebels of Buckinghamshire and Oxfordshire.

Partly responsible for the government's initial attitude towards the summer risings of 1549 was its earlier success in quelling the spring risings without the use of force. Instead of raising troops, it had alerted and instructed local authorities,[37] and dispatched members of the government who had landed interests in the troubled areas to organize the local gentry: Lord Riche, for example, in Essex, the earl of Arundel in Surrey and Sussex, and Lord St John and the earl of Southampton in Hampshire.[38] Somerset, a substantial landowner in the trouble-spots of Hampshire, Wiltshire and Somerset, remained in London, but operated locally through his servants, John Thynne, Richard Fulmerston and Robert Crouch.[39] By winkling out the ringleaders, hearing grievances, promising remedy and offering a pardon for the rebels who returned home, the risings were pacified unobtrusively and economically and without the mobilization of troops.[40] As a result of its success the government on 4 July could assure the anxious William Paget, then serving as ambassador at the imperial court: 'there is no likelihood of any

---

Philip Hoby, 23 August (BM MS Harley 523, f. 50); to Hoby, 24 August (*ibid.*, ff. 52*ff*, partially printed in Strype II (2), EE); to Hoby, 1 September (BM MS Harley 523, ff. 53b *ff*, partially printed in Strype II (2), FF); to Russell, 18 September (Pocock, p. 74); to Russell, 25 September (Pocock, pp. 74*ff*).

[35] Woodman, *op. cit.*, pp. 79 *f.* The number of troops under Grey's command are probably exaggerated, see n. 60 and n. 61, p. 92. The number was possibly nearer 500.

[36] Pocock, pp. 26*f* and 29.

[37] E.g., PRO SP10/VII/31, Anderson, *op. cit.*, pp. 66 and 68, and SP10/VIII/9.

[38] See Jordan I, pp. 446 and 351*f*, and Anderson, *op. cit.*, p. 68.

[39] *HMC* Bath IV, pp. 109 and 111.

[40] For the activities of Sir Thomas Wyatt in Kent and of Lord Riche in Essex, see Jordan I, p. 446, and of Lord Arundel in Sussex, see *ibid.*, pp. 451*f*, and of John Thynne in Hampshire, see *HMC* Bath IV, p. 111, and Lord Stourton and the bishop of Bath in Somerset, *ibid.*, p. 109; Hughes and Larkin, 334; Wriothesley, *op. cit.*, p. 13, and Pocock, p. 14 (SP10/VII/44). For a contemporary comment on the methods employed and their success in pacifying the spring risings, see Rose-Troup, *op. cit.*, pp. 489 *f.*

great matter to ensue thereof', a fair prediction since the troubled counties of
the spring—Kent, Essex, Sussex, Surrey, Wiltshire, Somerset and Hampshire—
remained comparatively quiet for the rest of the year except for a brief and easily
extinguished flare-up in Kent and Essex in mid-July.[41] This initial success heavily
influenced the government's approach to the summer risings. It proceeded against
the first of them, the western rising, in a similarly discreet and indirect manner.
Local gentry received instructions to put themselves secretly in order, but, in the
meantime, to persuade the rebels to disband, probably with the offer of a pardon.[42]
Court aristocrats with local connections, first Sir Peter and Sir Gawen Carew, and
then Lord Russell, were dispatched westward to organize resistance and to negotiate with the rebels.[43] The emphasis was upon appeasement by verbal persuasion
and concession, and, for this reason, both Somerset and Riche criticized Sir
Peter Carew for provoking a conflict with the rebels at Crediton.[44] Russell's
charge was to convince the rebels that false rumour had misled them, and, while
ordered not to make any concessions in religion, he was instructed to discover
the social and economic causes of unrest and to seek a remedy. To aid him in this
respect he was provided with an enclosure commission and with the price-fixing
proclamation of 2 July, which had been instrumental in appeasing the spring
rebels.[45] The government's dependence on promises of remedy and pardon was
forcefully expressed in the government's printed reply to the rebel's demands of
8 July which stated: 'We would ye were . . . quietly pacified than rigorously
persecuted.'[46] Until this policy had been tried and tested, the government refrained from supplying Russell with troops and instructed him to avoid combat
and to wait upon events.[47]

This policy could not be termed a gentle wooing. From the start the government acted positively and with proven means to restore order. Military arrangements, moreover, were quickly made in case the policy of appeasement failed,
and Russell was soon dispatched to the west with a commission of array for the
counties of Devon, Cornwall, Dorset and Somerset.[48] The government sought to
pacify by terror as well as by clemency. The printed letter of 8 July warned the
rebels that, if they failed to submit, 'we will forthwith extend our princely power
and execute our sharp sword against you, as against very infidels and Turks.'[49]

[41] Pocock, p. 24 n. (a); *ibid.*, p. 32, *SP Span.* 1547–9, p. 405 and *HMC* Hatfield I, 237 (misdated).

[42] PRO SP10/VII/42. The draft of a proclamatory pardon dated 20 June exists (SP10/VII/37).
The instructions of 26 June which refer to earlier instructions appear to suggest that a pardon had been
offered (Pocock, pp. 12 *f*); and the existence of a pardon which could be used seems to be the assumption
of the instructions issued to Russell on 29 June (Pocock, pp. 15 *ff*).

[43] John Vowell, alias Hooker, *The Dyscourse and Dyscoverye of the Lyffe of Sir Peter Carew*, ed. John
Maclean (London, 1857), pp. 50–52; *CPR* 1548–9, p. 251. The order to send Russell thither had been
made before 22 June (PRO SP10/VII/38), and by 26 June Russell was on his way (SP10/VII/42).

[44] John Vowell alias Hooker, *op. cit.*, pp. 50–52.

[45] PRO SP10/VII/40 and Pocock, pp. 17 *f*.

[46] Foxe V, p. 734.

[47] Pocock, p. 11, and PRO SP10/VII/41. Jordan condemns Somerset for this, regarding it not as a
stratagem but an expression of his lofty idealism (Jordan I, p. 462).

[48] See n. 43.

[49] Foxe, *op. cit.*, p. 736.

A proclamation of 11 July threatened rebels after a certain day with treason and the forfeiture of their possessions.[50] The government was prepared neither to concede any of the rebels' religious demands, nor to relinquish the sword if appeasement by policy failed, as Russell's instructions indicated.[51] It is true that the government appeared less willing than Russell to resort to a large-scale military exercise against the rebels. But these differences of opinion only expressed Russell's exposure to the rebels and his need for protection, and the realism of a distant government which had other military schemes in the forefront of its mind. They did not indicate a difference in attitude towards rebellion. When the protector told Russell on 12 July: 'We assure you such care we have to the repression of the most rank traitors', he was speaking his mind.[52]

Appeasement in the spring manner held a special appeal for the government, not because of a tender regard for rebellious subjects, but because of its lack of funds and its military schemes elsewhere. In spite of the emptiness of the treasury and no likelihood of revenue until late in the year,[53] Somerset planned to send an army into Scotland with the purpose of establishing another garrison to serve as a replacement for Haddington. In this way he hoped to regain the initiative in Scotland which had been lost in the previous winter.[54] Urgently requiring troops and funds for this project, as well as to counter the likelihood of French aggression, Somerset was not disposed to waste them on rebels if, as it had been proved, they could be restored to order in other ways. The connection between the rebels and foreign affairs was made by the government on several occasions. The printed letter of 8 July, for example, demanded of the rebels: 'What greater evil could ye commit than even now when our foreign enemy in Scotland and upon the sea seeketh to invade us, to rise in this manner . . . and to give us occasion to spend that force upon you which we meant to bestow upon our enemies, to begin to slay you with that sword which we drew forth against the Scots and other enemies, to make a conquest of our own people which otherwise should have been the whole realm of Scotland?'[55] This was no mere propaganda. It declared the government's current intentions and fears. The government's consequent behaviour to peasant rebels was described by John Hooker, an eye-witness of the western rising. He attributed the government's early response to the western rebels to its preoccupation with 'the weighty causes concerning the state of Scotland', which, he thought, caused Somerset to send 'very courteous letters, gracious proclamations and many merciful offers unto all the commons of these parts to have pacified and satisfied them if they had had so much grace so to have accepted it.'[56]

---

[50] Pocock, p. 24, and Hughes and Larkin, 339.   [51] PRO SP10/VII/40.

[52] Pocock, p. 27. Russell seems to have interpreted Somerset's policy as one of unnatural leniency based upon an unusual sympathy for the rebels (implied in Somerset's reply to a letter from Russell which is now lost, see Pocock, pp. 25–7). This interpretation of Somerset's actions has been accepted as standard (see A. Fletcher, *Tudor Rebellions* (London, 1968), p. 52, Jordan I, p. 462, and Rose-Troup, *op. cit.*, *passim*).

[53] See PRO SP10/VII/38.   [54] See above, pp. 16 f.

[55] Foxe, *op. cit.*, p. 736.   [56] J. Hooker, *Description of the City of Exeter*, II, pp. 59 and 66.

In the face of peasant insurrection the government, certainly by 22 July, had called off the Scottish project.[57] Yet it continued to question Russell's need for a substantial army royal.[58] This was not because it persisted with a policy of non-violent appeasement. The decision to crush the rebellion had been made by 10 July when, in response to Russell's demands for reinforcements, the government prepared to dispatch to him 150 Italian hagbutters, 300–400 horsemen under Lord Grey of Wilton, 400 foreign mercenary horse and 1,000 Almain footmen. It also instructed William Herbert to prepare himself with a force raised in Wiltshire and Gloucestershire. Two days later Somerset assured Russell that he could levy locally 2,000 footmen and 'if it be 4,000 we stick not at it.'[59] But other considerations, particularly risings nearer London, intruded to delay the arrival of these troops. The Buckinghamshire and Oxfordshire rising diverted Lord Grey.[60] New outbreaks in Kent, Essex, Norfolk and Suffolk led to the withdrawal of the Almains and delayed a further move to satisfy Russell's demands for reinforcements, the sending of a main force under the earl of Warwick.[61] In view of the new risings, and the taking of Norwich by Ket, the government naturally felt that its own safety was more seriously threatened from other quarters than by rebels in the distant west who appeared to be laboriously involved in the siege of Exeter. In the meantime the government could only offer Russell a force under Lord William Herbert drawn from South Wales and Gloucestershire.[62]

Russell's military problems in the west originally stemmed from an inability to raise within the sphere of his commission of array men who were willing to oppose the rebels.[63] This left him dependent upon what the government could provide. The latter's unwillingness to supply troops as quickly and as generously as Russell required was not only due to its other priorities, but also to its realistic grasp of the limited resources at its disposal. The government's plight was made evident when soon after the relief of Exeter, it required Russell to dismiss most of his troops in order to lighten the massive burden of the government's military commitments which involved an army of 10,000–12,000 engaged against the Norfolk rebels, a force of 8,000–10,000 men raised to defend the person of the king, the occupation of the Scottish Lowlands 'which is no small charge', and the war with France.[64] Just as the earlier unwillingness to supply Russell with troops showed no sympathy for rebellion, neither did this later willingness to withdraw them. At this late stage, having commended Russell for executing the ringleaders, the government had to reprove him for hesitating in Exeter when the task of mopping up the retreating rebels awaited him.

The government's attitude towards the western rising finally rested upon practical military sense. It questioned Russell's requirements on the grounds of

---

[57] See Pocock, pp. 31 f.   [58] E.g., Pocock, p. 44.
[59] Pocock, pp. 23 and 25. Some of the figures are wrongly given in Pocock, see Inner Temple, MS Petyt 538, 46, f. 436.
[60] Pocock, pp. 26 f.
[61] *Ibid.*, p. 29; *SP Span.* 1547–9, p. 405, and Pocock, p. 31 f.
[62] Pocock, p. 35.
[63] *Ibid.*, pp. 32, 40 and 47.   [64] *Ibid.*, pp. 47, 54 and 56 f.

victualling difficulties. After receiving Russell's news that he had arranged for Lord Herbert to provide him with 10,000 men, the council remarked: 'if seeing now ye complain for want of victual, if such a number of men come unto you, the one of you should be ready to eat another for want.' It pointed out that with unfed troops turning to mutiny 'ye should be in more danger of your own company than of the rebels themselves.'[65] The council justified the rapid dismissal of Russell's forces after the relief of Exeter on the same realistic grounds, as well as for reasons of economy.[66] The government's other military reason for opposing Russell was its belief that small numbers of horse and hagbut could contain the rebels more adequately than large numbers of foot. The government thought that the rebels could be defeated by skirmishing and 'by interruption of their victual' and that as Exeter was most likely to fall to the rebels, in this event, horsemen would serve most effectively to confront and harry the rebels as they proceeded eastward.[67] This preference for small numbers of well-equipped troops to deal with what was assumed to be an ill-equipped rabble dominated government thinking from late June until late July when Russell's entreaties for massive numbers of foot were conceded.

The final military consideration in the government's response to the westerners owed something to Somerset's own military experience. The military advice the council conveyed to Russell closely resembled the strategy and tactics which Somerset had successfully employed in the previous seven years against the Scots. In the course of the eight years war, Somerset had continually advocated other means than a mighty army royal for the subjection of Scotland. In 1542 he had thought of controlling the Scots by impeding the trade of the Forth; in 1545 he played a waiting game with a small holding force while relying upon a lack of provisions to drive a large Scottish army into retirement; in 1547-9 he constructed a network of forts in Scotland in order to dispense with armies royal.[68] Russell's instructions from the council to employ devious means of combat, to skirmish and deny access to victuals, to found a garrison at Sherborne, to wait for time to break the rebels down, to avoid putting an army royal in the field, all strongly echoed Somerset's Scottish experience.[69] Also reflected in his approach to the western rebels and to the Norfolk rebels as well, were some of the problems he had and still encountered in Scotland. At a time when the victualling of the Haddington garrison was the government's main headache, Somerset was understandably inclined to safeguard against victualling difficulties in the war against the rebels and to attempt their overthrow by depriving them of supplies.[70]

From first to last the government's main aim was to end the western rising in the quietest and most economical manner possible, not for the sake of the rebels, but to conserve its own interests, reputation and resources. When the actions of local gentry and the offers of pardon and promises of remedy failed to bring

[65] *Ibid.*, pp. 44 f.
[66] *Ibid.*, pp. 47 and 54.
[67] *Ibid.*, pp. 15, 22 f, 30 f, 34 f and 40.
[68] See above, pp. 12 f, and Thesis, pp. 355 ff.
[69] Pocock, pp. 11 and 30 f, and SP10/VII/41.
[70] See above, n. 65 and n. 67.

results, it resorted without compunction to military force. A similar procedure was followed in East Anglia.

The government's approach to these two outstanding risings of the year was far from identical. Because the demands of the East Anglian rebels were not religious, the government could make concessions which were more relevant to the rebels' main demands.[71] However, it was not prepared to show the rebellion more tolerance or gentleness of treatment. Somerset ordered the mayor and vice-chancellor of Cambridge: 'if by gentleness the offenders do not cease their evil, let them cease . . . by your execution', and he warned the Norfolk rebels that if they failed to disband, the king would use 'sharper means to maintain both his own dignity and the common quiet.'[72] The failure of appeasement, the persistence of Ket's rebellion, its proximity to London and the defeat of a royal force under Lord Parr at the end of July which made reprisal a point of honour,[73] steeled the government in its determination to crush the rising. It dissipated the resources of men and money originally reserved for the Scottish project principally against the East Anglians.[74] Neither the Scottish consideration nor the priority of other risings influenced the government's behaviour towards Ket. Consequently there was less delay in sending troops. Military action, moreover, became an urgent necessity following France's declaration of war upon England on 8 August. This news convinced the government that, at the earliest opportunity, the rebels had to be crushed so that 'we shall the better attend foreign doings.'[75] Otherwise the approach to the two risings was much the same. Just as Lord Russell had been quickly commissioned to array the militia of the western shires against the rebels of Devon and Cornwall, Lord Willoughby was soon made captain-general of Lincolnshire and Norfolk and authorized to levy the subjects there for action against the rebels of East Anglia.[76] His instructions, like Russell's, were to proceed harshly if military action became necessary. However, at first the government again sought to do without military intervention, receiving the rebels' demands, making offers of pardon, extending promises of remedy, announcing enclosure commissions, proclaiming the fixing of certain prices, and threatening 'sharper means' if the king's clemency was ignored.[77] Following the rejection of the offers of pardon, and the rebels' success in taking the provincial capital, the government prepared for sterner action, but, as in the west, fought shy of a substantial force, and sought to evade head-on conflict with the rebels. Since Willoughby was involved in the defence of King's Lynn, Lord Parr with 1,400 troops, mainly cavalry, marched on Norwich with instructions 'to avoid the fight', to present

[71] Russell, *op. cit.*, pp. 58 f.

[72] *Ibid.*, and App. K.

[73] For the impact of Parr's defeat on the government's deliberations, see Lodge I, p. 133.

[74] The government explained to the citizens of Yarmouth on 6 August that it was dispatching a main force against the rebels now that the risings had 'taken from us all opportunity to follow our entire and good proceedings in Scotland' (Russell, *op. cit.*, pp. 108 f).

[75] Pocock, p. 59.

[76] PRO E351/217: by 21 July, twelve days after the original outbreak.

[77] Russell, *op. cit.*, pp. 58 f. The first offer of pardon was made on 20 July, the second a day later (Mayors Court Book, 1534–49, Norwich City Record Office, f. 67).

the royal pardon, and if necessary, to persuade the rebels to accept it by cutting their supply lines.[78] Parr's defeat in the streets of Norwich caused the government to put a main force in the field. Somerset himself intended to lead it,[79] but was then replaced by Warwick.

Circumstances such as the abandonment of the Scottish project, the outbreak of war with France, and the rebels' success in taking Norwich and in repelling Parr dictated a somewhat different approach to the Norfolk rebels. But running through the government's policy towards the risings as a whole was a thread of consistency which rendered the treatment of the East Anglians and the westerners remarkably alike. The differences certainly cannot be seen as a victory of a hard-line policy over one of gentleness which replaced Somerset by Warwick as leader of the force directed against Ket.[80] Somerset's replacement seemed a consequence of Russell's victory over the western rebels which released Warwick for action in the east.[81] Moreoever, Warwick's leadership produced no radical change in the approach to peasant rebellion. His primary aim was fully consistent with former policy—to secure a simple surrender by means of a pardon.[82] With the pardon again rejected, he sought to starve the peasants out of Mousehold Heath by impeding their supplies of victuals. Employing the tactics which Parr had been instructed to use but had failed to apply, Warwick succeeded in driving the rebels from the heath where they had been safe against cavalry attack.[83] Furthermore, even when the rebels formed in battle array on the exposed plain of Dussin's Dale, he did not conduct a slaughter. To deal with them he deployed only the newly arrived Almains and his horsemen, a force of 3,000 men.[84] Before the first engagement, he offered another pardon. After the first sortie, a round of hagbut fire followed by a cavalry charge which shattered the rebels' ranks, he offered it yet again. The rebellion came to an end when his own personal presentation of the pardon ensured its acceptance.[85]

Ket's rebellion ended in a slaughter of peasants.[86] But the responsibility did not

---

[78] PRO E351/217; Parr had been dispatched by 27 July (see Pocock, p. 28 (misdated by Pocock) and Bindoff, *op. cit.*, p. 5). Edward VI's journal suggests a preponderance of horsemen (*The Chronicle and Political Papers of King Edward VI*, ed. W. K. Jordan (London, 1966), p. 15. Also see Pocock, pp. 58 *f*.

[79] Lodge I, p. 133, and Strype II (1), pp. 272 *f*.

[80] For the suggestion that tougher members acquired dominance and dictated a change in policy, see Jordan I, p. 444.

[81] Somerset had been appointed by 6 August (Strype II (1), pp. 272 *f*). Within the next twenty-four hours, during which time the news of the relief of Exeter must have reached the government, Warwick's commission to lead an army against the Scots was at last revoked and instead of the plan to send him to Russell (Pocock, p. 30), he was commissioned to lead the shires of Cambridgeshire, Bedfordshire, Huntingdonshire, Northants, Norfolk and Suffolk against Ket (PRO E351/215, APC II, p. 309, and Tytler I, p. 193).

[82] Russell, *op. cit.*, pp. 123–5.

[83] Strype II (2), pp. 426 *f*, and Russell, *op. cit.*, pp. 142–4.

[84] *Ibid.*, p. 144. For the numbers of horsemen, see PRO E351/215, 217 and 221. The total force numbered 8,000 (E351/215, 217 and 221, PRO SP15/III/52 and APC II, p. 316). It fell considerably short of the 10,000–12,000 reported by Somerset to Russell (Pocock, pp. 56 *f*).

[85] Russell, *op. cit.*, pp. 144–8.

[86] Jordan I, pp. 492 *f*.

lie with Warwick who, according to Somerset, tried to prevent a massacre.[87] Instead it lay with the intransigence of the rebels, and also the determination of the gentlemen, who had cringed away earlier, to prove and to reassert themselves in acts of revenge.[88] In the military treatment of peasant rebels Somerset and Warwick saw eye to eye. Warwick's suppression of the East Anglians, with its reliance on horsemen, hagbutters and cutting supply lines, followed and justified the advice which the government had earlier pressed upon an unwilling and uncomprehending Lord Russell.

The treatment of rebellion clearly displayed the hand of Somerset, but was not necessarily his sole responsibility. In the spring there was criticism in the council of the government's handling of rebels. This originated probably in the disapproval of Somerset's earlier public announcement of a campaign against agrarian offences which had been responsible for sparking off the disturbances.[89] Paget recorded this opposition in the council in a letter from the imperial Court early in July. He accused Somerset of showing too much leniency and of ignoring the council, and declared that 'in this matter of the commons every man of the council hath misliked your proceedings and wished it other ways.' Certain inconsistencies in the government's behaviour confirmed Paget's impression.[90] The May proclamation which threatened force against enclosure rioters temporarily closed Somerset's campaign against agrarian offences,[91] and probably marked a victory for Somerset's opponents in the council. But the government took no harsh action against rebellious subjects[92] and finally, to close the proceedings against the spring rebels, the second proclamation criticized at Somerset's trial was issued, which confirmed an earlier pardon with a grant of immunity for crimes committed by the rebels during the risings.[93] This seemed to mark a victory for a policy not of force but of conciliation.

A struggle appeared to be in progress in the spring between a party keen on pacification by means of promises of remedy and pardon, and a party which saw remedy as an encouragement to disobedience and called instead for a show of force. The struggle resulted in Somerset treating rebellion in a way which ran counter to the wishes of his colleagues.[94] In contrast, signs of division within the council are not so evident for the summer risings.[95] By the summer, a policy of concili-

[87] Strype II (2), pp. 426 *f* ; for contemporary comments on Warwick's restraint of the local gentry, see Jordan I, p. 491.

[88] For the attitude of the gentry, see PRO SP10/VIII/55 (1).

[89] See above, p. 76 and n. 10, p. 85.

[90] Strype II (2), pp. 431–3. Paget was referring not to the immediate past, but to the period before mid-June when he left England for the imperial court.

[91] Hughes and Larkin, 333, and see above, p. 76.

[92] Herbert acted harshly in Wiltshire (E. K. Jordan, ed., *The Chronicle and Political Papers of Edward VI*, p. 12), and Riche in Essex (see above, n. 40), but, apparently, on their own initiative.

[93] Issued on 12 July (Hughes and Larkin, 340). The text refers to ex-rebels, and clearly relates to the spring risings.

[94] Paget's statement that every member of the council was against Somerset in this matter is not necessarily true. Warwick was most probably against (see above, n. 185, p. 76), but Lord Arundel's actions in dealing with the rebels of Sussex indicated an appeaser, not a chastizer (Jordan I, pp. 451 *f*).

[95] Most of the charges brought against Somerset in October which concerned the 1549 risings

ation had proved that it could reduce peasants to order. Furthermore, in the summer Somerset declared himself to be thoroughly conventional in his abhorrence of rebellion and showed his willingness to use force. There is no evidence that this behaviour was dominated by his colleagues. The insistence on conciliation and pardon remained and the decision to use force seemed a logical consequence of enduring rebellion and of the availability of troops. In view of the consistency of a policy which seemed a response to practical considerations not radical ideas, and also considering the fact that the government's instructions on rebellion usually took the form of conciliar dispatches in which St John, Riche and Cranmer regularly deliberated,[96] the government's response to the summer risings seems to have rested on a consensus of opinion in the council and on shifting circumstances rather than upon the idealism of one man who in the later stages of the risings happened to be overborne.

Outcome

In quelling disorder, the government's policy towards the rebellions of 1549 was eminently successful. Most of the risings were dispersed as the government intended, with minimal effort and expense. This was true both of the spring risings and the summer ones. The Yarmouth, Landbeach, Cambridge, Suffolk, Yorkshire, Kent, Essex and Midland stirs of the summer were all pacified without the government's military intervention.[97] Plenty of evidence continued to justify the government's initial policy of delaying direct military action, and the year demonstrated that the traditional offer of a royal pardon and promises of remedy was the most effective way to subdue peasant rebels. Furthermore, in the exceptional cases where the government applied the sword, it easily accomplished its objective without heavy losses of capital and men. The total cost of coping with the risings of 1549 came to £28,122, a substantial but not an astronomical sum, and was a demonstration that the government had succeeded in its urgent attempt to economize.[98] In addition, the military tactics favoured by the government proved correct with the Norfolk rebels starved onto the plain by a lack of

---

appeared to relate to the handling of the spring risings, and seemed to represent a raking up of former grievances in the search for charges to bring against him (Foxe VI, p. 291 (x, xii, xiv, xv and xvi)). The exceptions are charges iii and xiii which might relate to the grievance of a number of gentlemen in September concerning the granting of individual pardons to certain rebels, and the dismissal of charges brought against others (PRO SP10/VIII/56), possibly suggesting a revival of conflict over the treatment of rebels following the suppression of the summer risings.

[96] For the western rebellion these outnumbered instructions from Somerset alone by 17 to 2. Fifteen councillors at various times applied their signature, in the following order of frequency: Somerset (17), St John (16), Riche (12), Petre (11), Cranmer (10), Wingfield (6), Paget (5), Southampton, Sadler, Warwick, Smith (3), North (2), Wotton, Denny, Northampton (1). Paget signed regularly after his return from the imperial court. The dispatches are printed in Pocock.

[97] Cambridge: Russell, *op. cit.*, App. K, and App. L; Landbeach: J. R. Ravensdale, *op. cit.*, pp. 108–12; Suffolk: Jordan I, pp. 446 f; Yarmouth: Russell, *op. cit.*, p. 46 and n. 6; Yorkshire: Dickens, *op. cit.*, pp. 167 f; Midlands: Lodge I, p. 134; Kent: *HMC Hatfield* I, 237; Essex: *SP Span.* 1547–49, p. 405, and *APC* II, pp. 313 f.

[98] BM MS Harley 353, f. 102.

victuals and defeated by hagbut and horse, while the crucial defeat of the western-ers at Fenny Bridges occurred before any reinforcements had reached Russell.[99] The government's failure was to prevent the risings from dictating the rest of its policy. Because of them and in spite of the government's efforts, the Scottish project had to be postponed at least for another year. The risings, moreover, al-lowed the French to seize a ring of forts surrounding Boulogne without difficulty or fear of immediate reprisal, and thus to dishonour the English Crown.[100] They left the government even more impoverished not only because of the sums spent in subduing them but also because of their disruptive effect upon the col-lection of revenue.[101]

Somerset's effective, efficient and flexible treatment of rebellion contrasted sharply with his disastrous Scottish policy and his ineffectual programme of social reform. Nevertheless, the aristocracy did not allow it to count in his favour. They failed to appreciate its subtlety and practicality, and because of it they branded him as a radical. He did not have this reputation before the risings. It cannot be seen as a simple product of his programme of social reform. Men only came to see him in this light when his social programme proved to be a cause of insurrection, and when it seemed that Somerset was prepared to allow the in-surrections some licence. The charge of unwarranted leniency towards the risings was made by Paget, Smith and Russell, who criticized the reliance on pardons and proclamations and advocated the application of force.[102] The next step was to explain this supposed leniency in terms of sympathy. Russell did so by implication, as did Van der Delft, the imperial ambassador, in his capacity of purveyor of Court rumour.[103] The charge was made again at his trial.[104] Because of the aris-tocracy's extreme conception of rebellion, sympathy for it implied support for revolution. The final step was, in the light of this leniency, to re-assess Somerset's social programme as an attack on the traditional order. In July Paget reported to Somerset the rumour that 'you have some greater enterprise in your head that lean so much to the multitude.'[105] By late 1549, as a result of his policy towards insurrection and the new light it seemed to throw upon his social aims, Somerset had acquired a widely accepted public reputation as a radical. In September Sir Anthony Aucher reported that the gentry were 'in jealousy of my lord's friend-ship, yea, and to be plain, think my lord grace rather to will the decay of the gentlemen than otherwise'.[106] In October, at the time of his overthrow, circulated handbills proclaimed him as the particular friend of the poor commons,[107] and in November the peasantry of Norfolk expected the protector's tenantry to

[99] See above, p. 95, and Rose-Troup, *op. cit.*, pp. 255 *ff.*
[100] For Somerset's account of these disasters and the blame he attached to rebellious subjects for causing them, see *SP Span.* 1547-9, p. 232, and BM MS Harley 523, f. 55.
[101] *SP For.* 1547-53, 196.
[102] See n. 90, PRO SP10/VIII/33, and Pocock, pp. 25 *ff.*
[103] *SP Span.* 1547-9, p. 395.
[104] Foxe VI, p. 291 (xii, xiii, xiv and xv).
[105] Strype II (2), p. 431.
[106] PRO SP10/VIII/56.   [107] Tytler I, pp. 209 and 210 *f.*

come to their assistance if they rose again.[108] Because of this reputation, his overthrow was easily accomplished.

There was no question of Somerset deserving the reputation. While sympathetic towards certain of the grievances which the rebels professed, his attitude towards rebellion was one of conventional antipathy. His policy towards rebellion stemmed not from radical sentiments but from his urgent need to wage war in Scotland and to withstand the French, as well as to demonstrate the efficacy of redressing social ills as a means of quelling disorder. When conciliation failed, he proceeded to use force. The 'sword' was as much a part of his armoury for dealing with rebellion as 'policy'.

[108] See Mayors' Court Book, 1549–55, Norwich City Record Office, f. 3. As this occurred after Somerset's fall, it is possible that the implied radicalism resulted from rumours generated by Somerset's fall and the charges brought against him.

5

Religious Policy

Measures

In the brief period of the protectorate the anglican church was transformed by means of the Homilies' assertion of sole faith; the Order of Communion's eviction of compulsory auricular confession; the statutes for communion in two kinds, clerical marriage and a new vernacular service which allowed the abolition of the catholic mass; and the council's orders for the complete destruction of images, the liming of churches and for the prohibition of Ash Wednesday ashes, Palm Sunday palms, and Good Friday creeping to the cross. So positive and extensive were the changes in religion that Bishops Bonner and Gardiner preferred prison to conformity, Dr Richard Smith fled the country, Princess Mary forsook the Court and in 1548 and 1549 peasants and priests resorted to rebellion. At the same time protestants were troubled by the persistence of popery.[1] What was achieved in such a short time makes nonsense of any charge against the government of tardiness or even caution in changing matters of religion; but, like the conservatives in religion, the dissatisfied protestants had a case. Obscuring the settlement was a pervasive discretion which produced an air of ambiguity and compromise. This applied not only to the well-known instance of the Prayer Book which removed the elevation of the host and sacrificial language, and emphasized the mass as a thanksgiving and a memorial rather than a sacrifice and a work, but retained the canon, traditional vestments, the altar, candles, chrism and a prayer for the dead and failed to deny overtly catholic doctrine.[2] The same discretion is also evident in the act for communion in two kinds which sheltered behind the disarming declaration that there was no 'condemning hereby the usage of any church out of the king's majesty's dominion'.[3] The Order of Communion, moreover, tactfully moderated its replacement of private auricular confession with a general confession in the eucharistic service when it permitted the communicant the choice of an additional private confession, an arrangement which was incorporated in the Prayer Book.[4] Through ambiguity, compromise and tact, the impact of change was muffled, its definition blurred, and it was possible to think that the past had been modified, not reformed.

[1] E.g., see the reports of Hooper and Dryander to Bullinger (*Original Letters* I, pp. 71 f, and C. Hopf, *Martin Bucer and the English Reformation* (Oxford, 1946), p. 57).

[2] A. H. Couratin, 'The Holy Communion 1549', *Church Quarterly Review* 164 (1963), pp. 150 ff, A. G. Dickens, *The English Reformation* (London, 1964), pp. 218 f, and Hopf, *op. cit.*, p. 56.

[3] 1 Edward VI, c. 1.   [4] Couratin, *op. cit.*, p. 148.

The second outstanding characteristic of the settlement was its moderate enforcement. Victims were relatively few, martyrs at the stake were non-existent, and the conservative bishops tumbled from office in any number only after Somerset's fall.[5] Nevertheless, the lack of rigour in the settlement's enforcement did not allow all that much tolerance. Richard Smith, for example, lost his professorship of divinity at Oxford because of his conservative opinions, and was made to recant.[6] Both Bonner's and Gardiner's imprisonment followed a process of hounding them into making a declaration of their non-conformity.[7] The first session of parliament forbad the public discussion of the mass.[8] In time, and under the pressure of critical circumstances, the protectorate became an oppressive regime. By September 1548 preaching had been prohibited;[9] by August 1549 no book could be printed without the permission of the government, and no play whatsoever could be performed.[10] During the protectorate commissions were issued to test the conformity of the clergy and the members of colleges and universities;[11] and in April 1549 the laity came under surveillance with a commission to search out heretics and contemners of the Prayer Book.[12] Princess Mary was allowed some freedom to celebrate the old mass, but only as a temporary concession.[13] The repeal act abolished the heresy laws but essentially to relieve protestants of a former source of oppression.[14] Furthermore, although the first act of uniformity failed to make penal provision for lay attendance at church, it did not grant the laity a new liberty, since, in the traditional manner, it left the task of enforcing attendance to the ecclesiastical authorities.[15] The protectorate witnessed no departure from the principle of conformity, which the government diligently upheld.[16] However, while the degree of moderation in the settlement's enforcement has been exaggerated, the regime certainly showed a noticeable leniency in the persecution of religious dissent when placed within the context of the age.

Neither of these generally accepted characteristics seemed the simple realization of beliefs and principles.[17] Somerset's responsibility for the settlement is undeniable, but the settlement did not bear much relation to his religious views. Like the rest of his policy, the changes in religion are inexplicable if seen in a void and separated from the rest of the government's business. It is the familiar story; in his direction of the reformation, Protector Somerset responded to a political

[5] Only Bonner was deprived under Somerset, while Gardiner, Heath, Day, Tunstall, Veysey and Rugge were either deprived or forced to resign under the Northumberland regime (L. B. Smith, *Tudor Prelates and Politics, 1536–1558* (Princeton Studies in History, 8 (1953), p. 256 n. 9).

[6] R. W. Dixon, *History of the Church of England* (Oxford, 1872–1902), III, pp. 114.

[7] See below, pp. 113–16.

[8] 1 Edward VI, c. 1.

[9] Hughes and Larkin, 313. Earlier in the year all unlicensed preaching was banned (*ibid.*, 303).

[10] *APC* II, p. 312, and Hughes and Larkin, 344.

[11] Jordan I., pp. 163–6, and T. Rymer, *Foedera*, XV, pp. 178 *f* and 183 *ff*.

[12] *Ibid.*, pp. 181 *ff*.   [13] See below, pp. 116 *f*.

[14] See below, p. 136.   [15] Dickens, *op. cit.*, p. 220.

[16] W. K. Jordan provides the evidence but imposes upon it contrary conclusions (Jordan I, pp. 146 *f* and 219–29).

[17] For the opposed view, see Jordan I, pp. 126 *f*.

situation created by his primary desire to pursue war. In this respect, the settlement was heavily influenced by his political ambitions.

Somerset's Religious Beliefs

In 1539, shortly after the passing of the act of six articles, Somerset entertained Latimer at his house, indicating that when he became protector his protestant sympathies were of long-standing. However, until the death of Henry VIII, his association with protestantism was understandably shadowy and provided no precise clues to the nature of his beliefs.[18] The opening of the new reign produced reports of Somerset's positive protestantism; Hilles informed Bullinger that Somerset was 'well disposed to pious doctrine' and 'not very favourable to the priests', and the imperial ambassador revealed that in December 1547 the old mass had ceased to be celebrated in his house.[19] By 1549 protestants regarded him as a driving force of religious change. Peter Alexander, for example, recommended Somerset to Martin Bucer as 'a very pious man and one exceedingly desirous of extending and adorning the christian religion.[20] Furthermore, he became sufficiently advanced in his beliefs for Peter Martyr and Stumphius to enthuse over his early release from the Tower in 1550 and for Calvin to be distressed by his death.[21] However, while bearing witness to his anticlericalism, his piety, his desire for change, and, while suggesting that his protestantism was far from mild, this evidence fails to define either the character or the course of his beliefs in the crucial period of the protectorate. His own writings and statements on religion hardly remedy this deficiency. From his correspondence it is clear that, early on in the protectorate, he expected bishops not to have 'cure and charge out of their diocese', preferred changes in religion to be determined by laymen as well as clerics, believed in the superiority of scriptural authority, sole faith, and the necessity of services in the vulgar tongue and regarded images as idolatrous.[22] Furthermore, he saw the reformation as one of the government's main tasks, declaring in June 1548 that it was 'no small part of our charge under the king's majesty to bring his people from ignorance to knowledge and from superstition to true religion'.[23] His own devotional writings indulged in pious sentiments about the humility of man before God, but, as with the correspondence, do not admit a substantial definition of his beliefs during the protectorate.[24] Of

[18] Seymour Papers, Box 5, 18 (23 May); see Thesis, pp. 477–81.

[19] *Original Letters* I, pp. 256 and 258; *SP Span.* 1547–9, p. 221.

[20] G. C. Gorham, *Gleanings of a Few Scattered Ears during the Period of the Reformation in England* (London, 1857), p. 75.

[21] *Original Letters* II, pp. 464 f and 737, and see below, p. 111.

[22] Muller, App. 3; Burnet II (2), 28 (bk I); Foxe VI, pp. 28 f; Muller, 136; H. C. Porter, *Reformation and Reaction in Tudor Cambridge* (Cambridge, 1958), p. 67, and PRO SP10/V/12.

[23] Burnet II (2), p. 220.

[24] These include a prayer (Strype II (2), B), a preface to the published tract *A Spiritual and Most Precious Pearl* (London, 1550), prayers composed prior to his death (BM MS Stowe 1066) and his own published translation of a letter Calvin sent to him in October 1549 (E. Somerset, *An Epistle from Calvin* (London, 1550)).

greater help is the contribution he made to the Lords' debate on the Prayer Book in December 1548. At one point he ruled out a reference to Erasmus as an authority because of an original agreement not to cite recent writers, a possible indication of proper chairmanship but also a suggestion that his beliefs lay none too close to humanism. He also threatened Thirlby with dire punishment for accusing the government of tampering with the Prayer Book after the bishops had given their consent to it in September, a sign of temper, but also of the limited extent of his gentleness and tolerance. In response to Thirlby, he declared that the consultation with the bishops had been 'for unity', suggesting that the exact realization of one belief was not his major concern. The debate also revealed something of his attitude towards the eucharist. He opened the debate with the disputing point as to 'whether the bread be in the sacrament after the consecration or not', and later, following an assertion by Bonner of the verity of the presence, he declared that 'there is bread still'.[25] The debating point was a subtle choice because, as the debate revealed, it allowed catholic doctrine to be questioned by focusing discussion on the role of consecration and faith, while keeping it away from the minefield of the real presence.[26] It certainly allowed the believers in transubstantiation to be separated from the rest, but it did not differentiate the believers from the disbelievers in the real presence. In the ensuing debate the latter distinction came to be made when certain bishops ignored the point of debate and declared the omission of the adoration to indicate a wish to present the bread and wine as signs. But this did not draw Somerset into the open, although it produced statements of disbelief in a real presence from Ridley, Cranmer and Smith.[27] Consequently, Somerset declared his disbelief in transubstantiation but not in the real presence. Nevertheless, the debate added another fact about Somerset's attitude towards the sacrament of the altar. The imperial ambassador's statement that mass was no longer celebrated in Somerset's household was probably more indicative of the repeal of the act of six articles, which had shortly preceded it, than a true statement of the date at which Somerset became disenchanted with the old mass, but it does reveal that Somerset abandoned the catholic mass for his own personal use long before the Prayer Book caused the nation to follow suit. In addition, the Lords' debate revealed that, as early as 1548, Somerset had abandoned a view of the eucharist which the Prayer Book appeared to accept.

While the evidence does not permit an insight into what Somerset precisely felt about doctrine, forms of worship or the organization of the church at any particular time, it would be wrong, even in the absence of more specific and systematic evidence, to regard his protestantism as a form of moderate and cautious piety which the official religious changes of the protectorate mirrored.[28] The

[25] F. A. Gasquet and E. Bishop, *Edward VI and the Book of Common Prayer* (London, 1890), App. V, p. 423; *ibid.*, p. 406 and T. F. Shirley, *Thomas Thirlby, Tudor Bishop* (London, 1964), pp. 98–100; Gasquet and Bishop, *op. cit.*, p. 404; *ibid.*, pp. 397 and 407.

[26] The real presence became the subject of the debate only because of the refusal of certain bishops to abide by Somerset's debating point.

[27] Gasquet and Bishop, *op. cit.*, pp. 397 and 405; *ibid.*, pp. 434–5 (Ridley), p. 440 (Cranmer), and pp. 423*f* (Smith).   [28] For a representation of this view, see Jordan I, pp. 125–7.

H

key to his religious beliefs in the period of the protectorate lies in his protégés and associates rather than in his words and reputation. They reveal him as much more than pious and anticlerical, far from moderate or ambiguous in his religious affiliations, and far removed from 'the Erasmian tradition'.[29]

During the protectorate Somerset associated closely with John Hooper, William Turner and Thomas Becon, three men notable and notorious for their religious works, and fiercely committed, extreme and uncompromising in their religious opinions. All of them had been victims of the Henrician government. In taking them into his house, Somerset made explicit his inclination towards radical protestantism.

John Hooper returned to England in May 1549, having fled from the Henrician government five years earlier. He spent the first three years of his exile in Strasbourg, and the remainder of the time in Zurich. In Zurich he had lived with Bullinger, studying theology under his tutorship and Hebrew and the Old Testament with his disciple Pellican. In this period Hooper became thoroughly captivated with Zwinglian doctrine and the liturgy of the 'templa Tigurinorum' with its exclusion of images, altars, statues, banners and organs. Before returning to England he plainly declared his devotion to the Zwinglian school in *An Answer to the Bishop of Winchester's Book* and *A Declaration of Christ and his Office*. Because of this close association with Zurich, he was heralded as 'the future Zwingli of England' upon his arrival in the country accompanied by his wife, a former sacramentarian and a refugee in her own right, and his daughter Rachel, the godchild of Bullinger.[30] William Turner had also taken refuge in Zurich, as well as in Basle, Cologne and Emden. During his exile he came under the particular influence of John a Lasco, a later friend of Hooper and a subscriber to similar Zwinglian views.[31] Summoned by Somerset, Turner returned to England soon after Edward VI's accession.[32] Thomas Becon escaped Henry VIII not by going abroad but by retreating beyond the reach of Westminster into the Midlands and the Peak District.[33] Nevertheless, although his wanderings failed to bring him into contact with continental reformers, by the time of his return to London in 1547, he held views which fall into the same category as those of Hooper and Turner.

For Hooper the real presence was 'but a yesterday's bird', and the sacrament of the Lord's Supper, like the other sacraments, was basically 'a testimony of God's

---

[29] A case is made for the humanist connection by J. K. McConica in his *English Humanists and Reformation Politics under Henry VIII and Edward VI* (Oxford, 1965), pp. 238 f.

[30] C. H. Smyth, *Cranmer and the Reformation under Edward VI* (Cambridge, 1926), pp. 97 f, and C. W. Dugmore, 'The First Ten Years, 1549–59', in *The English Prayer Book, 1549–1662* (London, 1963), pp. 16–18.

[31] See *DNB* under William Turner. For a Lasco's relationship with Hooper, see *Original Letters* I, p. 61 and II, p. 675.

[32] In the dedication of his work *A Book of the Nature and Properties as well as of the Baths in England as of other Baths in Germany and Italy* (London, 1562), which was dedicated to Somerset's son, Turner stated: 'after that I had been in Italy and Germany . . . and was called by your father's grace . . . into England to his service. . . .'

[33] D. S. Bailey, *Thomas Becon and the Reformation of the Church in England* (Edinburgh, 1952), ch. 5.

promise unto all such as believe'.[34] However, as a true son of the later Zwingli and of Bullinger, and in reaction to bald sacramentarianism, he carefully refrained from the complete rejection of 'presence': 'True it is,' he wrote, 'that the body is eaten and the blood drunken, but not corporally. In faith and spirit it is eaten, and by that sacrament the promise of God sealed and confirmed in us, the corporal body remaining in heaven.'[35] These views inclined towards the standpoint which Bullinger and Calvin embodied in the *Consensus Tigurinus* of May 1549. Yet even in this company, Hooper was distinguished by his need to emphasize the memorial aspect, and to regard the bread and the wine basically as 'seals of God's promises in Christ', and as 'a badge and open sign of God's favour'.[36] In contrast, Calvin stressed the vital role of the eucharist in refreshing or strengthening frail faith, largely in an attempt to make the Lord's Supper more than a mere testimony of faith and a thanksgiving. Even Bullinger appeared keener than Hooper to elevate the sacrament in importance, stressing like Calvin and also Zwingli its function as an exercise in faith and its value to 'admonish us of brotherly love'.[37]

Turner and Becon also dismissed the Lord's Supper as a sacrifice and a work, and admitted an encounter with Christ for those with faith, while rejecting the idea of Christ's corporal presence. Becon's point of view seemed particularly close to Hooper's. In 1550 he wrote: 'The Lord's Supper is a holy and heavenly banquet, in the which the faithful christians, besides the corporal eating of the bread, and the outward drinking of the wine, do spiritually through faith both eat the body of Christ and drink his blood unto the confirmation of their faith, the comfort of their conscience and the salvation of their souls.'[38] Turner was less explicit in his characterization of the presence, and failed to relate it to the faith of the communicant except by implication; but he was forthright by this time in his rejection of its corporal nature: 'The Supper hath in it bread and wine outwardly and mystically the body and blood of Christ. Bread is not wine, neither bread is Christ's body, neither is wine Christ's blood.'[39] Both Turner and Becon, unlike Hooper, presented the Supper as more than a memorial, essentially by regarding it as a reminder of social obligation. As Turner expressed it: 'the end of Christ's supper is to remember Christ's death, to give thanks for our redemption and to remember that we all are members of one body, and ought therefore one to love another.'[40] Becon made the same point, carrying it a little further: communion was a reminder of community and the need for 'all to be beneficial

---

[34] John Hooper, *Early Writings*, pp. 112 and 76.

[35] A. Barclay, *The Protestant Doctrine of the Lord's Supper* (Glasgow, 1927), pp. 9*f*; Hooper, *op. cit.*, p. 62.

[36] *Ibid.*, pp. 513 and 128.

[37] F. Wendel, *Calvin* (London, 1963), p. 312; Barclay, *op. cit.*, pp. 9*f*; J. T. McNeill, *The History and Character of Calvinism* (New York, 1954), p. 87.

[38] Thomas Becon, *The Catechism*, pp. 508*f*. Becon may have become a sacramentarian (see C. W. Dugmore, *The Mass and The English Reformers* (London, 1958), p. 234), but was certainly not one in the reign of Edward VI.

[39] See *The Rescuing of the Romish Fox . . .* (Zurich, 1545), and *A New Dialogue Wherein is contained the Examination of the Mass . . .* (London, 1548), both unpaginated.

[40] *A New Dialogue.*

one to another' and, in recalling Christ's sacrifice, obliged man to alleviate the lot of 'the poor members of Christ'.[41]

Although far from identical, the three views of the Lord's Supper differed only in emphasis and corresponded on essentials. In regarding it as the testimony of a historical sacrifice which was necessary for the sustenance of faith, and in rejecting the magic of priestly consecration while preserving the mystery of Christ's presence, with the onus for his appearance resting on the faith of the communicant, all were on the same side of the fence and moving in the same direction. Basically this view derived from the double reaction against sacramentarianism and the body of sacramental doctrine which preserved the real presence. Though totally objectionable to lutherans and catholics, it commanded the following of Bullinger, Calvin, a Lasco, Peter Martyr and eventually Bucer.[42] On the other hand, it bore no relationship to the overt doctrine of the Order of Communion, the Catechism of August 1548 or the first Prayer Book.

The three men were also closely allied during the protectorate in their attempt to revalue the role and importance of good works. All were preoccupied with christian conduct. While rejecting good works as a means of securing grace, Hooper, for example, was eager to emphasize the need for repentance and charity. Both were vitally necessary, he argued, to avoid falling out of God's grace. 'Such as be sanctified by Christ,' Hooper threatened, 'must live an honest and holy life, or else his sanctification availeth not. As God forsook the children of Israel for sin, so will he do us.'[43] The special importance he attached to conduct led him to support the idea of an imposed discipline, which he thought could be effected through the instrument of excommunication.[44] Neither Turner nor Becon held exactly this view, and their deep concern with christian conduct was for different reasons. Turner in more of a Calvinistic manner was less concerned with salvation than Hooper and more concerned with the need to avoid dishonouring Christ by repudiating his example.[45] Becon possessed Hooper's concern with salvation, but regarded good works first and foremost as an exercise in faith: through good works, according to Becon, one could 'labour to confirm thy faith'. He argued that charity 'maketh thee sure that thy faith is true and livish' in a similar manner to those seeking to present the Lord's Supper as something more than a simple testimony and thanksgiving. In *Solace of the Soul*, he even asserted that the ability to be virtuous could be taken as 'testimonies and signs that thou art elect of God.' Good works thus became a distinct sign of grace.[46] In their different ways, all were deeply concerned with the role of conduct. Having denied the traditional efficacy of good works as a means of grace, all needed to wrestle with the problem of finding a new function for good works so that men could be kept up to the mark. In other words, all three were critically

---

[41] Becon, *op. cit.*, pp. 509 f.

[42] P. Brooks, *Thomas Cranmer's Doctrine of the Eucharist* (London, 1965), ch. 3.

[43] Hooper, *op. cit.*, p. 76.

[44] *Ibid.*, p. 183.   [45] *A New Dialogue.*

[46] Thomas Becon, *The Early Works*, p. 473; Becon, *The Catechism*, p. 574; also see *ibid.*, p. 640.

aware of the practical defects of the sole faith doctrine, and their barbs were not only against papists, but also 'our new evangelists' who, according to Hooper, 'dream of faith that justifyeth, the which neither repentance precedeth, neither honesty of life followeth', and who, according to Becon, think 'thou are so thoroughly justified by faith alone . . . that thou needest not do any good works.'[47]

In addition they seem to have had emphatic views on liturgy and the organization of the church, although such matters did not figure prominently in their writings. In his *The Hunting and Finding out of the Romish Fox*, an attack on Bishop Gardiner which was printed in 1545, Turner exposed what he considered to be papal doctrine: 'Ye hold still vestments and copes, incense and altars, organs and descant in the church.' Later his objection to vestments caused him to train a dog to snatch the square cap from a visiting bishop.[48] However, in the reign of Edward VI it was left to Hooper to provide the action when, upon his appointment as bishop of Gloucester in 1550, he refused at first to comply with the ceremony of episcopal consecration or to adopt episcopal dress because they were unscriptural.[49] Becon later adopted vestarian views, although the subject failed to figure in his Edwardian works.[50] The condemnation of clerical dress was part of a desire for an extreme liturgical simplicity which both Turner and Hooper had contracted from a Lasco and Bullinger during their period of exile. Another concern was church organization. None of them questioned the subjection of the church to the state. Hooper's need for a church discipline did not incline him towards an autonomous church on the Genevan model. Hooper was particularly explicit on this point. Having cited the example of the Israelites he added: 'no general council, no provincial assembly, no bishops of any realm or province may charge the subjects thereof with any law or ceremony, otherwise than the prince of the land by the word of God can give account to be good and godly. For the people are committed unto the prince to sustain the right of them all, and not only to defend their bodies, but also their souls.'[51] Of the three men, Turner proposed the most radical reorganization of the church. It imposed a Calvinist system with bishops preserved but elected and deprived of their lands, and with pastors elected by their congregations. But this view was published in 1554.[52] There is no evidence that it was held during the protectorate. The reforms proposed then were much more modest, although as far as Hooper was concerned they involved putting to other uses three-quarters of the bishops' lands.[53] Both Becon and Hooper seemed to believe that an additional clerical officer was required to oversee the clergy.[54] No objection, however, was voiced against the authority of the bishops. The objection to them concerned their secular distractions, not their ecclesiastical function.

[47] Hooper, *op. cit.*, p. 33; Becon, *Early Works*, p. 473.
[48] See *DNB* under William Turner.
[49] See F. D. Price, 'Gloucester Diocese under Bishop Hooper, 1551-3', *Transactions of the Bristol and Gloucestershire Archaeological Society* 60 (1938), pp. 54 f.
[50] Bailey, *op. cit.*, p. 118.   [51] Hooper, *op. cit.*, p. 141.
[52] W. Turner, *The Hunting of the Romish Wolf* (Basle, 1555), unpaginated.
[53] Hooper, *op. cit.*, p. 396.   [54] Bailey, *op. cit.*, p. 60.

What is clear is that during the protectorate the three men held a body of religious opinion only part of which was incorporated in its reformation. Noticeably Turner's tract *The Rescuing of the Romish Fox* (1545), which condemned communion in one kind, services in the Latin tongue, the celibacy of priests and images, bore a remarkable affinity with the changes actually realized by the Somerset government. But unrealized were their views on the mass, the liturgy and the clergy which the government made no real effort to apply, and which must have made the culmination of its reforms, the first Prayer Book, a disappointing document.

Of the three, Turner was with Somerset the longest, serving him for more than three years as his physician and daily waiter, but not as his chaplain.[55] Somerset's interest in him possibly related to his other occupations, since he was a herbalist and lawyer as well as a physician and a protestant propagandist, who wrote about baths, herbs, fish, wines, birds and metals as well as writing religious tracts.[56] However, Somerset summoned from exile this man whose religious works had been banned by proclamation in the previous reign,[57] and employed him during a period in which he continued to publish his forthright and radical views. It is therefore very likely that Somerset knew about these views and sympathized strongly with them. His commitment to the beliefs of Becon and Hooper is more obvious and indubitable, since both of them performed a religious function in the household. Becon was employed as chaplain, possibly from late 1547, and by late 1549 and early 1550 was closely involved with Somerset's family in religious matters. He dedicated his *Governance of Virtue* to one of Somerset's daughters and his *Flower of Godly Prayers* to Somerset's wife. Somerset himself supplied a prefatory epistle to the tract *Spiritual and Most Precious Pearl* which was appended to the 1550 edition of Becon's *Humble Petition to the Lord*.[58] The relationship between Somerset and Hooper began when Hooper dedicated to him his *Declaration of Christ and his Office*, and shrewdly found the way to Somerset's heart by complimenting him in the dedication on his victory over the Scots.[59] Nevertheless, Hooper did not return to England specifically to enter Somerset's household, and was only admitted when the outbreak of peasant risings prevented him from visiting his native Somerset. Furthermore, he only resided temporarily with Somerset 'till things become more settled'.[60] Thus Hooper did not enter Somerset's service, but he did become his protégé and also an intimate of his family.[61] Somerset clearly approved of his views since he authorized him to preach at Court and in London.[62] His appreciation and support continued in 1550 when,

[55] See the preface of *A New Herbal* (London, 1551). Turner stated that Somerset had favoured him earlier, but he did not specify in what way.

[56] The only work he dedicated to Somerset was *A New Herbal*.

[57] Hughes and Larkin, 272.

[58] W. S. Hudson, *John Ponet (1516?–1556), Advocate of Limited Monarchy* (Chicago, 1942), p. 22 n. 10, and Bailey, *op. cit.*, pp. 54 *f* and 142–3.

[59] Hooper, *op. cit.*, p. xi.   [60] *Original Letters* I, pp. 66 and 68.

[61] He referred to Somerset as his patron (*ibid.* I, p. 69) and of the family, Hooper claimed to have 'much used their company' (Foxe V, p. 764).

[62] *Original Letters* I, p. 75.

restored to some authority, he fought against most of the bishops for Hooper's elevation to the bishopric of Gloucester.[63] This appreciation was reciprocated. Becon, for example, later eulogized: 'What shall I speak of that godly and mighty prince Edward Duke of Somerset which, in the time of his protectorship, did so banish idolatry out of this our realm, and bring in again God's true religion, that it was wonder so weighty a matter to be brought to pass in so short a time'; and Hooper commented upon Somerset's first fall from power: 'We hope that his life will be spared . . . for the glory of His name and the benefit of His church.'[64] His patronage of Hooper and his employment of Becon and Turner, the proximity he allowed them to himself and his family and their appreciation of him as a reformer, strongly suggest that Somerset possessed affinitive religious beliefs, and was a radical protestant who, in the Lords' debate on the Prayer Book, concealed his disbelief in the real presence.

His dealings with continental reformers substantiate this impression. Considering his closeness to Hooper, his lack of correspondence with Bullinger is a surprise. Also odd was his apparent failure to take into his household any of the refugees fleeing to England during the protectorate, even for the temporary period between arrival and employment. Nevertheless, the bent of his beliefs is evident in his patronage of the Flemish calvinist, Valerandus Pollanus, his cool association with Martin Bucer and what seemed to be a much warmer relationship with John Calvin and Peter Martyr.

The nearest Somerset came to offering hospitality to continental reformers was to provide a home for a number of Flemish weavers under the leadership of Pollanus at Glastonbury. Pollanus was related to Hooper by marriage, and the establishment of his community in Somerset presumably owed something to Hooper's promotion of a Lasco's schemes for founding autonomous churches in England for foreign refugees.[65] Pollanus, who had earlier succeeded Calvin as minister of the French church at Strasbourg, inclined towards Geneva rather than Zurich, corresponded with Calvin, not with Bullinger, and referred to himself in his letters to the former as 'your ever most attached pupil'.[66] At this time, in view of the proximity of the churches of Geneva and Zurich which the *Consensus Tigurinus* established, this did not mean much of a difference. Somerset could therefore patronize Pollanus without betraying the beliefs upon which his patronage of Hooper appeared to rest. The noticeable feature of his dealings with Pollanus was their belatedness. In May 1549 Pollanus returned to Strasbourg, having failed to establish himself in England. It was only upon his return in the next year that he came under Somerset's wing, and only in 1551 that, under Somerset's auspices, he succeeded in establishing his foreigners' church at

[63] *Ibid.* II, p. 410.

[64] T. Becon, *Prayers and other Pieces*, ed. J. Ayre (Parker Society, 1844), p. 205; *Original Letters* I, p. 71.

[65] Dugmore, 'The First Ten Years, 1549–59', *op. cit.*, p. 17, and Smyth, *op. cit.*, pp. 190–223.

[66] *Original Letters* II, p. 739. For the extent of his calvinism and his debt to a Lasco, see Valerandus Pollanus, *Liturgia Sacra, 1551–1555*, ed. A. C. Honders (Leiden, 1970), preface, and its review by C. W. Dugmore in *Journal of Ecclesiastical History*, 24 (1973), pp. 81 f.

Glastonbury.[67] It seems that, as time went by and probably not during the protectorate, Somerset turned firmly towards Calvinism, as did Turner. This did not mean a change in direction for his religious beliefs, but essentially a further development.

Somerset's direct dealings with Calvin support this impression. Significantly, they began only after his first fall from power. Earlier the duchess of Somerset had presented Calvin with a ring which prompted Calvin to write to Somerset's daughter, Ann.[68] Moreover, in 1550 Thomas Norton who later became the first English translator of Calvin's *Institutes of the Christian Religion* was tutor to Somerset's children.[69] Clearly, there were undercurrents in the household pulling in the direction of Reform. But direct contact between Somerset and Calvin only came with Martin Bucer's request to the latter to 'give the lord protector such advice as the present state of things demanded'. Calvin responded in a letter of 22 October 1549, composed in ignorance of Somerset's fall from power earlier in the same month.[70] The letter was not a statement of religious belief. It called upon Somerset to proceed harshly against rebels, to shun the use of moderate measures in promoting the reformation, and 'to hold the bridle short' in punishing adultery, whoredom, drunkenness and blasphemy. For this reason Somerset's enthusiasm in receiving the letter, which caused him to publish his own translation of it, did not necessarily indicate a confirmed Calvinism, although the presence of sympathy is unquestionable. Perhaps more significant is the approval it denoted of an attack on moderation. Calvin was quick to capitalize upon the letter's good reception. A second letter reached Somerset soon after his release from the Tower, and a further two arrived in 1551.[71] Calvin had a high opinion of Somerset,[72] and Somerset earned it by bestowing favours upon Calvin's followers and by channelling his works through to the king.[73] Upon Somerset's final fall, Francis Bourgoyne told Calvin: 'greatly did he esteem you'.[74] Somerset may well have ended a Calvinist, but during the protectorate, he seemed to be only reaching in that direction, and was essentially at one with the Zurichers.

Martin Bucer was the bridge which intellectuals used to cross the gulf between lutheranism and the advanced protestantism of Zurich and Geneva. Somerset's relationship with him is important for suggesting the state of his religious development in the period of the protectorate. In the first instance, upon Bucer's arrival

---

[67] See Smyth, *op. cit.*, p. 222, and L. A. Williams, 'The Alien Contribution to the Social and Economic Development of England and Wales in the Sixteenth Century' (unpublished University of Wales M.A. thesis, 1953), pp. 8–11.

[68] *Original Letters* II, pp. 702 f.   [69] *DNB*, see under Thomas Norton.

[70] Gorham, *op. cit.*, p. 115; *An Epistle from Calvin to the Duke of Somerset* (London, 1550).

[71] *Original Letters* II, pp. 704 ff ; see Gorham, *op. cit.*, n. (k) p. 55 (not extant); and J. Strype, *Memorials of the Most Reverend Father in God, Thomas Cranmer*, II (Oxford, 1840), pp. 892 ff. Gorham's account of five letters is inaccurate and due to misdating the eventually printed letter of 22 October 1549, attributing it to 1548, which led him to suppose that an additional letter was composed in September 1549, particularly in the light of a remark made by Calvin in a letter to Bucer. But this related to the letter which Gorham misdated (Gorham, *op. cit.*, p. 55, n. (k)).

[72] *Original Letters* II, pp. 710 f.

[73] *Ibid.* II, p. 734, and Strype, *op. cit.*, p. 892.   [74] *Original Letters* II, p. 735.

in England in 1549, Somerset with Cranmer had welcomed him, and he presumably helped to secure for him the regius professor of divinity at Cambridge.[75] Bucer, moreover, had not been long in England when he established contact with two of Somerset's daughters by means of a gift of books.[76] However, after the original reception, Bucer and his followers ceased to make favourable comments about Somerset, and the signs of favour shown by Somerset to Bucer stopped. The reports of the Zuricher group in England to Bullinger, which remarked upon Bucer's pernicious influence upon Cranmer but said nothing of his influence upon Somerset, also suggest the distance between the two men. Certainly, by Whitsun 1550 Bucer had come to hold such a low view of Somerset that he instructed Calvin to 'seriously admonish him respecting this desolation and betrayal of the churches which with very few exceptions are entrusted to those who neither know nor care to know anything about Christ.'[77] The lack of attachment probably owed much to Somerset's connection with Hooper, with whom Bucer was in profound disagreement.[78]

Bucer's low view of Somerset contrasted with Peter Martyr's elevated view of him. In terms of favours received, the two men were on an equal footing, Martyr acquiring the regius chair of divinity at Oxford in March 1548, a few months after his arrival in the country. Again, as with Bucer, there are no later signs of Somerset extending friendship, hospitality or patronage. Where Bucer and Martyr differ in this period is in the latter's rapid conversion to a form of Zwinglianism and his euphoric appreciation of Somerset as a man of religion, while Bucer remained aloof, communicating with his friend Calvin but repudiating the Zurichers, and remaining comparatively conservative in his beliefs. On his arrival in England Martyr was a Buceran, having spent the previous five years with Bucer in Strasbourg. However in June 1548 Bullinger was informed that Martyr did not 'differ at all, or [only] very little, from you' in his view of the eucharist.[79] A year later their views coincided as Martyr admitted himself when, in response to Bullinger's congratulations for his performance in the Oxford disputation of 1549 on the mass, he attributed the credit for it to Bullinger 'since you have for so many years both taught and maintained that doctrine which I there undertook to defend'.[80] The outcome of his rapport with Zurich appeared to be his rapturous welcome of Somerset's release from prison in early 1550 which he expressed to Somerset in a lengthy Latin epistle.[81] At the time he told Bullinger: 'these things are very pleasing to godly persons because they know him by experience to have been a most firm supporter of religion.'[82] He clearly saw Somerset not only as responsible for the earlier changes, but also as a mover of further

---

[75] *Ibid.* I, p. 333.   [76] *Ibid.* I, p. 2.

[77] *Ibid.* II, p. 548.

[78] Hopf, *op. cit.*, pp. 51 and 145.

[79] See Smyth, *op. cit.*, pp. 114 and 125 *f.*

[80] *Original Letters* II, p. 478.

[81] The epistle was translated by Thomas Norton and printed: see Vermigli, *An Epistle to the Duke of Somerset* (London, 1550).

[82] *Original Letters* II, p. 480.

advances at the time of his fall. Martyr's expectation and appreciation of Somerset, coupled with Bucer's dissatisfaction, underline the Zwinglian standpoint of the protector.

At his death Somerset was criticized for his abandonment of the gospel and for his spurious christianity.[83] But these strictures related to the period after his first fall from power when he was no longer protector. During the protectorate, in contrast, he gained a reputation for being a keen and advanced protestant, and nothing detracts from it. Measured by the standards of the time, he inclined in this period towards an extreme protestantism, a fact which rendered the actual religious changes of the protectorate something other than a simple impression of his religious beliefs, and only explicable in more complicated terms.

Somerset's Principles

Somerset certainly believed in a form of international toleration. He told Gardiner that in the matter of religion he 'would not condemn other countries', and he was responsible for the passage in the act allowing communion in two kinds which professed no desire to criticize the practice elsewhere.[84] He also believed in the classical principle of measure as the touchstone of conduct. As he put it to Gardiner: 'There be some so ticklish, and so fearful one way, and so tender stomached, that they can abide no old abuses to be reformed, but think every reformation to be a capital enterprise against all religion and good order, as there be on the contrary side some too rash who, having no consideration what is to be done, headlong will set upon everything. The magistrates' duty is betwixt these.'[85] However, in making this point, Somerset was not defining the nature of the beliefs and ambitions which man could responsibly hold. He was not agreeing with Paget when the latter said: 'I never loved extremes.'[86] In Somerset's mind was the consideration of how man should conduct himself. He was declaring a desirable tactic, the best means to an end, not the perfect goal. For this reason, it was possible for him to hold advanced religious views and to amass enormous wealth without being justly accused of inconsistency. In matters of religion, he appreciated measure as the means whereby far from moderate religious beliefs could be implemented 'with good and politic order of the commonwealth, without any contention and strife among the king's subjects'.[87]

Neither of these principles was unusual nor objectionable. Even Gardiner found Somerset's belief in toleration between nations palatable;[88] and the appreciation of measure as the ideal code of conduct was common coin.[89] Furthermore, neither principle accepted religious non-conformity within the state. Such toleration, which the age associated with chaos rather than enlightenment, was, in contem-

---

[83] See Smyth, *op. cit.*, p. 271, and J. Bradford, *Letters, Treatises, Remains*, ed. A. Townsend (Parker Society, 1853), pp. xxviii *f.*

[84] Muller, 143.   [85] Foxe VI, p. 30.
[86] Tytler I, p. 24.   [87] Foxe VI, p. 30.
[88] See Muller, 143.   [89] Jones, *The Tudor Commonwealth*, pp. 94–6.

porary terms, the very opposite of measure;[90] and in advocating toleration between nations Somerset was not proposing that it should be allowed within them. In keeping with his contemporaries, Somerset seemed to value religious uniformity as the linchpin of order. His comment to the imperial ambassador on the peasant risings of 1549 was: 'You see what comes of all these divergencies in religion.'[91] Personally, he ordered uniformity of worship in Oxford and Cambridge.[92] When the council in May 1548 instructed licensed preachers to assert the duties of obedience and to condemn the idea that 'every man should choose his own way to religion', there is no reason to believe that its action went counter to Somerset's beliefs.[93] His reverence for religious uniformity is clearly expressed in the proceedings his government conducted against religious dissent. The persecution of Bonner and Gardiner, and the treatment of Princess Mary depended heavily upon Somerset's intervention and direction, and demonstrated unequivocally where he stood in the matter.

Within a month of the new reign Gardiner had established the standpoint of dissent which he was to maintain throughout. Because of the kingdom's vulnerability in a time of minority, he reasoned, it was essential to mark time until the king came of age. The minority, then, had to be regarded as 'a time rather to repair that needeth reparation than to make any new buildings'.[94] As the changes occurred, Gardiner and the government came into conflict. Within eight months of the accession, Gardiner had been confined to the Fleet because of his opposition to the Homilies and Injunctions. He was released on 8 January 1548 in response to his promise to comply, but within a month he had been confined to his London house following his failure to subscribe to certain articles of doctrine which the government compiled for his approval. A promise of good behaviour soon placed him at liberty, but this was short-lived. In April 1548, alarmed by his behaviour in the diocese of Winchester, the government again sought to restrain him. Because of his troublemaking in Hampshire, he was confined to London, and then, for failing to preach a sermon according to the government's instructions, he was placed in the Tower in early July.[95] He remained there awaiting trial for the next two and a half years. Somerset was absent in Scotland when Gardiner was first imprisoned, and mediated successfully against his internment in the Tower in May 1548. Moreover, he was not so antagonistic as perhaps other councillors were to a man who, after all, had been his friend.[96] None the less, he

---

[90] Conrad Russell, 'Arguments for Religious Unity in England, 1530–1650', *Journal of Ecclesiastical History* 18 (1967), pp. 201 *ff*.

[91] *SP Span.* 1547–9, p. 408.   [92] Porter, *op. cit.*, p. 67, and PRO SP10/V/(12).

[93] Burnet II (2), 24 (p. 190).   [94] Muller, 117.

[95] J. A. Muller, *Stephen Gardiner and the Tudor Reaction* (London, 1926), pp. 166 and 170–82.

[96] For the previous friendship, see Muller, 120, 138 and 140. For Somerset's intervention in Gardiner's favour in May 1548, see Foxe VI, p. 152. Warwick, at least, who had struck Gardiner in 1546, was more antagonistic towards him. In June 1548 he wrote to Cecil 'being desirous to hear whether my lord hath proceeded with the arrogant bishop according to his deservings', and commented: 'I rather fear that his accustomed wiliness, with the persuasions of some of his dear friends and assured brethren, shall be the cause that the fox shall yet again deceive the lion' (Tytler I, p. 108). Somerset again favoured Gardiner in 1550 (Muller, pp. xxxi *f* and PRO SP10/X/9) by pleading for his release from the Tower.

was an active participant in the process of persecution. The responsibility for Gardiner's final internment in the Tower lay as much with Somerset as with anyone else.

Somerset's particular responsibility for Gardiner's downfall lay first in his dispatching two of the king's chaplains to Winchester in May 1548 to declare the government's proceedings in religion to the locality. Gardiner lacked the self-discipline to withstand this act of provocation. The chaplains reported his abuse of them to Somerset whose complaint caused Gardiner to be summoned before the council.[97] In addition, Somerset had a hand in requiring Gardiner to deliver the public sermon which led directly to his imprisonment in the Tower. Somerset was not solely responsible for making this requirement of Gardiner. The witnesses examined at Gardiner's trial in 1551 appeared to agree that the responsibility lay with Somerset and the rest of the council.[98] But Gardiner was not put away simply because of being required to preach. His imprisonment in the Tower was due to the instructions issued to him on the subject of his sermon, some of which he ignored. In this respect, Somerset was heavily responsible for Gardiner's fall since the particular instructions which Gardiner incriminated himself by ignoring were the ones imposed upon him by Somerset personally. In the first instance, the government reached an agreement with Gardiner that, instead of giving it a preview of his sermon, Gardiner should incorporate within the sermon certain articles determined by the council.[99] However, between the time that Gardiner received these articles and delivered the sermon, between 18 and 29 June, Somerset on his own initiative produced further articles for Gardiner to include. Influenced by the western rebellion of April 1548 and fearing for the security of the realm, Somerset ordered Gardiner to declare in his sermon that the king's commandments were not impaired by his minority and to avoid any discussion of the Lord's Supper. Gardiner's immediate refusal to comply with the latter instruction caused Somerset to warn him that 'we be desirous to defend and advance the truth determined or revealed, and so consequently we will not fail but withstand the disturbers thereof.'[100] Gardiner's failure to comply on 29 June, when he delivered a sermon which omitted to mention the minority and discussed the eucharist, seemed to alienate completely an already infuriated Somerset, compelling him to fulfil this threat.[101]

The extent of Somerset's responsibility for the persecution of Gardiner is uncertain. However, it is clear that he took a leading part in his downfall, and, in all likelihood, the earlier proceedings against Gardiner did not go against the protector's will. From the early days of the reign Gardiner had angered him, to such a pitch that in November 1547 Gardiner had to complain that 'your grace's letters return every word of my letters in my neck and take my fly as it were a

[97] See Foxe VI, pp. 154 and 133.

[98] *Ibid.*, p. 78, and PRO SP10/IV/20; and the depositions of Paget (Foxe VI, pp. 162*f*), of North (*ibid.*, p. 157) and of Chaloner (clerk of the council) (pp. 146*f*).

[99] Muller, *op. cit.*, pp. 174*f*.

[100] Foxe VI, p. 145, and Burnet II (2), 28 (p. 220).

[101] Muller, *op. cit.*, pp. 178–81, and Burnet II (2), 28 (bk I).

bee, which I thought should have stung no man.'[102] Early in 1548 they met two or three times and Somerset appeared to recover some of his former friendliness, but by March a further conflict was building up and by June Somerset was so alienated that he was no longer prepared to give Gardiner an audience, except to make him comply with the council's requirements for the sermon.[103] Somerset's hostility had been present for a long time. By mid-1548 his patience had reached its limit[104] and he appeared ready to dispose of Gardiner in the quickest and most convenient manner. Basically, Somerset and his colleagues had insisted on conformity. Gardiner's refusal to comply had caused him to be hunted down with no more than a faint show of clemency.

The government's treatment of Bonner was along similar lines. It also forced him to declare his conformity with a public sermon. The government, in fact, seems again to have goaded its victim into making a stand of open defiance. Bonner showed a greater readiness to submit. In view of it, his persecution stands out even more so as the expression of an intolerant government inciting a recalcitrant subject to commit an act of obvious disobedience so that its repressive actions could be presented as necessary rather than savage. In Bonner's case, Somerset's actions were not complicated by any previous friendship with the victim.

Bonner fell into serious trouble in August 1547 by refusing unreservedly to accept the Injunctions and Homilies. Hauled before the council, he was convicted of showing contempt for the king's authority in church matters and of acting in a manner likely to breed sedition. Bonner made a simpler submission than Gardiner. He renounced his former protestation and signed a formal submission. This did not save him from a spell of imprisonment in the Fleet, but it did ensure a much shorter sentence than Gardiner initially received: imprisoned on 12 August, he was released on bail on 27 September and set completely at liberty a month later.[105] Besides his greater readiness to submit, Bonner appeared less prone than Gardiner to martyrdom. Throughout 1548 and in the early months of 1549, he formally acquiesced, except as a member of the House of Lords.[106] He carried out the government's instructions for the abolition of candles, ashes and palms in January 1548; and he celebrated communion in the officially approved manner in 1549.[107] He consequently enjoyed a respite from government pressures until June 1549. In that month the council reprimanded him for allowing the celebration of private masses in St Paul's, and also insisted on communion taking place only in the chancel. Bonner meekly complied; within two days he had ordered the dean and the chapter of St Paul's to obey the council's instructions. A month later the government reprimanded him for his dilatory promotion of the new church service. Bonner again acquiesced. Soon afterwards he ordered the

[102] Muller, 136 (p. 420).

[103] Foxe VI, p. 246, *SP Span.* 1547-9, p. 238, and BM Add. 28,571, f. 15a; Muller, App. 3, Foxe VI, p. 152, and Muller, *op. cit.,* pp. 174 f.

[104] Burnet II (2), 28 (bk I).,   [105] Alexander, pp. 436-8.

[106] *Ibid.,* p. 438.   [107] Foxe V, 716 f, and Alexander, p. 435.

archdeacons of London, Colchester and Essex to act upon the council's letter. In August, the government blamed him for the people's failure in his diocese to attend prayer and communion, accused him of permitting the celebration of the traditional mass and ordered him 'to abide and keep residence in his house'.[108] The final fall came when, after this badgering, the government imposed upon him certain tests: to administer communion on specified occasions at the high altar of St Paul's, to deliver a sermon which emphasized obedience and asserted the validity of the king's authority in spite of being a minor and to punish non-attendance of the services prescribed in the Prayer Book. In addition the government insisted that he reside in London until 'otherwise licensed by us'.[109] Under the weight of this interference Bonner's sense of self-preservation snapped. In his prescribed sermon he asserted transubstantiation and omitted to declare that the king's authority was as complete now as it ever would be.[110] Thus, in response to his goading by the council, Bonner finally abandoned his slack conformity, announced his defiance and fell victim to the government which, by the beginning of October, had deprived him of his bishopric and had committed him to prison.[111]

Somerset participated in Bonner's downfall both as a member of the government and as an individual making a special contribution. When the instructions for the content of the sermon were presented to Bonner at a council meeting on 10 August 1549, Somerset discovered the omission of the crucial article concerning the king's minority and the validity of the laws made during it—the very article he had personally imposed upon Gardiner—and commanded its inclusion. Bonner's failure to comply with this article was the major charge brought against him at his trial and the grounds of his conviction for disobedience.[112] When Bonner in late October declared Thomas Smith and Somerset to be 'my deadly enemies', and claimed that they 'hath sundry ways studied and laboured my ruin and destruction', it seems likely that he not merely sought to make a scapegoat of a man who by this time had fallen himself but also made a genuine accusation.[113]

The problem of Mary's non-conformity became evident at Christmas 1548 when, in her discussions with the government, she stubbornly upheld her father's religious settlement and refused to countenance further changes until her brother attained his majority.[114] For a time the government held its hand, hoping that she would keep her religion to herself; but, provoked by Mary's newly acquired habit of hearing between two and four masses daily in the company of her household, by June it had decided to take action. On the grounds that she 'did use to have mass said openly in her house', the council ordered her to conform and to send up for examination certain of her servants.[115] Mary at first refused, but then complied

108 Alexander, pp. 438 f, and PRO SP10/VIII/36.
109 Foxe V, pp. 728–30, and Alexander, pp. 439–41.
110 BM M485/52, 198, ff. 34–46b (Hatfield MS).
111 Alexander, pp. 446–50.
112 Foxe V, pp. 778 f, and Alexander, pp. 448 and 450.
113 Foxe V, p. 797.   114 See Strype II (1), pp. 92 f.
115 *SP Span.* 1547–9, pp. 101 and 407, and *APC* II, pp. 291 f.

to the extent of dispatching the wanted servants to the Court. In July the government again pressed Mary to conform, alleging that her open dissidence fanned the flames of insurrection. Then in August the government granted her a dispensation to hear mass in private with no more than twenty of her household whose names would have to be reported to the privy council. In this manner Mary received a measure of licence. But this had nothing to do with the principle of toleration. It was no more than an exceptional and temporary concession. The government intended it to last only until certain prelates and other learned men appointed by it had discussed the religious settlement with Mary. The Somerset regime did not provide Mary with a permanent licence to celebrate mass.[116] Furthermore, it granted her a temporary licence essentially because of practical considerations. The basic aim was to placate the emperor, who required that 'our close relative' should be allowed to worship the old religion, and to preserve the imperial alliance at a time when England found itself at war with France and Scotland. The government also aimed to prevent Mary from becoming a figurehead of rebellion at a time when insurrection was rife.[117] The treatment of Mary, although dissimilar to the persecution of Bonner and Gardiner, likewise expressed the government's belief in religious uniformity.

Somerset undoubtedly approved of the concessions made to Mary. Moreover, as with Gardiner, his former friendship with the victim probably compelled him to be gentler towards her than other members of the council.[118] But it cannot be said that the differences which developed within the council over the treatment of Mary rested on the issue of whether or not concessions should be made, or upon a principle of toleration which was respected by Somerset and repudiated by his colleagues.[119] There seemed to be no dispute over granting her a temporary concession. For this reason Mary's fortunes were affected not by Somerset's fall but by the passing of time and changing circumstances, particularly the peace with France and Scotland and the ending of the insurrections. As the imperial alliance became less vital and rebellion was contained, Mary became a less explosive charge and the government could therefore bring greater pressure upon her to conform. At the root of the discord within the council over the treatment of Mary, seemed to be Somerset's indiscretion in promising the imperial ambassador that Mary should have the licence to celebrate mass without first seeking the consent of his colleagues.[120]

The treatment of Mary and the persecution of Bonner and Gardiner thus demonstrated Somerset's reverence for religious unity, his belief in the persecution necessary for its maintenance and the conventionality of his attitude towards toleration. Undoubtedly Somerset's religious policy was a reaction against the repressiveness

[116] Foxe VI, pp. 8 and 10; PRO SP10/VIII/30, 31 and 51.
[117] Foxe VI, pp. 11–15, and *SP Span.* 1547–9, pp. 330, 381 *f*, 406–8 and 430. For the imperial consideration and its importance, see below, pp. 119–22.
[118] See Thesis, p. 479 *f*, and Tytler I, pp. 51 *f* and 60 *f*.
[119] The difference was recorded in 1551 by John ab Ulmis in a letter to Bullinger (*Original Letters* II, p. 439).
[120] Implied by Van der Delft, the imperial ambassador (*SP Span.* 1547–9, p. 447).

of the Henrician regime; he seems to have felt that, as the reformation had been formerly stemmed by repression, what was needed was merely the removal of this impediment for it to flow naturally in the right direction. Hence the support for the repeal act and his remark to Gardiner in 1547 that, while he wanted to reform 'all lightness and lewdness', he would not carry it out 'so cruelly and fiercely as some peradventure would wish'.[121] But a concern for the reduction of repression was far from an acceptance of toleration. Furthermore, the repeal of the heresy laws was not the action of a government moved by liberal principles so much as of victims throwing off the instrument of their former persecution. Somerset in time became less squeamish and more appreciative of the necessity of repression. A parallel exists between his attempt to persuade his own brother, the Scots, peasant rebels and enclosure offenders to conform by a policy of forgiveness before proceeding to their chastisement. Just as the gentleness he showed in these quarters cannot be regarded as the outstanding feature of his policy, neither can the liberality he showed to religious dissent. Long before its end the government had become an illiberal regime, and this was not in spite of Somerset. As with the Scots, his brother, offenders against the agrarian laws and peasant rebels, the government adopted tougher measures without scruple towards religious dissent when gentleness failed to work. It is true that the government never imposed the death penalty for the offence of religious non-conformity. But this seemed the result of a high incidence of recantation. The lack of martyrs derived not from the government's enlightened mentality, but from the sense of self-preservation of those it persecuted. The strong conservatism of the universities, for example, was probably restrained by the recantation and flight of Smith and the submission of Redman. The conservatives, Perrin and Asheton, also recanted as did the anabaptists, Thombe, Puttoe and Champneys.[122] The exception was Joan Butcher who presumably would have been burnt by the Somerset government if it had not fallen before punishment could be administered.

Other than the special case of Mary, the only non-conformity Somerset was prepared to tolerate was that of foreign immigrants whose advanced protestant-ism probably resembled his own beliefs and whom he allowed, as did the following regime, to establish their own autonomous churches in England.[123] In addition Somerset tolerated the occasional subject, such as Thomas Dobbe and John Hancock, whose views on the sacrament of the altar were probably not far from his own, and whose dissension he pardoned.[124] A degree of tolerance seems to have stemmed from the fact that the reformation was not fulfilled overnight. Its fluidity allowed a measure of forbearance to be shown towards those moving in advance of it and in the direction that Somerset wished it to go. Political and personal considerations probably contributed to the lack of heavy-handedness and

[121] See below, p. 135. and Foxe VI, p. 35.

[122] R. W. Dixon, *History of the Church of England*, III, pp. 39 *f* 42 and 106 (n.), PRO SP10/VII/23 and Wriothesley, *Chronicle* II, p. 13.

[123] Smyth, *op. cit.*, pp. 191–4, 219 *f* and 222 *f*, and see above, p. 109.

[124] Foxe V, pp. 70 *f* and *Narratives of the Days of the Reformation*, ed. J. G. Nichols (Camden Society, old series, 77 (1859)), pp. 71–9.)

rigour in persecution. Somerset's desire for the reputation of being a good ruler which, according to the traditional formula, was attainable by acts of clemency, and also his ambition to solve the Scottish problem may have inclined him to stay his hand in making subjects conform. Finally, the descretion of the settlement which safeguarded against a head-on conflict with the conservative bishops and the ending of the regime, before the April commission for the suppression of heresy had proceeded very far, all added to the air of tolerance.

The tolerance of the regime thus derived from a mixture of circumstances and inclination, but in no way from principles alien to the age. Somerset's devotion to religious conformity made him the enemy of the principle of toleration. Moreover, except for purposes of personal esteem, he seemed to value tolerance only as a means of furthering the reformation. There was nothing idealistic about his approach since persuasion by gentleness was essentially a prelude to persuasion by force. Neither the settlement itself nor the treatment of religious dissent can be explained in terms of the protector's appreciation of liberalism.[125]

Circumstance

Although of such great importance that delay was out of the question, the reformation was not the government's chief priority. For this reason other considerations directed its course, chiefly the need to maintain good relations with the emperor and the government's fear of popular insurrection and civil discord. Acting in a period of minority, the government pursued a religious policy which respected the natural vulnerability of a state in that condition. Acting for the most part in a time of war, the government allowed diplomacy to determine the declaration and development of the official religion. It consequently produced a settlement which was essentially determined not by religious beliefs but by circumstance.

In these years the government urgently required the friendship of the emperor, first because it feared him, and secondly because of the Scottish war. Although in reality the emperor's problems were not so neatly solved as his victory at Muhlberg and his peace with both the French and the Turks suggest, for a period of time which coincided with the protectorate the emperor seemed freer than ever before to avenge his aunt, Katherine of Aragon, and to crush heresy in England.[126] William Thomas, clerk of the council, asked, 'Where shall he end his fury but against us?' once he had reduced Germany to order. The same fear moved William Paget who believed the emperor to be now in a supreme position for the subjection of England, not simply because of his lack of distractions elsewhere but also because, if he crusaded against the English, he would find allies among them.[127] Such fears cautioned the Somerset government to appease the emperor. In addition, Charles V could seriously trouble the English even

[125] For the counter-view, see Jordan I, pp. 126 f.
[126] G. R. Elton, *Reformation Europe* (London, 1963), pp. 250 ff.
[127] Strype II (2), p. 383; PLB, Paget to Somerset, 2 February 1549.

I

without taking military action against them. In the Scottish war, the emperor was England's only possible ally. His goodwill was needed for the supply of foreign mercenaries and naval resources, to avoid the economic disruption which his closure of the cloth market in Flanders could cause, and to prevent French ships engaged in dispatching supplies to Scotland from using the Netherlands ports.[128] Moreover, if England ever planned counteraction against France, it would require imperial friendship to gain the necessary access to military supplies in Flanders.[129] England's hope of victory in Scotland, after the intervention of the French in June 1548, came to rest on the distant possibility of neutralizing or distracting the French by persuading the emperor to declare war upon them. In time, principally because of its dependence upon foreign mercenaries, its hope of any success in Scotland came to lie in retaining the imperial favour. Thus, for reasons of national security and the Scottish war, it became essential not to alienate the emperor and to acquire his active support. These aspirations culminated in the diplomatic bargaining of June and July 1549, and resulted in the ratification of the Anglo-imperial treaty of 1543.[130]

The English failed to secure the emperor's active support, but managed to preserve the amity in spite of the reformation. This was achieved by complying with the emperor's wishes, by mollifying him with compliments, by declarations of devotion and by prevaricating in matters of religion. Thus in 1548 the Renegat affair was settled in the imperial interest, the commercial treaty of 1522 was ratified in spite of the opposition of the English wool merchants, and in 1549 the emperor's complaint against the English seizure of some of his subject's ships soon resulted in apology and restitution.[131] So eager were the English to please the emperor that the government informed him of its pleasure at his victory over the German princes and expressed its wish to see Germany the devoted subject of the emperor. It also turned a blind eye on the plight of the German protestants, never wavered in reiterating its devotion to the emperor, and, having provided the German princes with secret help in March 1547, thereafter had nothing to do with them.[132] In the process of appeasement religion played a crucial part. Continually the government sought to avoid offending the emperor's religious scruples. It did so by misrepresenting the changes to him, by accompanying the changes with a smoke-screen of apparent counter-measures and ambiguity, and by complying with his wishes, all of which helped to give the religious settlement its particular character.

William Paget expressed the influential role of the emperor in the religious

128 See Paget's survey of the international situation in his letter of 2 February 1549 (PLB), and for the extent of England's imperial dependence, BM MS Harley 523, ff. 27 and 29b*ff*, *SP Span.* 1547–9, pp. 106*f* and 367, and *SP For.* 1547–53, 50, 133 and 136.

129 C. S. L. Davies, 'Provisions for Armies, 1509–60; a Study in the Effectiveness of Early Tudor Government', *Econ. HR* 2nd ser., 17 (1964), pp. 239 and 244.

130 PRO SP68/III (*SP For.* 1547–53, 160 and 176), *ibid.*, 185 and 187, BM MS Cotton Galba B XII, f. 42*f* (Strype II (2), CC), and Burnet II (2), 40 (bk I).

131 *SP Span.* 1547–9, p. 244; PRO SP 68/II (*SP For.* 1547–53, 100) and *SP Span.* 1547–9, pp. 195, 261 and 527; *ibid.*, p. 329, and BM MS Harley 523, ff. 21b*f*.

132 *SP Span.* 1547–9, pp. 103 and 218; *APC* II, pp. 60*f*; *SP Span.* 1547–9, pp. 120*f*, 292*f* and 387*f*.

considerations of the English government when on 25 December 1548 he advised Somerset to present the recent changes in religion 'as God be pleased and the world little offended', a remark he elaborated upon in a letter of 2 February 1549. Stressing the need not to alienate the emperor, he wrote:

> wherefore me thought yesternight your grace began to devise well, to fain friendship with the emperor, to seem to yield to him and to dally with him, to win time of him by putting him in hope that you will give ear to him, and you have good means to do it yet. For the things that hitherto you have passed be but forms and fashions of service and ministration of the sacrament which is and hath been diverse in divers places in Christ's church, and ordered and altered as pleaseth the governors. So as there is no cause why the emperor should be indeed offended with this, if the matter were well debated with him; and there-fore have you hereby (if you stay going further) good means to practice with him and to induce him to think that as you might alter these ceremonies from their former fashion to this they be now at, so he may fortune to induce you to alter them from this fasion to that they were at before . . . by this means . . . it is possible to win a respite to breathe and to make yourself able after to run the better.[133]

Somerset subscribed to this policy both before and after Paget advised its use. Whenever it informed the emperor of any changes in religion, the government tended to stress their moderate nature or sought to escape the responsibility for them by declaring the changes to be the outcome of decisions made in the pre-vious reign or contrary to its exact wishes. Thus, Somerset showed pleasure in July 1547 when the ambassador told him how he had reported home that mass and confession in England were still administered in the old manner. In November he assured the ambassador that the Injunctions were the work of Henry VIII; in December he informed him that 'he will always hold in profound reverence the holy sacrament', and in August 1548 he professed to the ambassador a wish for a form of worship and doctrine close to that of the Interim. At this time he also confessed to the ambassador that he was none too happy with all the religious changes taking place. A year later, in conversation with the ambassador, Somerset presented the religious changes of the second session as forced by the demands of the realm upon the government which otherwise would have waited for the deliberations of the Council of Trent before making any liturgical alterations, and as little more than the translation of the traditional service into the vernacular. In the same conversation he again appeared to proclaim his conservatism by stating his lack of objection to priests communicating alone.[134] In the light of his con-nections with advanced protestantism, such evidence cannot be safely regarded as statements of actual belief. It squares with the rest of the evidence only if seen as a ploy to conciliate the emperor.

[133] PLB, Paget to Somerset, 25 December 1548 and 2 February 1549.
[134] *SP Span.* 1547–9, p. 120 f; *ibid.*, pp. 205, 221 and 285 f; *ibid.*, pp. 381 and 429 f.

For the same reason, the government complied with the emperor's demand that Mary be allowed to celebrate the traditional mass, a clear indication of the weight of his influence in English affairs. Furthermore, it avoided blatantly provocative measures. The act for the communion in two kinds seemed to have the emperor in mind when it declared an unwillingness to criticize the practice in other countries, and, if Paget's fears were representative, it is likely that the Prayer Book was also influenced by the imperial consideration. The general behaviour of the government in matters of religion, the ambiguity of the changes, the counter-measures which accompanied them, particularly the proclamations preserving fast days, protecting the clergy from public assault, silencing disputes on the eucharist, forbidding unofficial innovations in worship, restricting and then prohibiting preaching, and the lack of official change after the second session in accordance with Paget's recommendation,[135] must be seen in the context of a growing need for imperial support as the French and the Scots became firmly allied and a war on two fronts became a fact.

This sustained policy of deceit in matters of religion succeeded in its object. Although alarmed at times, the imperial ambassador remained capable of reporting hopefully to the emperor that the changes were neither radical nor irreversible;[136] and the emperor, with no pressing political need to show England friendship, could overlook its rapid drift into heresy and continue to offer assurances of amity[137] and even assistance. With Mary tolerated and the protector apparently so moderate in his beliefs that he seemed not wholly in sympathy with the changes in religion, the emperor promised both to close his ports to the French shipping engaged in the Scottish war and to prevent the French from raising troops in his territories, while allowing the English to hire his subjects as mercenaries and to convey others through his territories.[138] But this diplomatic achievement was at the expense of the reformation. Because of the means used to preserve the imperial friendship, the appearance and probably the rate of development of the Edwardian reformation was affected. Significantly, only in the new circumstances of the Northumberland regime when a radical change in foreign policy reduced the dependence upon the emperor and the emperor again became distracted by wars with the German princes, the French and the Ottoman Turks, did

---

[135] Hughes and Larkin, 297, 292, 296, 299, 303 and 313. Paget thought that the changes in religion could only be presented as unobjectionable to the emperor 'if you stay going further' (PLB, Paget to Somerset, 2 February 1549).

[136] The changes of the first session were clearly sugared by the proclamations and official orders which followed (*SP Span.* 1547–9, pp. 245, 253, 261 and 262). In April and May 1548 the ambassador grew concerned (*ibid.*, pp. 263 and 265), but in June 1548 government measures to curb innovations and preaching restored his faith in the English government's attitude to the mass (*ibid.*, pp. 272 *f*); and in August he was assured of Somerset's conservatism following a conversation in which Somerset showed himself to be respectful of the Interim (*ibid.*, pp. 285 *f*). In 1549, in spite of the abolition of the mass, the ambassador continued to make calm and collected reports as a result of being wooed by the licence allowed Mary to practise the old religion, and Somerset's assurances that the changes had not actually abolished the mass (*ibid.*, pp. 375, 381, 381 *f* and 429 *f*).

[137] *SP For.* 1547–53, 100, and Strype II (1), pp. 244.

[138] PRO SP68/II, f. 500 (*SP For.* 1547–53, 100) and *ibid.*, 91; BM MS Cotton Galba B XII, ff. 16b–19; e.g. SP68/II (*SP For.* 1547–53, 100) and *ibid.*, 133.

the government finally cast off its disguise, and declare an unequivocal religious settlement.

The government's religious policy was also subjected to the consideration of domestic harmony. It deliberated in religious matters partly in the light of its own religious inclinations and diplomacy, but also to preserve order. In addition to the chance of civil war, the likely concomitant of a minority, was the fear of popular revolution, the traditionally accepted bed-fellow of heresy. In its attempt to avoid such disasters the government bent in both directions, but inclined in the direction forced upon it by the need to please the emperor, that is, towards moderation.

It would be misleading to think that the driving force behind the official religious changes was simply the government. The government itself was, to some extent, driven and spurred on by the people it governed. This clearly happened, for example, in the matter of images. The reign opened with sermons against images and acts of iconoclasm. In July 1547 the government's order for the selective destruction of images aroused an upsurge of iconoclasm which sought to sweep the country clean of them. With Somerset in Scotland, the government temporized, requiring offenders to be punished while forbidding the re-erection of the fallen images.[139] Finally, in February 1548 the council complied with popular demand. Because the order for the partial destruction of images had caused 'much strife and contention [and] considering . . . that almost in no place of this realm is any sure quietness, but where all images be clean taken away', the government ordered the bishops to remove all images, and to see that the removal was 'quietly done, with as good satisfaction of the people as may be.'[140] Popular initiative also played a part in the authorization of services in the vulgar tongue. In December 1547 the imperial ambassador reported that the common people were beginning to sing psalms in English. In May 1548 several churches in London including St Paul's, conducted the whole service in the vernacular.[141] In these circumstances the government, which had originally opened the door by minor allowances in the Injunctions of 1547,[142] was finally persuaded to order the general public to receive the whole service in English. The act of uniformity, like the earlier order for the removal of all images, realized what in parts was a *fait accompli*. The government was also subjected to considerable pressure from the realm to abolish the mass. By the time of the first parliamentary session, the question of the mass had become a subject of such heated debate among the people, that, to preserve order, public disputes on the subject were forbidden by an act and a proclamation.[143] In spite of the prohibition, the public debate on the mass continued in 1548. Ballads, sermons and plays exposed and ridiculed it. In May certain

[139] Jordan I, pp. 147*f* and 151, J. G. Ridley, *Nicholas Ridley* (London, 1957), p. 118, Muller, 119, and *APC* II, p. 25; G. Constant, *The Reformation in England*, II, pp. 48*f*; *APC* II, p. 518, and *SP Span*. 1547–9, pp. 148 and 222.

[140] Foxe V, pp. 717*f*.

[141] *SP Span*. 1547–9, p. 222, and Wriothesley, *Chronicle*, II, p. 2.

[142] C. W. Dugmore, *The Mass and the English Reformers* (London, 1958), pp. 112*f*.

[143] Hughes and Larkin, 296, and 1 Edward VI, c. 1.

London churches dispensed with the traditional mass, and, according to the imperial ambassador, there was 'open contempt of the holy sacrament' among the people.[144] In these circumstances the government's moderate measures only caused disobedience and disorder, the very opposite of their intention. Cranmer's Lutheran catechism, for example, 'occasioned no little discord, so that fightings have frequently taken place among the common people.'[145] Only under pressure from the realm did the government find the courage of its protestant convictions, and the act of uniformity authorized what in some churches was already taking place.

This popular pressure placed Somerset and his colleagues in a peculiar position, not because they were forced to act contrary to their religious beliefs, but because they were made officially to comply with them. Privately, Somerset and others had disposed of the mass long before they deprived the country of it; vernacular services were used in the royal chapel well before they were authorized for the realm.[146] The destruction of all images was something Somerset had proposed to Gardiner as a measure to restrain disorder almost a year before it was finally ordained. The government found itself withstanding its own beliefs in order to prevent political disruption, as well as to avoid offending the emperor. As Somerset declared to Gardiner: 'We do study to do all things attemperately with quiet and good order.'[147] In its actions the government responded to traditional assumptions and to recent evidence. Somerset could cast scorn on those who 'think every reformation to be a capital enterprise against all religion and good order'; and he could question the ancient connection between heresy and disorder by asserting that the true religion was the foundation of obedience and that dissidence was the result of resisting its establishment.[148] But in view of the Pilgrimage of Grace, the disturbances which occurred during the protectorate and the prevalence of the traditional assumptions about heresy—predictably asserted by the conservatives, Gardiner and Mary, and not completely repudiated by the reformers—the government could not escape the cold, prickling sensation that it was handling an explosive charge, or the knowledge that, especially in a time of minority and because of its war aims, it needed to proceed with caution.[149] Essentially it approached the problem of changing the official religion by seeking to prevent outbreaks of disorder and disobedience. In order not to outrage conservative feeling, it produced moderate and guarded reform; in order not to out-

[144] Wriothesley, *Chronicle*, II, p. 2, *SP Span.* 1547-9, p. 265, Hughes and Larkin, 299, 300, 303 and 313, and Burnet II (2), 24 (bk I).

[145] *Original Letters* II, pp. 642 f.

[146] See above, p. 102; in April 1547 complin was first sung in English in the king's chapel (Jordan I, p. 146); by late 1548 a communion service completely in the vernacular had become the rule in the king's chapel and was being enforced upon the university of Oxford and Cambridge by Somerset as a temporary measure, presumably until parliament had authorized the Prayer Book (see Porter, *op. cit.*, p. 67, and PRO SP10/V/12).

[147] Foxe VI, pp. 28, 30 and 35.   [148] *Ibid.*, p. 30, and Burnet II (2), 15 and 28 (bk I).

[149] See Somerset's own account of the problems of Henry VIII in his letter to Mary (Burnet II (2), 15 (bk I)). For his consideration of the western rebellion of 1548, see Foxe VI, 145. For the assertions of the conservatives, see Muller, p. 308 and Burnet II (2), 15 (bk I).

rage reformed feeling, it presented the changes as interim measures rather than as final statements.[150] Basically the government proceeded towards the reformation of the church by continually applying a brake out of fear of a conservative backlash and by releasing it occasionally to appease the protests its moderation aroused.

The government's religious changes, then, have to be seen not only in an international situation of imperial supremacy and of English dependence upon the emperor, but also in a domestic situation of imminent and actual dissension, the result of both too rapid and too limited a process of religious change. The principles upon which Somerset acted were a response to these particular circumstances; his concept of international toleration seemed designed to appease the emperor, while his principle of measure was aimed to quieten disruptive forces within the state. Only his religious beliefs were born independent of circumstances, and they were not allowed to direct the religious programme. The connection between the circumstances which his responsibility as a ruler and the priority of the Scottish war made him respect, and the degree of reform allowed by the government, cannot be precisely measured or mapped. But these circumstances seemed to be the basic elements conditioning the development of the settlement. Somerset was a zealous and advanced protestant, but also a governor with a sense of responsibility and with overriding political ambitions. He presumably aimed to allow his beliefs scope for unpersecuted practice and the opportunity to become the official religion, but not at the expense of his foreign schemes and domestic order. In this respect the settlement was very much the product of secular circumstances.

In his formulation of religious change, Somerset had essentially to comply with his political designs and anxieties. But to what extent was the settlement influenced by the religious beliefs of his colleagues? With the collapse of the house of Howard, the removal of Gardiner, the death of Anthony Browne and the relegation of Wriothesley, it is likely that the council was not seriously divided in the matter of religion and as a body was dominated by a variety of protestantism. Paget was certainly dissatisfied with the slack enforcement of religious change,[151] but not the religious settlement itself. Somerset's readiness, in spite of his advanced protestantism, to introduce moderate changes for political reasons seemed to prevent conflict with his less advanced protestant colleagues over the degree of religious change required. For these reasons it seems unlikely that the settlement was a compromise between the religious beliefs of Somerset and his colleagues. Of the other members of the council, Thomas Cranmer was clearly important to this stage of the reformation, but there is no certainty that he determined its character. The first Prayer Book may have reflected the hesitation of his own standpoint, but its acceptance was in all likelihood the outcome of political considerations rather

[150] This applied both to the Order of Communion (Hughes and Larkin, 300) and the new service (Couratin, *op. cit.*, pp. 150*f*).

[151] PLB, see his letters to Somerset of 25 December 1548, 2 February and 7 July 1549 (printed in Strype II (2), HH).

than of the weight of his influence. Cranmer certainly kept the hope of concord among protestants alive and was important for attracting eminent foreign divines to England. He may well have played a vital role in securing a slight majority among the bishops for the first Prayer Book. But there is no evidence that his presence determined the character of the settlement. Probably no individual was that decisive. Dominating the whole process of religious change seemed to be circumstances which related neither to discord nor compromise in the council, but to the likelihood of discord with the emperor and between the subjects of the realm. There appeared to be no dispute over the need to respect these circumstances. A protestant government could therefore develop a religious programme which bore no simple relationship either to the beliefs of a particular individual or to the amalgamated beliefs of the ruling group, but which was directed by the undeniable need for change and the government's fears about its political repercussions.

6

The Policy towards Government

Novelty and Change

In a period of government change, the Somerset regime was remarkable for its conservation of the existing system. This was not surprising considering its short and hectic life. In local government it passed on the conciliar system of regional government which it inherited, and the establishment of lord lieutenants throughout the realm, although inclined towards during the protectorate, and possibly proposed by Paget in February 1549, was only realized after Somerset's first fall.[1] Moreover, in spite of the pressures to produce a new military machine and new financial resources, both for the sake of domestic security and foreign war, the Somerset government fell back on the employment of foreign mercenaries and, except for an ill-fated excursion into indirect taxation, resorted to conventional financial expedients such as the sale of church and chantry lands and the exploitation of the mint.[2] In the circumstances of a minority, the privy council became, inevitably, more formalized in its procedure and larger in its membership, a feature of both the Somerset and Northumberland regimes, yet seemed to acquire

[1] The civil disorders of 1549 may well have prompted the idea of extending the function of the office, which was traditionally confined to military emergencies, to allow for the regular policing of the shires. But no contemporary evidence indicates that the system, which came fully into operation in the closing years of Edward VI's reign, when the country was divided into areas each with a lieutenant performing military and police duties, operated before Somerset's fall from power. Strype claimed to have found a mention of several commissions of lieutenancy for 24 July 1549 in a now irretrievable manuscript in the Cotton collection (Strype II (1), p. 278). But the commission quoted by Strype closely resembled the Northumberland commissions and was, in all probability, misdated by him (see G. Scott Thomson, *Lords Lieutenants in the Sixteenth Century: a Study in Tudor Local Administration* (London, 1923), pp. 24 *f* and 30 *f*). The lord lieutenancies appointed in 1549 seemed to have the limited function of raising troops and quelling the rebels: see the Willoughby commission (PRO E351/217), the Warwick commission (E351/215), the Russell commission (*CPR* 1548–9, p. 251) and the Shrewsbury commission (Lodge I, p. 133). The first mention of the system of lord lieutenancy, which was explicitly in operation in 1551, seemed to occur in Edward's chronicle for May 1550 (*The Chronicle and Political Papers of King Edward VI* (W. J. Jordan, ed.) (London, 1966), p. 29). For Paget's proposal to dispatch important figures to the localities to supervise the changes in religion and to maintain order, see PLB, Paget to Somerset, 2 February 1549.

[2] Schemes for the better provision of troops were in the air: see Wyatt's plan for a standing army (D. M. Loades, ed., *The Papers of George Wyatt, Esq.* (Camden Society, 4th series, 5 (1968)), pp. 163 *ff*), Hoby's plan for an army financed by confiscated bishoprics (Strype II (1), p. 139), and the scheme mentioned by Van der Delft for raising a large number of horsemen by relating their provision to tax assessment (*SP Span.* 1547–9, p. 270). None of these schemes appeared to be applied. For the system of finance, see Jordan I, pp. 391–7, and C. E. Challis, 'The Debasement of the Coinage 1542–1551', *Econ. HR* 2nd ser., 20 (1967), p. 454.

no new role nor further powers.[3] Parliament's recent encroachment into the spiritual sphere by means of the act for the restraint of appeals, the succession act of 1536, the annates act and the act of six articles, was furthered during the protectorate by the enactment of the Prayer Book, of the mass in two kinds and of clerical marriage, but, as in the previous reign, religion was not subjected completely to statutory authority.[4] In 1549 the government planned to use parliament to ratify a treaty with the emperor, but as part of a diplomatic bargain, rather than to include within the sphere of parliament a traditional preserve of the king's prerogative.[5] The administration of government finance was a pressing problem and a source of anxiety because of its expensiveness, unnecessary duplication and lack of co-ordination. The Somerset government, however, merely enacted the Henrician decision to fuse the courts of general surveyors and augmentations, and left it to the Northumberland regime to provide the eventual solution.[6]

In the history of governmental development, the protectorate offered nothing of substance and quality comparable either to the developments of the 1530s, particularly the achievement of national sovereignty, the extension of statutory competence, the rise to prominence of the principal secretary and the conciliar changes of that decade, or to the developments of the Northumberland regime with its notable advances in local government and financial administration. Nevertheless, in the personnel, instruments and financing of government, the protectorate was responsible for some significant innovations, as well as for several notable changes which tended to further developments already under way, while in the government of Ireland Somerset made a contribution which, for a time, broke with the past.

The personnel of government was affected by the removal of bishops from secular office. This development complemented the work of Henry VIII who had deprived the clergy of their traditional possession of the secretariat but had continued to depend heavily upon bishops as diplomats, privy councillors and as governors of outlying regions. In contrast, by 1549 Cranmer remained the only bishop in central government; the bishops had lost the presidency of the council of the Welsh Marches;[7] and they had ceased to figure on ambassadorial commissions. Their removal under the protectorate was by no means sudden. Cuthbert Tunstall served for a time as a privy councillor, and Thomas Thirlby survived until April 1548 as English representative at the Court of Charles V.[8] Nor was the removal complete since Cranmer persisted in the privy council, while Tunstall remained an important secular official in the north and Holgate clung to the

---

[3] PRO SP10/I/15 and G. R. Elton, *The Tudor Constitution* (Cambridge, 1965), p. 43.

[4] A. G. Dickens, *The English Reformation*, pp. 120 f. Issued without parliamentary consent were the Injunctions of 1547 and the Order of Communion of 1548.

[5] See below, p. 143.

[6] G. R. Elton, *The Tudor Revolution in Government* (Cambridge, 1953), pp. 229 f and 239.

[7] See Penry Williams, *The Council in the Marches of Wales under Elizabeth I* (Cardiff, 1958), p. 36.

[8] C. Sturge, *Cuthbert Tunstal* (London, 1938), p. 271; T. F. Shirley, *Thomas Thirlby, Tudor Bishop*, p. 93.

presidency of the council of the north.[9] Nor did the Somerset regime's exclusion of bishops from matters of government establish a point of no return; bishops made a slight comeback under Northumberland with the appointment of Goodrich to the lord chancellorship and achieved a restoration in the following reign. However, by the close of the protectorate, the episcopal bench was more exclusively restricted in its function to ecclesiastical matters than ever before. In this respect the protectorate marked a further stage in the secularization of government.[10]

Inevitably, the recently created peers of Henry VIII ran the government of Edward VI. The circle of civil servants and military leaders who had dominated and survived the Henrician government, with the exception of Wriothesley, ruled that of his son, and took their reward. However, a distinguishing feature of the protectorate was the government's employment of, and attitude towards, the nobility of ancient lineage. In certain respects, the protectorate can be regarded as a period of resurgence for this class. Lord Arundel established himself as a foremost privy councillor, although appointed only as an assistant executor in Henry VIII's will, and the earl of Shrewsbury performed also in the privy council and prominently as a military commander in the Scottish war.[11] Essential to the military leadership of the Somerset regime was Lord Grey of Wilton, Somerset's lieutenant in the far north until 1549, and Lord Clinton, admiral of the fleet, who was involved in the establishment of garrisons in Scotland both in late 1547 and late 1548.[12] Considering the prime importance of the northern war and their military duties in it, members of the old nobility must be regarded as playing an outstanding part in the Somerset government. In addition, under Somerset the older nobility reclaimed the wardenries, Lord Dacre replacing Lord Wharton on the West March and an earl of Rutland reappearing as warden of the East and Middle Marches.[13] Furthermore, during the protectorate, the houses of Stafford, Percy, Fitzgerald and Darcy were revived. Although the Fitzgeralds had to wait until Mary's reign for their reinstatement, the process of recovery began under Somerset when Gerald Fitzgerald, heir to the fallen earldom of Kildare, received permission to return from exile and was granted a pardon for treason and an annuity of £300.[14] The Staffords, the Darcies and the Percies had their attainders reversed and benefited from a substantial restoration of their family estates.[15] The protectorate is not distinguished by any exclusion of the old nobility, as Jordan asserts.[16] Instead it must be noted both for the use it made of peers of ancient

[9] Sturge, *op. cit.*, pp. 271–5, and A. G. Dickens, *Robert Holgate, Archbishop of York and President of the King's Council in the North* (St Anthony's Hall, York, Publications, 8 (1955)), pp. 16 f.

[10] See Pollard, pp. 80 f.

[11] Shrewsbury was not included in the list of councillors which was drawn up in December 1547 (*CPR* 1548–9, pp. 96 f); but served regularly on the council early in 1549 (see R. C. Anderson, *Letters of the Fifteenth and Sixteenth Centuries*, pp. 57, 61, 64 and 65, PRO SP10/VII/18 and Pocock, p. 7).

[12] See above, pp. 15 ff.

[13] Bush, 'The Problem of the Far North', *Northern History* 6 (1971), pp. 55 and 58.

[14] *APC* II, pp. 163 f, *CPR* 1553 with an Appendix, p. 406, and *ibid.* 1549–51, p. 119.

[15] 1 Edward VI, Original Act, 18, 2/3 Edward VI, Original Act, 41, and *ibid.*, 47.

[16] Jordan I, pp. 90–95.

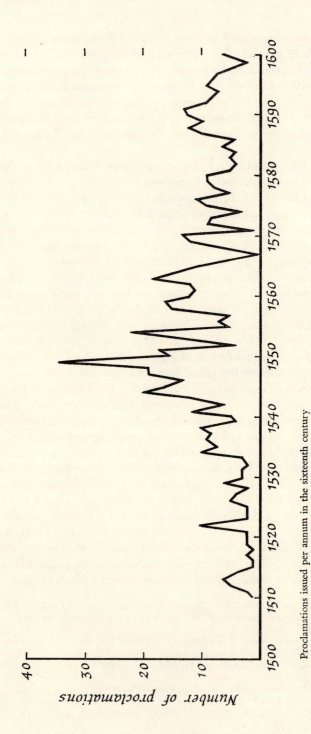

Proclamations issued per annum in the sixteenth century

lineage and for the permission it granted for the recovery of those magnate families who had been the victims of Henry VIII. Behaviour of this sort was not peculiar to Somerset's government, but was a feature of the Northumberland and Marian regimes as well.

The second important area of change concerned the declaration and enforcement of the government's will. The protectorate saw the making of a remarkably large number of royal proclamations. In the space of two and three quarter years, over seventy were made, a rate of use unrivalled for any comparable period in the sixteenth century. However, this does not mean that proclamations were being used for new purposes, and, to be seen in true perspective, it needs to be related to the large numbers issued before and afterwards in similar emergency situations.[17]

In addition the character of government was affected by the repeal act, 1 Edward VI, c. 12, which reduced the means of legal action at its disposal by abolishing all the laws relating to religious opinion, and much of the treason and felony legislation of Henry VIII. In the 1530s the first major addition to the law of treason had been made since the reign of Edward III.[18] Some of this was swept away. But there was not a simple return to a pre-Henrician past. The repeal act preserved many of the statutory enlargements which the Henrician government had made to the traditional law of treason. Writing and words as well as overt deeds, the denial of the king's title to the headship of the church and the state of England, as well as attempts to destroy the royal family, remained statutory grounds for high treason as did the treasons of forging the seals and counterfeiting.[19] What changed was that words became treason only in the third instance, and subject to an accusation which was supported by the evidence of two witnesses or the unaided confession of the accused, and made within thirty days of the offence.[20] Treason by words thus remained, but safeguarded against misuse and applied with less severity. In addition, because of the repeal act, a conviction of treason at law did not entitle the forfeiture of all possessions, only those held in fee simple, unless by act of attainder. In this respect the status quo ante was merely enacted.[21]

Sweeping away the heresy laws removed the more important felonies created by Henry VIII: those connected with the act of six articles.[22] The repeal of the additional felonies of Henry VIII's reign was consequently of less significance than

[17] See graph, p. 130.

[18] G. R. Elton, *Policy and Police* (Cambridge, 1972), ch. 6.

[19] 1 Edward VI, c. 12 (v–viii).

[20] *Ibid.*, v, xix and xxii.

[21] It was traditionally possible in exceptional circumstances, such as levying war against the king, for the Crown to forfeit lands in tail as well as in fee simple as a result of a conviction of treason without act of attainder, but not as a result of trial by common law (J. G. Bellamy, *The Law of Treason in England in the Later Middle Ages* (Cambridge, 1970), pp. 192–4).

[22] Some of the felonies, those relating to the sexual activities of clerics and the women associating with them as wives and concubines, had been repealed in the same reign (see 32 Henry VIII, c. 10). Remaining to be repealed was the felony of refusing confession and to receive the sacrament, and the felony of opposing any one of the six articles (31 Henry VIII, c. 14).

the repeal of the treason and heresy legislation. In fact it only erased superficial details of the crime which, as it might be expected, had been defined and substantiated long before. Furthermore, some of the Henrician felonies, those relating to military desertion or unlicensed military leave and to buggery, were re-enacted in the following session,[23] while the Henrician felony of servants robbing masters of goods and chattels was preserved by a proviso in the repeal act.[24] In addition, the statute, 23 Henry VIII, c. 16, concerning the unauthorized export of horses, was quickly re-enacted in the session of its repeal, no longer as a felony, but with stiff penalties of fine and imprisonment.[25] The felonies in force which the repeal act removed were a small and peripheral collection, some of them undeniably harsh and anomalous.[26] Their removal relieved without affecting the basic character of the criminal law or the government's means of action. The repeal act, for example, did not deprive the government of an adequate instrument for dealing with the insurrections of 1549. It is true that it lost the power to convict as felonies such offences as the robbing and draining of fishponds, the killing of privately owned deer and rabbits, the burning of unfinished houses and dyke-breaking in Norfolk and Ely. But it seems unlikely that, as a result, the government's hands were tied for dealing with the specific problem of riot, although some of the rioters' actions fell within the scope of the repealed Henrician felonies. The government was at a particular disadvantage in 1549, not because of the laws it had abrogated in 1547, but because of the absence of legislation to condemn generally riots which did not aim directly at the king, his officials and installations.[27]

More remarkable than the deletion of the Henrician felonies was the permission granted by the act for the removal of felonies from the due process of law. To a small degree, this involved the act's extension of the right of sanctuary. Rape and arson were readmitted to the privilege which they had lost in 1540. But otherwise the major crimes were prevented from escaping the law in this manner, in accordance with tradition and Henrician legislation.[28] A much more profound change stemmed from the act's legislation on benefit of clergy. The act stood the earlier legislation on its head. The Henrician government had increased the restrictions upon the privilege first by confining it to those in orders for the major

---

[23] 2/3 Edward VI, c. 2 and c. 29, re-enacting 3 Henry VIII, c. 5, and 25 Henry VIII, c. 6.

[24] 1 Edward VI, c. 12 (xviii).   [25] 1 Edward VI, c. 5.

[26] 22 Henry VIII, c. 11 (breaking dykes in Norfolk and Ely), 23 Henry VIII, c. 11 (clerks convict breaking prison of the ordinary), 31 Henry VIII, c. 2 (robbing and destroying fishponds), 31 Henry VIII, c. 12, and 32 Henry VIII, c. 11 (poaching privately owned rabbits and deer, and stealing hawks' eggs and young hawks), 33 Henry VIII, c. 12 (xiii) (stealing the king's goods above 12d. and entering his house with intent), 33 Henry VIII, c. 8 (attempting to practise sorcery), 37 Henry VIII, c. 6 (burning the timber frames of houses), and 37 Henry VIII, c. 10 (dispensing slanderous bills accusing others of treason).

[27] W. S. Holdsworth, *A History of English Law* (London, 1922–52), IV, p. 497.

[28] See John Bellamy, *Crime and Public Order in England in the Later Middle Ages* (London, 1973), pp. 109 and 111; I. D. Thornley, 'The Destruction of Sanctuary', *Tudor Studies*, ed. R. W. Seton-Watson (London, 1924), pp. 203 f; and Holdsworth, III, p. 307. The relevant statutes are 32 Henry VIII, c. 12, and 1 Edward VI, c. 12 (ix). Pollard was quite wrong in thinking that treason was readmitted to the privileges of benefit and sanctuary (Pollard, p. 61).

felonies and later by depriving the whole clergy of the privilege for these crimes. While the repeal act with slight modifications upheld all these restrictions, in addition it allowed a select group of laymen, the peerage, with no necessary clerical qualifications of literacy, to enjoy the privilege for all felonies of the first offence except murder and poison. By retaining the Henrician restrictions upon the clergy and by giving the privilege to a class with no clerical pretension, the act seriously breached tradition. However, this new opening for the laity to escape from the law was in future to be blocked off gradually by the use of the already established practice of enacting statutes which refused in specific matters to countenance the privilege for anyone.[30]

The act's generosity towards the peerage went even further in the matter of crime, since it extended the noble privilege of trial by peers, traditionally confined to treason, to compass 'any offence limited in this act'. The act thus allowed the peerage the option to remove itself completely from the common-law process in criminal matters.[31] In this way, as T. F. T. Plucknett first noticed, the rise of the peerage, a phenomenon of the late middle ages, which by the early seventeenth century had produced a substantial class of noblemen distinguished from the rest of the aristocracy with their own parliamentary house and unshared privileges and offices, proceeded a step further.[32]

A final outcome of the act was the repeal of the act of proclamations. This removed the complicated machinery enacted in 1539 for the making and trial of proclamations. It also ended a system which had allowed for the use of two distinct types of proclamation: one type possessed closely restricted powers which were possibly less and certainly no more than proclamations had traditionally exercised, but was unencumbered by the machinery of the act; the other was subjected to this machinery, but possessed powers beyond the legitimate reach of the traditional proclamation. Its repeal did not transform the role of proclamations as an instrument of government, but since the act had had some practical effect, its removal was a landmark in the history of the royal proclamation.[33]

The Somerset government made its most decisive alteration to the existing system in Ireland where it sought to impose a more direct form of rule than had operated in the past. In response to the unrest and the rising of the O'Connors and the O'Mores, and as a result of the ideas of Sir William Brabazon and Sir Edward Bellingham, it adopted a policy of control in Ireland based on the establishment of garrisons, rather than on the traditional negotiation with local magnates which the Henrician regime had accepted even in the 1530s as its main source of government. As the Somerset government planned to man the garrisons with Englishmen, schemes of colonization accompanied their establishment.[34]

[29] Holdsworth III, pp. 299 f; 1 Edward VI, c. 12 (ix and xiii).
[30] Holdsworth III, p. 300.   [31] 1 Edward VI, c. 12 (xiv).
[32] T. F. T. Plucknett, 'Some Proposed Legislation of Henry VIII', *TRHS*, 4th ser. 19 (1936), pp. 123–125, and see K. B. McFarlane, *The Nobility of the Later Medieval England* (Oxford, 1973), ch. 8.
[33] See below, pp. 136–40.
[34] D. G. White, 'The Reign of Edward VI in Ireland: some Political, Social and Economic Aspects', *Irish Historical Studies* 14 (1965), pp. 197 ff.

Control through strategically placed garrisons was applied in Ireland before it was attempted in Scotland. In March 1547 the privy council instructed the deputy and council in Ireland to establish garrisons 'in most meet places of service without the English pale', which were to be 'furnished all of Englishmen, saving four in every hundred to be Irishmen serving for guides'.[35] In the following two years four garrisons were founded, fortified and manned. Situated in Nenagh, Athlone and Leighlin Bridge, Offaly, and with Fort Protector in Leix, these garrisons subjected the whole midland area to the direct rule of the government. The garrisons were manned by leasing to Englishmen estates confiscated from the O'Mores, O'Connors and Kavanaghs. In this sense the policy in Ireland proceeded much further than in Scotland where the Crown hesitated to assert any right of actual landownership and, faced with the problem of manning the forts, used foreign mercenaries for the purpose.[36] But, nevertheless, the basic means of control, by garrisons of aliens to the region, was the same in both cases.

In Ireland, as in Scotland, garrisons were not applied without precedent. Traditionally, English rule in Ireland had consisted not only of alliances with Gaelic chieftains and princes and with Anglo-Irish lords, but also of garrisoning the English pale. Furthermore, in Henry VIII's closing years, the equivalent of the English garrisons in Scotland at Jedburgh and Langholm were established beyond the pale in Ireland, at Daingean, Offaly, and Ballyadams, Leix, both of them the result of an expedition led by Brabazon in 1546 against the O'Mores and the O'Connors. But only under Somerset did the garrisoning of Ireland beyond the traditional pale become the main aim of the government, the core of its policy, the means of permanent assertion rather than the ephemeral response to a crisis. This innovation in the government of Ireland did not wither with Somerset's fall. It was yet another aspect of Somerset's policy which Edward VI's other government took over lock, stock and barrel.[37] Moreover, while garrisoning was brought to an end by its costliness, the idea of controlling Ireland by settlement, already conceived and with medieval precedents, but first applied in the sixteenth century by Somerset, ripened into a major feature of future policy.

Finally, in the second parliamentary session, the government produced a new fiscal device, a tax on the production of wool and the manufacture of cloth. Larger claims have been made for the tax than it deserves. It was essentially regarded as a means of tapping new wealth, but this was foiled with two provisos inserted by the Commons which allowed sheep-masters and cloth-manufacturers to set their liability for the relief on sheep and cloth against their liability for the accompanying subsidy on personality, paying tax only on the higher assessment.[38] It proved an inadequate tax, having to be delayed and mitigated

---

[35] *APC* II, p. 76.

[36] White, *op. cit.*, pp. 203 f; and see above, pp. 19 and 35.

[37] White, *op. cit.*, p. 199; *ibid.*, pp. 204 ff.

[38] 2/3 Edward VI, c. 36. The bill was first introduced in the Commons where it lodged for a month, in which time the two provisos (vii and ix) were presumably inserted (*Commons Journals*, 1, 14, 25 February, and 2 March). The Lords passed it without much delay and without addition (*Journals of the House of Lords*, 5, 6 and 12 March). They seemed to accept the Commons' draft without demur.

while in operation, and for this reason and probably in a bid for popularity it was quickly repealed by the Northumberland regime.[39] However, it demonstrated the government's willingness to try new devices, and, by requiring a survey of the nation's sheep in connection with the sheep tax, the government revealed a modern mindedness, also evident in the government-sponsored milch-kine bill, which corresponded with the novel order of the 1530s for the keeping of parish registers.[40] The relief on sheep and cloth was of significance in the history of taxation, not for representing the deliberate creation of a fiscal means of social control, but for marking an entry into what was for England the grossly under-worked and obvious field of indirect taxation.

None of these changes, except for the military occupation of midland Ireland, can be explained simply in terms of a novel attitude towards government. They occurred because of the government's need to react against past excesses and to respond to present circumstances. In this respect, the changes owed very little to concepts and theories of government, and a great deal to what contemporaries felt had happened under Henry VIII, and was happening under his son.

The Impact of Past and Present

Somerset was undoubtedly a firm supporter of the repeal act, 1 Edward VI, c. 12. At the time of its enactment, he told the imperial ambassador: 'Some of our laws . . . are at present extremely rigorous and indeed almost iniquitous in their sever-ity', and later John Mason held him personally responsible for the changes in the law which centred on terminating the first offence by words as treason.[41] But in holding this view, Somerset stood neither alone nor on liberal principles.[42] Paget directly condemned the Henrician government as extreme: 'Then all things were too straight', he wrote, 'then it was dangerous to do or speak though the meaning was not evil.'[43] What is more, while the passage of the act through parliament was complicated, this was, in all likelihood, because of the measure's ambitiousness, not because of the vigour of any opposition to the idea of repeal.[44] If the parlia-mentary objections to it had been against the removal of laws, the many pro-visos appended unofficially during the passage of the act would have re-inserted the laws which the blanket repeal evicted *en bloc*, but instead they tended to insert

and added no provisos (see Original Act, 2/3 Edward VI, 37). The delay in the readings between 6 and 12 March was, apparently, to allow the accompanying concessions (see above, pp. 49*f*) to be concluded first (see *Journals of the House of Lords*, 9 March (purveyance bill), 11 March (sheriffs bill and escheators bill). The fee-farms bill was read on the same day as the final reading of the bill for the Relief, but got into difficulties and was committed.

[39] See SP10/VII/42 and Pocock, pp. 61 and 75.

[40] See above, p. 78.

[41] *SP Span.* 1547–9, p. 205, and Jordan I, p. 175.

[42] For this traditional view, see Pollard, p. 58, and Jordan I, pp. 172–5.

[43] PLB, Paget to Somerset, 25 December 1548.

[44] See *Journals of the House of Lords*, 10, 11, 15 and 16 November; *Commons Journals*, 21 and 30 November, and 6 and 12 December; *Journals of the House of Lords*, 16, 20, 21 and 22 December and *Commons Journals*, 23 December; and n. 85, p. 145.

K

measures of further mitigation.[45] In future years the critics of the act were few and far between. Other than catholics objecting to the freedom allowed protestantism by the repeal of the act of six articles, only Thomas Seymour during the protectorate attacked it explicitly and for no other reason than that it was his brother's measure and because he thought it licensed subjects to slander his wife.[46]

By means of the repeal act, the new government condemned the old regime, although it excused the rigorous measures of the Henrician government as dictated by former circumstances, and thus avoided calling Henry VIII a tyrant.[47] The Somerset government acted for a number of reasons. One was a new government's automatic need to react against the one it had replaced. The repeal act emphasized the repressiveness of the Henrician regime; enacted measures which, except in religion, changed little, but strongly expressed the need for less rigour and more clemency; and disposed of acts which had previously met with disapproval. All this suggests to some extent, that the government regarded the act as a means of achieving popularity. The act seemed to arise from the need of a new government to establish rapport with the realm. Thirty-eight years earlier, the new government of Henry VIII had seized upon the financial exploitation associated with his father's regime and had proceeded against the ministers held responsible in what must have been a similar search for popularity, and in the same cause, the second government of Edward VI seems to have removed several of the measures associated with Somerset.[48]

But it would be incorrect to explain the repeal act simply as a government's attempt to foster goodwill, and a reaction against what had gone before. The wholesale abolition of 'all acts . . . concerning religion or opinions' was more than a device for attracting popularity.[49] Inevitably, a government run by protestants was bound to abolish the measures previously enacted to crush them and their kind. The abolition was initiated by men whose religious beliefs had made them potential victims. This part of the repeal statute, then, has to be seen as an act of revulsion against a history of oppression in the cause of self-preservation. It certainly was not the declaration of a belief in toleration nor an abandonment of the traditional reverence for religious unity, nor did it rest on a feeling that religious dissent should always be pacified rather than exterminated.[50] Sustaining it was a strong current of self-interest.

The act of proclamations was also an anti-heresy measure because of its excep-

[45] The crimes reinserted in this way were the felony of servants robbing their masters (xviii) and possibly the treasons of counterfeiting coins and forging the king's seals (vii), and the crime of poison, which the repeal act deemed murder not treason (as the statute, 22 Henry VIII c. 9, had anomalously enacted), and replaced death by boiling with the more normal form of execution for murderers (xii). In all a mild tally, the last mentioned insertion being one of amelioration. Otherwise, the insertions were preponderantly mitigatory (see xiv, xv, xvi, xvii, xix, xx, xxi and xxii). For the unofficial nature of the provisos, see below, p. 145.

[46] F. Rose-Troup, *op. cit.*, p. 213, and S. Haynes, ed., *Collection of State Papers . . . left by William Cecil, Lord Burghley* (London, 1740-59), I, p. 76.

[47] See the preamble, 1 Edward VI, c. 12.

[48] See above, pp. 181*f*.

[49] 1 Edward VI, c. 12 (ii).   [50] See above, pp. 112*ff*.

tion concerning religion.[51] But this was probably not the basic reason for its inclusion in the repeal act which seemed to be a matter of practical government. The repealed act had created one type of proclamation with a highly doubtful ability to modify statutes and to impose fearsome penalties except in matters of religion. It had also created another type so enlarged in its powers that it could contravene statutes (if made after the act), create offences punishable by informer actions in the courts of common law, and threaten unusually harsh penalties, involving the forfeiture of goods and chattels, for offences which fell outside the category of religion, rebellion and war.[52] The two types of proclamation were formally differentiated by an explicit reference in the text of the proclamation to the authority of the proclamations act. By quoting the authority of the act, a proclamation acquired special powers, while, at the same time, it became subject to the machinery set up by the act for the making of such special proclamations. At least eleven proclamations of this sort were issued, a small proportion (one in nine) of the proclamations made during the life of the proclamations act.[53] Their purpose was two-fold: first, to legislate on economic matters by creating informer actions enforceable in the courts of common law and by imposing heavy penalties enforceable in a special conciliar committee; and secondly, to infringe statutes. Thus, one special proclamation priced sugar and allowed informations 'in any of the king's courts'. Another priced meat and likewise allowed enforcement in the courts of common law. Another, in the same way, forbad the hoarding of grain. A lost proclamation, which is known to have rested on the act and to have forbidden the export of victuals and other commodities, threatened to penalize offenders with the forfeiture of goods and chattels, among other penalties, but not by trial in a court of law.[54] Other special proclamations went contrary to statute. Two, for a period of two years, provided an alternative penalty of fine and imprisonment to the harsh statute, 32 Henry VIII, c. 11, which made a felony of taking hawks' eggs.[55] Another simply breached the statute, 33 Henry VIII, c. 6,

---

[51] See Hughes and Larkin, pp. 545 *f*: an exception to the limitation placed on the powers of proclamations was allowed for 'such persons which shall offend any proclamation to be made by the king's majesty, his heirs or successors, for and concerning any kind of heresies against christian religion.'

[52] The distinction was finally imposed by an addition ('and in every proclamation which hereafter shall be set forth by authority of the same'), inserted by the Lords in the closing stages of the debate and, in all probability, a government move to free itself of the restrictions imposed upon the bill by the Commons and the Lords (see n. 65), so that some of its original intentions could be realised. That the phrase 'and in every proclamation' as well as the interlineation 'hereafter . . . same' (Hughes and Larkin, p. 546) were added by the Lords is made clear by the correction evident in the Original Act (31 Henry VIII, c. 8) and by the fact that without the interlineation the passage does not make sense. G. R. Elton refers to these changes as 'not world-shaking' ('Henry VIII's Act of Proclamations', *Engl. HR* 75 (1960), p. 217). However, at a stroke, they seem to have transformed the Commons' bill, bringing it more in line with what was probably the purpose of the original bill.

[53] Hughes and Larkin, 197.6 (omitted from vol. I and appended to vol. III), 201, 205, 211, 217, 218, 225.5 (omitted from vol. I and appended to vol. III), 231, 232, 242 and 271. Two of these proclamations merely voided or modified earlier proclamations resting on the authority of the act: 201 modified 197.6 and 271 voided 225.5. 217 extended the operation of 211 for a further year and 232 almost repeated 231.

[54] Hughes and Larkin, 218, 231, 232, 242 and (III) 197.6.

[55] *Ibid.*, 211 and 217.

(which forbad the use of handguns) by authorizing the whole community to use them subject to certain restrictions. In this case, the proclamation took away the grounds for informer actions which the statute allowed.[56] Thus, as a result of the proclamations act, proclamations acquired remarkable powers of legislation, but did not become the equal of statute since, among other restrictions, these powers did not include the authority to sanction new felonies, treasons and fiscal measures.

This use of the proclamations act seemed to correspond with the original intentions of the government. In framing the bill the government, in all probability, had not been thinking in terms of power for power's sake, or of finding a general alternative to statute, but—in addition to improving the effectiveness of its religious proclamations—of securing additional emergency powers mainly for the sake of regulating the economy and particularly to cope with inflation. The surviving evidence of the government's attitude towards the bill points firmly in this direction. Cromwell's remarks to Norfolk about proclamations having the effect of law in prohibiting the export of bullion, and Gardiner's statement that the proclamations act arose from the problem of enforcing proclamations prohibiting the export of grain, comply both in the character of their subject matter, and in their concern with enforcement.[57] Gardiner was presumably referring to the validity of common-law informer actions which rested on proclamation, and so was Cromwell. There can be little doubt that when Cromwell consulted the judges in 1531, as he recorded in his letter to Norfolk, he was not worried about the validity of prohibiting by proclamation the export of coin—this was self-evident—but about the validity of prohibiting the export of coin by means of a proclamation which allowed enforcement by informer action in the court of exchequer.[58] The favourable reply of the judges to Cromwell's enquiries about the validity of such a proclamation, even if it did not rest upon statute, remains a mystery, but the nature of the interest seems clear. If economic regulation by means of informer actions cognizable in the courts of common law was the government's intention, it makes sense of the act's final section which safeguarded the royal right to mitigate the penalties of proclamations involving sums of money. The clause acquires meaning in the light of the constitutional restriction upon the powers of the Crown in normal common-law informer actions when it could mitigate the penalty only by reducing the king's moiety of the forfeit.[59] This closing proviso seems to have been inserted to prevent the royal authority expressed through proclamations from becoming subject to the constitutional restrictions placed upon the king in relation to statutes, and indicates the act's purpose of equipping proclamations with a system of common-law enforcement.

The aims of the proclamations act are confirmed by the fact that the act was not

[56] Hughes and Larkin, (III) 225.5. It had a short life. Issued in February 1544, it was voided in July 1546 (*ibid.*, 271), with the result that the statute again became law.

[57] See Elton, 'Henry VIII's Act of Proclamations', pp. 219 *f*; Cromwell's remark relates to 1531, not 1535 (see Elton, *Reform and Renewal*, pp. 117*f*).

[58] Hughes and Larkin, 133. The related statute only stated vaguely that the informer should receive half the forfeit 'of the king's gift' (5 Richard II, c. 2).

[59] Hughes and Larkin, p. 549, and G. R. Elton, *Tudor Constitution*, p. 19.

so much a turning point as the culmination of a development. Statutes authorizing legislation by proclamation in specified matters are a feature of the 1530s. The subject, for the most part, was, predictably, price regulation. Thus 25 Henry VIII, c. 2, allowed proclamations to declare the prices of victuals taxed by a committee and to determine the penalty. Another act of the same session, 25 Henry VIII, c. 1, regulating meat prices, empowered proclamations to suspend the act and to alter the official price of meat in accordance with the economic situation. A statute of the following session, 26 Henry VIII, c. 10, permitted proclamations to abrogate and revive certain statutes relating to foreign trade, and a final statute, 28 Henry VIII, c. 14, authorized a committee to fix the price of wine by proclamation. As they allowed informer actions, these statutes established the precedent for proclamations, resting on the authority of statutes, to provide the specific ground for information laid in the courts of common law. They also established the precedent for committees on the authority of statute to implement their decisions by proclamation. The act of proclamations seemed part of a series of measures, all designed to deal with the problem of economic regulation which required for its solution greater flexibility than unaided statutes possessed.

Somerset seems to have had a statute repealed which in practice, and by design, had increased the powers of the Crown for the purpose of regulating the economy. His government not only proceeded against the act at the first opportunity, but also declined to rest any proclamations upon its authority. Repeal was necessary because by this time the special proclamation which the act had created had become a cumbersome and useless device. Earlier, in 1542, the awkwardness of the machinery for the enforcement of this type of proclamation had led to a modification of the act.[60] This modification, however, had expired on the death of Henry VIII. The new government was forced to do something, particularly as it was subject on account of Edward VI's minority to section viii of the act which required fourteen councillors to authorize by signature a proclamation with special powers.[61] The choice for the Somerset regime was either to modify the act or to have it repealed. The case for the latter was overwhelming. The attempt to enforce proclamations by common-law informer actions does not seem to have succeeded.[62] Moreover, by Edward VI's reign the experiment of beating inflation by fixing prices was in disrepute, and the device was resorted to only in moments of desperation.[63] Much of the *raison d'être* had gone, and consequently the advantages to be gained from the act no longer offset the disadvantages. What is more, as a result of the act no statute made before 1539 could be touched by proclamation, except simply for the purpose of enforcement. In addition, the cumbersome procedure for making special proclamations, which the act imposed during a minority, made it extremely difficult for the Somerset government to

[60] 34/35 Henry VIII, c. 23. It reduced the size of the council committee necessary for the legitimate enforcement of a proclamation.

[61] G. R. Elton, 'Henry VIII's Act of Proclamations', *Engl. HR* 75 (1960), pp. 213 f.

[62] See R. W. Heinze, 'The Pricing of Meat: a Study in the Use of Royal Proclamations in the Reign of Henry VIII', *Historical Journal* 12 (1969), p. 594 and n. 68.

[63] See below, pp. 151 f.

use them and forced it to rely wholly upon normal proclamations, the extent of whose powers had been rendered questionable by the act. Somerset's government seems to have had the act repealed in order to escape its restrictions and to allow the traditional type of proclamation to recover its traditional powers.

The act was not repealed because of Somerset's desire for personal pre-eminence. This is to read the situation of 1549 into that of 1547. In 1547, with the exception of Seymour and Wriothesley, the council appeared to be at one, or at least not seriously divided, and in conformity with Somerset's leadership. Nor was it repealed to solve a general problem of making proclamations, since the machinery of the act only needed to be used for making proclamations with special powers.[64] Furthermore, as the act had not been intended or used as a despotic measure, its repeal cannot be seen as an expression of genuine liberal sentiment. On the other hand, as the act had extended the possibilities of pro-clamation, and as Somerset did not appear before or after its repeal to misuse pro-clamations deliberately, neither can the repeal be regarded as an expression of aspiring despotism. The repeal probably owed something to the unpopularity surrounding the original enactment and to the compromise between the govern-ment and parliament which produced an act of little practical use.[65] Without doubt it also stemmed from changing opinion on the question of controlling inflation as well as from the knowledge of the act's defectiveness which had been acquired during its eight years in operation.

The Somerset government's remarkable reliance upon proclamations was like-wise compelled by the practical needs of the present. Their number cannot be simply explained as the culmination of a tendency for their more frequent use, although the number made in the closing years of Henry VIII's reign exceeded by far the number issued in the early years.[66] Nor can the presence of Somerset at the head of the government be considered as the answer since 1547's crop of pro-clamations, a remarkable number (19) for a period of peace and one which equalled the record numbers for the war years 1544 (19) and 1545 (18), seemed a response to the problems of the accession and the government's determination to pursue the reformation further,[67] while 1548 saw the issue of what was a normal number of proclamations for a time of war, inflation and religious change. The two outstanding characteristics of the quantity of the Somerset proclamations suggest another explanation. Almost half of Somerset's proclamations belonged to the first nine months of 1549, with heavy concentrations in January, April, July

[64] For the opposite view see Elton, 'Henry VIII's Act of Proclamations', p. 214.

[65] For the making of the act, see *ibid.*, pp. 208 *ff.* My opinion of the course of the bill is as fol-lows: first, the Lords unofficially added the restrictive machinery for the enforcement and issue of proclamations; second, the Commons unofficially added the restrictions on the powers of proclama-tions contained in section ii; thirdly, through the Lords, the government made the vital addition 'and in every proclamation which hereafter shall be set forth by authority of the same'.

[66] See G. R. Elton, 'Government by Edict?', *Historical Journal* 8 (1965), p. 268. In the first twenty-three years, which included two periods of war, the government issued 60 proclamations; in the last sixteen years, with one period of war, it issued 136 proclamations.

[67] The accession produced six proclamations (Hughes and Larkin, 275, 276, 277, 282, 289 and 290); while religious matters produced an additional four (*ibid.*, 281, 287, 292 and 296).

and August. The second notable feature is the number of proclamations dealing with political and economic emergencies, the former the outcome of religious change, war and civil discord, the latter the outcome of inflation.[68] In a time of crisis the government reached for its traditional emergency instrument. Just as the break with Rome and inflation helped to increase the number of proclamations in the 1530s,[69] and the prevalence of war and inflation worked with similar effect in the early 1540s;[70] in the same way the number of proclamations issued during the protectorate has to be explained in terms of contemporary circumstance. The large number reflected a crisis situation which was particularly acute in the

Table 6.1 **Emergency proclamations 1547–9**

Year	Political emergency[1]	Inflation	Total[2]
1547	6	2	19
1548	7	5	19
1549	21	5	34

[1] 'Political emergency' includes proclamations curbing disorder or relating to foreign war. For 1547 it includes two proclamations relating to the king's accession, and one relating to isolating the Court in a time of plague.

[2] Not all the items included by Hughes and Larkin are royal proclamations in the accepted sense of the term, and occasionally the same proclamation is printed twice. For suggestions about necessary deletions, see G. R. Elton, 'Government by Edict', *Historical Journal* 8 (1965), p. 268. In addition to these deletions, three items need to be removed since they are instructions to specific officials (Hughes and Larkins, 279, 283 and 305). A remarkable feature of the Somerset proclamations was the lack of compound proclamations incorporating a variety of matters in one proclamation—a feature of the proclamations issued by the Cromwellian and Northumberland governments. But this relative absence does not account for the differences in the numbers of proclamations which were made.

closing months of the regime when galloping inflation, war, insurrection and religious change necessitated the frequent use of proclamations.

Similarly, the government's permissive treatment of the old nobility was both a consequence of Henry VIII's reign, and a practical response to the present. In view of the traditional practice of restoring fallen noble families after a decent lapse of time, it was to be expected that Henry VIII's death would soon result in the forgiveness and restoration of the families he had felled; and not only of attainted houses but also of the disgraced magnate, Lord Dacre. Denied office and responsibility for the remainder of Henry VIII's reign after his unexpected pardon by trial of peers, Dacre's re-employment during the protectorate was undoubtedly the

[68] See table 6:1.
[69] Fifteen proclamations out of 47 for the Cromwell regime 1534–40.
[70] Thirty-eight proclamations out of seventy-eight.

natural repercussion of Henry VIII's death. Mary's reign was similarly affected and, in addition, was not restricted by the religious differences and personal antagonism which prevented the Edwardian governments from releasing the third duke of Norfolk from the Tower, and from restoring the houses of Howard and Courtenay. Otherwise, the protectorate and the Northumberland and Marian regimes are at one in expressing the reaction of governments unconstrained by Henry VIII's presence. Yet this was only one factor determining the Somerset government's attitude towards the old nobility. The government, for example, allowed Kildare to return from exile, partly because of the rumour that foreign powers were seeking to make use of him for raising rebellion in Ireland.[71] Furthermore, the re-employment of the old families in the far north sprang from a realization of their essential value, brought home by a decade of rule without them. The appointment of the earl of Rutland and of Lord Dacre to the wardenships, which, in the absence of a suitable Percy, represented the restoration of the traditional system of border defence, partly reflected the opportunity of the new regime to employ the formerly excluded Lord Dacre, but also an acceptance of reality, of the necessity of employing the old magnate families when they provided adequate candidates for the office of warden.[72] What seems certain is that the policy adopted towards the victims of Henry VIII owed nothing to a change in attitude towards the old nobility as a class, but was essentially a consequence of the past and a practical response to the pressure and needs of the present.

The government's fiscal devices seem to have similar origins. They sprang from the unusually heavy taxation of Henry VIII's closing years, the need of the new government to respect that fact for the sake of its own popularity, and its urgent need for further funds. In the first session it desisted from requiring supplies; and the chantry lands were granted on the understanding that the realm would be relieved of fiscal demands in the near future. In this delicate situation the government, in spite of its needs, hesitated to request supplies in the second session.[73] Its solution was to produce a tax which could not be labelled Henrician, and which was sugar-coated with concessions.[74] Sheep and cloth were taxed as a source of untapped wealth. Along with the plan to annex church ornaments and bells and to place them at the disposal of the state,[75] the relief on sheep and cloth was a device to extract revenue in a manner which would not impose too much of a burden on the realm. The government's main aim seemed the avoidance of another crushing subsidy; and the subsidy requested broke with Henrician habit and took the form of an assessment on goods, thus allowing lands to go untaxed.[76]

[71] PRO SP10/III/5, *SP Span.* 1547–9, pp. 348 *f* and 362, and *APC* II, pp. 163 *f* and 539–42.

[72] See Bush, 'The Problem of the Far North', *op. cit.*, 6 (1971), pp. 41 *ff.*

[73] See F. Dietz, *English Government Finance, 1485–1558* (University of Illinois Studies in the Social Sciences, ix (3) (1920)), p. 184; PLB, Paget to Somerset, 25 December 1548, in which Paget described Somerset to be 'in doubt to ask aid at home for your relief'.

[74] See the instructions issued to the commissioners for the Relief (Anderson, *Letters of the Fifteenth and Sixteenth Centuries*, pp. 62–4, and Bodley, MS Rawlinson D 1087, ff. 32–4), and above, pp. 49 *f.*

[75] See above, pp. 52 and 134 *f*, PL.B, Paget to Somerset, 25 December 1548 and 2 February 1549 and Paget's memorial of 25 January 1549, and PRO SP10/VI/25.

[76] For an appreciation of this concession, see the marquis of Dorset's alleged retort to Thomas

The factors determining the government's fiscal policy were the need to handle the realm carefully because of the heavy tax demands already made by Henry VIII in the last five years of his reign and, in addition, the pressing financial requirements of the Scottish war which made a request for supplies a necessity.

Finally, the plan to make a foreign treaty the subject of a parliamentary statute also seems to have been dictated by circumstances. When Paget was instructed to announce to Charles V the English intention to confirm by parliament the treaty which he had been commissioned to make with the emperor, the government was not declaring a desire to extend the function of statute, but was seeking to persuade the emperor of the need for his Estates to sanction the imperial part of the agreement.[77] The problem for the English was to make the treaty as binding upon an empire as upon a nation state, and to create a treaty which would not be undone by the emperor's retirement or death. More specifically, they aimed to bind the Netherlands and Philip II to accept a treaty made by Charles V. Far from asserting constitutionalism in foreign policy, the Somerset government merely desired to make a treaty effectively recognized by the emperor's subjects and his heir.[78] Nothing came of the plan. The emperor was shocked at the affront to his prerogative authority. Moreover, as proof of its diplomatic designs, the English government accepted the emperor's alternative suggestion that the treaty should be signed by his heir and the guardians of Edward VI, and failed not only to press parliamentary sanction upon him, but also to provide it unilaterally when the emperor refused to comply.[79]

In its approach to the system of government, as in its attitude towards Scotland, social and economic problems and to religious change, the government revealed a strong practical sense. It was driven by a need for popularity, and provided with the opportunity for acquiring it by the unpopularity of certain Henrician measures; at the same time it was moved by a concern to make government practical, to protect protestantism and to raise revenue. This practical sense was no safeguard against losing sight of reality; nor against failing to cope; but it tended to minimize the importance of ideas and the possible influence of idealism in the making of policy.

Principles and Plans

Early in 1549 Somerset discussed his theory of government with the imperial ambassador.[80] The ambassador, in his report of the conversation, did not reveal the nature of Somerset's views but, nevertheless, his account revealed Somerset's capacity to think about government in general, conceptual terms. But did this

---

Seymour's objection to the Relief: 'you were better grant such a subsidy than one out of your lands, and less charge it should be to you, for well I wot, it shall be less charge to me' (S. Haynes, ed., *Burghley Papers*, p. 76).

[77] PRO SP68/III (*SP For.* 1547–53, 160).

[78] PRO SP68/III (*SP For.* 1547–53, 177), Strype II (2), CC, BM MS Cotton Galba B XII, f. 91, and Burnet II (2), 40 (bk I).

[79] PRO SP68/III (*SP For.* 1547–53, 177) and Strype II (2), CC.

[80] *SP Span.* 1547–9, p. 352.

capacity for political thought mean that he planned a new system of government based on novel principles? Historians have tended to think so, regarding his policy as the product either of liberal or of despotic designs, and of a wish to demote the old nobility.[81] However, the only tenable evidence of principled planning is provided by the decline in the number of bishops holding offices of state, and by the garrisoning of midland Ireland.

The coincidence of the bishops' removal from affairs of state and the establishment of protestantism as the official religion was not purely fortuitous in view of the protestant feeling that bishops should confine themselves to their pastoral care.[82] Nevertheless, this idea concerned the running of the church rather than the state; it emphasized that bishops should serve their calling adequately rather than that non-churchmen should run the government. In this respect, it was more the by-product of a desire for ecclesiastical reorganization than an attempt at political reform. Moreover, application was not as simple as aspiration. Crucial to the bishops' removal from the government were not just the wishes of protestants, but also the disappearance of bishops capable of fulfilling secular tasks. The disgrace of Gardiner in the closing months of the previous reign and his differences with the Edwardian government, which prevented his recall to politics, were both of vital importance in altering the picture. Because of Gardiner's enormous experience in affairs of state, which initially the government was prepared to use,[83] it is difficult to see how Gardiner could have been excluded if he had behaved with more circumspection. Only in the special case of Ireland did a new scheme for political reform compel a change in the governmental system.

Without question, no new attitude towards government influenced the government's choice of its secular personnel. In spite of his conclusions, Jordan's findings indicate that if the small group of new nobility, which dominated the council of Henry VIII and Edward VI, is set apart from the rest of the nobility, no noticeable difference is discernible in employment and reward between the remainder of the new nobility and the old nobility.[84] Membership of the new nobility did not necessarily receive more government favour than membership of the old nobility. In fact, the government's capacity to conceive the nobility in the separate categories of 'old' and 'new' is highly dubious. The employment and reward of the nobility was, in the traditional manner, related to worth, ambition and good fortune, not to any social preference which the government was able to make within its ranks.

[81] See Pollard, pp. 57 *ff*, and Jordan I, pp. 172–4 for Somerset's 'experiment in liberty', and see G. R. Elton 'Government by Edict?', *Historical Journal* 8 (1965), p. 270, and his 'The Good Duke', *ibid.* 12 (1969), p. 705 for the view that the Somerset government had autocratic tendencies. Jordan, particularly, inclines towards the view that the Somerset government was noticeably opposed to the old nobility (Jordan I, pp. 90 *ff*).

[82] Somerset informed Gardiner: 'we do not think meet that bishops, having such charge of their flock as indeed they have, and require such presence, should have also cure and charge out of their diocese' (Muller, App. 3, p. 495).

[83] In a diplomatic matter (claimed by Gardiner at his trial (Foxe VI, p. 106), and confirmed by Paget's deposition (*ibid.*, p. 165).

[84] Jordan I, pp. 95–103.

The relationship between government planning and the changes which occurred in the method of government is demonstrated both by the repeal act and by the government's use of proclamations. While undoubtedly initiated by the government, the act was by no means the originally drafted bill. A large part of the act was unofficially created during its passage. After being introduced in the Lords who passed it with the addition of one proviso (either vii, x, xi or xii), the bill was redrafted by the Commons who accepted the preamble, sections one to eight, and the first half of section nine, added or amended sections nine to thirteen, and annexed a proviso of eight sections (xiv to xxi). All of this was accepted by the Lords who inserted a further proviso (section xxii). Thus, in an act of twenty-two sections only the preamble and the first eight and a half sections express with any certainty the government's original aims.[85] The government was responsible for the repeal of the Henrician treason and felony legislation, for making words a treasonable offence only in the third instance, for depriving the clergy of their traditional benefit for major crimes and possibly for transferring the benefit to the peerage.[86] But the sections which were not the work of the government added some of the more interesting and startling items, particularly the important provisos requiring in cases of treason by words that the accusation be made within thirty days of the offence, as well as insisting upon the unforced confession of the accused or the evidence of two witnesses in all cases of treason, and the restriction of forfeiture in major crimes to lands held in fee simple.[87] Because of the moderate changes in the law of treason and felony which the official part of the act effected, and the inevitable contribution which protestantism in power made to the abolition of the religious statutes, the basic 'liberalism' of the repeal act seemed to be heavily influenced by the modifications which parliament unofficially made to the original bill.

It would be perverse to deprive the repeal bill of all principle. After all, the government was moved like parliament by a concern for the anomalous harshness of certain Henrician statutes. However, generally the repeal act seems explicable only in more complicated terms. It resulted from several practical considerations, among which was the government's need to secure popularity in the realm and to release proclamations from the complications imposed by the proclamations act. It reflected the needs of protestants who, placed in authority and untrammelled by the presence of Henry VIII and other conservatives in religion, now had the chance to cast off the restraints which before had, so they could argue, withheld the Word from the people. It also realized the desire of

[85] See the Original Act (1 Edward VI, 12), which is on three separate pieces of parchment (in addition to the provisos annexed), the first two pieces containing the preamble and the first eight and a half sections, and indicating that the bill was dispatched from the Lords to the Commons, and the third piece containing the second half of section ix and sections x, xi, xii and xiii, and, in contrast, indicating that it was dispatched from the Commons to the Lords.

[86] Although in the part redrafted by the Commons, it seems unlikely that the Commons should have initiated the section allowing the peerage benefit of clergy. It seems reasonable to believe that this was part of the bill which received the original assent of the Lords and was adopted by the Commons.

[87] 1 Edward VI, c. 12 (xix, xxii and xvii).

laymen to wrench from the clergy their traditional privileges. Finally, it resulted from a pressure brought by parliament to react more strongly against the Henrician government than Somerset and his colleagues had at first intended.

Forced by circumstance, Somerset's government found no difficulty in re-imposing restraints and in acting harshly. This could not be said to have offended any principle. As Somerset informed the imperial ambassador, his government had intended the repeal act only to rid the realm of the unnecessary oppression of certain laws, not to free it of its traditional restraints.[88] Basically, the repeal act was not the principle of a man without the stomach for rigorous measures,[89] but the ploy of a man anxious to appear virtuous and prepared to practise policy before resorting to force.

In trying circumstances, as with the 1549 commission against enclosures, Somerset was capable of infringing the law. But it cannot be said that he designed to supplant the traditional policy with a despotic system of government. This is evident in his use of proclamations. Although his government issued them with greater frequency than its predecessors or successors in the sixteenth century,[90] it did not bestow upon them a wider range of function. The basic purpose of pro-clamations remained unchanged and mainly served either to enforce, suspend, anticipate and modify statutes, or to impose regulations in matters accepted as beyond the scope of statute. On several occasions Somerset used proclamations questionably, but not as part of a plan to use them in a new way. Generally, there was no blatant abuse of the instrument: the government made no attempt to repeal statutes by proclamations nor to use proclamations to tax the realm nor to create completely new felonies and treasons. Moreover, while relying heavily on proclamations, Somerset's government revealed its lack of interest in any alter-native system to the statute-based common law by making no attempt to increase the effectiveness of proclamations other than to use them *quoad terrorem populi*, and for offering rewards.

One third of the Somerset proclamations basically upheld statute, serving to provide it with additional flexibility and effectiveness. A small proportion of these proclamations simply enforced or anticipated statutes. The rest regulated the operation of statutes by altering their terms.[91] No matter whether they enforced or modified statutes, all these proclamations were similarly the flunkeys of statute, their function owing everything to the existence and supremacy of the latter.

The minor alteration of statutes by proclamation was established practice. None of the modifications made to statutes by the Somerset proclamations marked a new departure, and no Somerset proclamation encroached despotically upon a statute by denying its basic meaning. The Somerset government, for example, used proclamations to increase the severity of a statute but only by adding the pain of imprisonment to the statutory penalty of fine and forfeiture.[92] It also used

[88] *SP Span.* 1547–9, p. 197.
[89] See Constant, *op. cit.* II, pp. 35 *ff*, Jordan I, p. 351, and Pollard, pp 318 *f*.
[90] See graph, p. 130.   [91] See table 6.2, p. 147.
[92] Hughes and Larkin, 295, 315, 319, 326 and 331. The exception was the proclamation adding the pain of slave service in the galleys to the milder statutory penalties for rumour mongering (*ibid.*, 329).

proclamations to extend the range of a statute. More often than not, this latter practice involved the death penalty.[93] Thus proclamations imposed the penalty of treason upon persistent rioters who pretended in their actions to support the government, and upon officials encouraging, leading or equipping the insurgents.[94] Others imposed the statutory penalties for counterfeiting upon the

Table 6.2 **Statutory proclamations**

The figures in brackets represent the proclamations included in the adjacent figure, which relate to a number of statutes allowing regulation to be made by means of proclamation: 25 Henry VIII, c. 1 and 2; 26 Henry VIII, c. 10, and 28 Henry VIII, c. 14 (modified 34/35 Henry VIII, c. 7) and 27 Henry VIII, c. 26. The bracketed figures in the second column represent proclamations resting on these statutes but imposing penalties in excess of what the statutes specifically allowed, while the rest of the proclamations represented by the bracketed figures behave completely in accordance with statutory authority.

Proclamations	Simply enforcing statutes[1]	Extending statutes[2]	Regulating time of operation of statutes[3]	Mitigating the rigour of statutes[4]	Total statutory Proc.	Proc. issued[5]
Cromwellian regime 1534–March 1540	7 (4) +3*	5	10 (7)	2	27	47
Somerset regime	6 +2*	15 (4)	4 (3)	3	29	72
Northumberland regime	7 (3)	9 (3)	—	2	18	35

* These are anticipations of statutes (Hughes and Larkin, 145, 152 and 153; *ibid.*, 297 and 299). Only the Somerset proclamations which were enacted before his fall from power have been counted as 'anticipations'.
[1] Hughes and Larkin, 149, 168, 170, 172, 173, 183, and 187; *ibid.*, 306, 309, 324, 330, 337 and 339; *ibid.*, (*iii*), 356, 366, 375, 380, 381 and 383.
[2] Hughes and Larkin, 142, 161, 163, 171, 186; *ibid.*, 278, 281, 295, 304, 315, 319, 323, 325, 326, 327, 329, 331, 336, 342, 345; *ibid.*, 357, 359, 361, 365, 368, 371, 373, 377, 380, 386.
[3] Hughes and Larkin, 144, 148, 154, 159, 162, 164, 166, 175, 181, 193; *ibid.*, 280, 295, 296, 301.
[4] Hughes and Larkin, 143, 146; *ibid.*, 284, 286, 317; *ibid.* 381 and 387.
[5] The number of functions does not correspond to the number of proclamations because some proclamations had more than one function.

traffickers of counterfeited coin, and for piracy upon the abettors of piracy, while another extended the death penalty, recently enacted for soldiers departing without licence, to pilferers of military equipment, soldiers deserting their posts and to the unauthorized pillaging of assured Scots.[95] Proclamations could thus extend the

[93] For the two instances not involving the death penalty, see Hughes and Larkin, 278 and 281.
[94] *Ibid.*, 336 and 342.   [95] *Ibid.*, 326; *ibid.*, 323; *ibid.*, 325 (2/3 Edward VI, c. 2).

crimes of felony and treason, but not by creating completely new treasons and felonies. The cases where proclamation authorized the death penalty were closely related to existing statutes which already sanctioned capital punishment. Finally, proclamations extended statutes in the legitimate manner of withdrawing the royal right of remittance, particularly by forbidding licences for the export of victuals and other commodities, at times when such exports were placed under a general statutory prohibition.[96] Essentially these extensions by proclamation did not express any despotic deliberations but the ineffectiveness or inappropriateness of the statute book at a given moment, and the government's desperation in a time of crisis. Proclamations also suspended statutes temporarily or removed the suspension—a practice in accordance with legitimate procedure—while one proclamation brought forward the date of a statute's application which was another valid modification.[97] In these instances, proclamation, in response to changing circumstances, was merely making statutes flexible. The three proclamations which mitigated statutes were also in order. One merely granted a pardon to certain pirates for past crimes. The other two concerned the offence of deer poaching which in the previous reign had been made a felony. Before abolishing the felony in the repeal act, the Somerset government proclaimed unspecified punishments for hunting the king's deer in the honour of Grafton and the forest of Barnwood presumably in order to reduce the statutory penalty.[98] The two proclamations have an odd ring about them, as Somerset was authorized to determine the penalty. But as the matter was private and the penalty mitigatory, Somerset was presumably acting on the behalf of the infant king, rather than illegitimately overruling the law.

The above practice was by no means in complete conformity with the past. Distinctive departures were the small proportion of 'statutory' (as opposed to non-statutory) proclamations, and within that category the large proportion of extending proclamations.[99] Furthermore, compared with the proclamations of the 1530s and early 1540s, the Somerset proclamations show a remarkable unwillingness to suspend statutes, a feature shared by the proclamations of the Northumberland regime. However, this merely marked the running-down of a novel practice of the 1530s when a number of statutes were enacted which, in the interest of flexibility, permitted their operation to be regulated by proclamation.[100] Nor did the Somerset regime share the inclination of past governments to use proclamations which simply recalled, with the threat of the king's indignation, the existence of statutes worthy of enforcement. This habit, however, was reacquired by the Northumberland government. The distinction of the Somerset government's 'statutory' proclamations lies in their abandonment of earlier functions, as well as the government's greater use of them to extend the terms and penalties of statutes.

[96] Hughes and Larkin, 304, 319 and 345.

[97] *Ibid.*, 280 and 301; *ibid.*, 295; *ibid.*, 296 (which made 1 Edward VI, c. 1 immediately operable, thus overriding the starting point of 1 May 1548 which was laid down in the enactment).

[98] *Ibid.*, 317, 284 and 286, and 32 Henry VIII, c. 11.

[99] See table 6.2, p. 147.

[100] *Ibid.*

Neither change provided proclamations with a new role. As in the past, proclamations during the protectorate served the important task of being an adjunct to statute, with the specific purpose of remedying its clumsiness or ineffectiveness in the interests not of autocracy but of practicality.

Somerset's forty-three non-statutory proclamations, the remainder of those issued, rested purely upon the authority of the king's prerogative. Remarkably, the bulk of them arose from situations and dealt with matters which forced the government to issue an order resting solely upon its prerogative power. Proclamations were indisputably the proper and sole instrument for changing the coinage, regulating the king's private affairs at Court, adjoining law terms in emergency, summoning royal officials to the king's service, announcing the king's accession, declaring changes in the court of augmentation's methods of paying pensioners, ordering the payment of the king's debt, and countermanding or suspending prerogative orders.[101] Resorting to statute in these matters would have been outrageous, absurd or impossible. Such needs produced seventeen proclamations. Also beyond the scope of statute were the political emergencies of war and insurrection, another traditional matter for proclamation. Six non-statutory proclamations belonged to Somerset's wars against France and Scotland, and nine related to the risings of 1548 and 1549.[102] In these matters proclamations were no alternative to statute. They were the only instrument at the government's disposal.

In addition, the government issued eleven non-statutory proclamations whose subject matter was not the indisputable preserve of the king and where the government had something of a choice between resting its orders on statutory or prerogative authority, and selected the latter. The main feature of this group of proclamations is the predominance of proclamations which either deal with religious matters, repeat former proclamations or are compelled by emergency. Religion was a sphere of government activity which statute had invaded without annexing. Moreover, out of respect for the king's prerogative, the proclamations act had defined religion as a special field for proclamation.[103] Thus, Somerset had a clear choice of instrument for effecting religious change. In 1549, according to Paget, Somerset had considered changing religion by order rather than by statute, but, in fact, had used both statutes supported by proclamations, and non-statutory proclamations,[104] the latter being pure and legitimate assertions of the Crown's authority as head of the church. One of these non-statutory proclamations temporarily suspended preaching and was therefore hardly the concern of statute,[105] but the remaining four were common material for proclamation and statute alike. In practice, Somerset's approach to religious change was no different

---

[101] Hughes and Larkin, 302 and 321; *ibid.*, 290, 293, 320 and 347; *ibid.*, 312; *ibid.*, 277; *ibid.*, 275, 276, 289, 307 and 316; *ibid.*, 282; *ibid.*, 313, 322 and 332.

[102] *Ibid.*, 291, 298, 314, 318, 349 and 350; *ibid.*, 308, 333, 334, 340, 341, 343, 346, 348, 351.

[103] See above, pp. 136 f, and 31 Henry VIII, c. 8 (Hughes and Larkin, p. 546).

[104] PLB, Paget to Somerset, 25 December 1548. This was probably intended if parliament refused to enact the measures; Hughes and Larkin, 281, 296, 297, 299; *ibid.*, 287, 292, 300, 303, 313.

[105] *Ibid.*, 313.

from that of Cromwell and Northumberland. His method of using a combination of statutes, circulars, commissions and proclamations to impose changes in doctrine as well as in discipline and ceremony, accorded with existing habit.

Three of these common-ground proclamations repeated earlier proclamations and therefore cannot be regarded as innovations.[106] A further two have to be seen in a situation of economic and political crisis since they were issued in 1549 when the government was faced with extensive peasant risings and a price rise which was no longer alleviated by a glut of corn. In these circumstances, the government called upon proclamation in a traditional manner to prevent the hoarding of victuals, and to deal with players who were held partly responsible for the insurrections.[107] These cases were rendered non-statutory not only by the inadequacy of the law and the need for immediate action, but also by Somerset's fall, prior to the third session of the first Edwardian parliament which denied him the opportunity to secure statutory confirmation of recently issued proclamations, a practice used by his government on two earlier occasions.[108] Somerset's fall may have determined the character of another proclamation in this category, since a proclamation regulating the manufacture of woollens was enacted almost word for word, but with a milder penalty, in the session which followed the termination of the protectorate. This enactment cannot be regarded as proof of the Northumberland regime's greater reverence for statutory authority, since fairly late in the previous session a bill for the false-making of cloth had been introduced to the Commons.[109] In all likelihood, the Somerset government had proceeded by proclamation as a result of the failure to enact this bill, and as a temporary measure until the enactment could take place, and the non-statutory character of the proclamation was only the accident of a political event which brought the regime to a close. The same may well have happened with the victuals proclamation which had been thwarted as a bill in the second session and was enacted under the Northumberland regime.[110] What is certain in these cases is that the use of proclamation did not indicate a preference for proclamation over statute. The same can be said for the remaining proclamation which opposed the killing of the king's deer in Waltham Forest, a subject for statute which was issued in the interval between the repeal of the relevant Henrician law and its re-enactment by the Northumberland regime.[111] It was clearly an emergency matter. The text reveals that the offenders were acting upon the rumour, presumably generated by the official disparking of Hampton Court Chase, that Waltham Forest was to be dissolved. In the circumstances the government needed to act with speed, but had no statute to enforce, and therefore proceeded with a non-statutory proclamation. None of this evidence indicates an unusual preference for prerogative authority.

---

[106] Hughes and Larkin, 288, see 179; *ibid.*, 294, see 270; *ibid.*, 310, see 184.

[107] *Ibid.*, 336 and 344.

[108] *Ibid.*, 297 and 299.

[109] *Ibid.*, 328 and 3/4 Edward VI, c. 2; *Commons Journals* (31 January).

[110] Hughes and Larkin, 336; see above, p. 51 and n. 189, p. 77, and 3/4 Edward VI, cc. 19 and 21.

[111] Hughes and Larkin, 311; see above, p. 132, and 3/4 Edward VI, c. 17.

Somerset's non-statutory proclamations were certainly massive in number and, as a proportion of the proclamations his government issued, well in excess of the norm for the early sixteenth century.[112] But it would be rash to conclude or intimate from this evidence a wish to rule in a new manner, or even to regard it as indicating a breach with the past in the method of government. Many of the non-statutory proclamations could only have been given statutory authority by a highly unorthodox use of statute. Furthermore, the character of the Somerset proclamations owed much to circumstance. Political crisis naturally spawned an excess of proclamations of a non-statutory nature. This is exemplified by the excess of non-statutory proclamations in the warring forties and by the greater proportion of 'statutory' proclamations in the peaceful years of the 1530s and the 1550s. At a time when war and insurrection were superimposed upon rampant inflation and religious change, purely prerogative proclamations and those exercising the prerogative to regulate statute, were bound to tower over proclamations which merely recalled and asserted individual statutes, especially when, in addition, the habit had been lost of framing statutes which authorized their future modification by proclamation.

Both the general and specific functions of the Somerset proclamations were in keeping with tradition, and determined by circumstance. Rather than enabling the government to rule without statute or to reduce its dependence upon parliament, their general function was (1) to regulate the law in accordance with present needs, (2) to meet emergencies, (3) to exercise the royal prerogative in matters belonging to the prerogative, (4) to make announcements to the realm and (5) to administer matters too trivial for statute. In particular, Somerset's main uses of proclamations—to prepare for war, to cope with insurrection, to change religion, to alter the coinage and to regulate the export and internal market—was a natural consequence of the way in which proclamations had been previously used.

As there was no change in the purpose of proclamations, the differences between the subject matter of Somerset's proclamations and those of Henry VIII and the Northumberland regime are explicable in terms of governmental experience and of prevailing circumstance. Thus, the lack of price-fixing proclamations was the outcome of the Henrician failure to limit prices by price-fixing statutes and proclamations.[113] Driven by the force of inflation, Northumberland revived the practice of price-fixing by proclamation, but abandoned the measure as a result of the protests it aroused and the government's own misgivings about the effectiveness of employing such primitive remedies for a highly complicated problem.[114] This feeling was probably not newly acquired. Somerset used a price-fixing proclamation once only, again resulting in criticism,[115] and

[112] See Elton, 'Government by Edict?', *Historical Journal* 8 (1965), p. 269.

[113] Between 1534 and 1547 the attempt to fix prices produced twenty-one proclamations; Edward VI issued five.

[114] Hughes and Larkin, 366 and 380; he also used the old price-fixing committee on wine (383), *ibid.*, (III) 382. 5, and Tytler I, p. 341.

[115] Hughes and Larkin, 336: this was the first use to be made of the statute 25 Henry VIII, c. 2,

Table 6.3 **The penalties of proclamations**

A tabulation of the specified penalties which proclamations authorized, calculated as a percentage of the total specified penalties imposed by the proclamations of each regime. Penalties which are mere enforcements of statutes are not included: with the exception of those penalties resting on the act 25 Henry VIII, c. 2, which allowed proclamation to determine the penalty. Figures in brackets represent the number of penalties imposed.

Penalty	Death	Imprisonment	Corporal pain	Fine or confiscation	Forfeiture of goods, chattels, lands	Removing royal pardon	Forfeiture of goods and chattels
Cromwell (46) regime 1534–40	13 (6)	39·1 (18)	2·1 (1)	13 (6)	4·3 (2)	18·6 (8)	10·9 (5)
Somerset (53) regime	17 (9)	45·3 (24)	3·8 (2)	20·6 (11)	5·7 (3)	5·7 (3)	1·9 (1)
Northumberland (39) regime	2·6 (1)	46·1 (18)	5·1 (2)	38·3 (15)	—	—	7·9 (3)

this measure was a device for quietening peasant insurrection rather than a sincere attempt to curb inflation.[116] In fact both Somerset and Northumberland appear to have resorted to it when circumstances were beyond their control and they needed to demonstrate their concern by means of a token. It seems, then, that in the 1530s an experiment in controlling prices by statutes and proclamations was tried, which by the late 1540s was known to have failed, and that this realization explains the lack of price-fixing proclamations. The other noticeable alteration in the subject matter of proclamations was clearly the product of changing circumstances. War and insurrection during the protectorate explain the numbers of proclamations dealing with these matters, while the remarkable glut of corn until the failure of 1549 probably explains the lack of proclamations against regrating and forestalling. Furthermore, the relatively few proclamations on the coinage, compared with the number issued by the Northumberland government, seem to reflect the unwillingness of the Somerset government to abandon debasement.[117] On the other hand, the plethora of proclamations regulating the export of victuals and other commodities expressed the inflation of the time, as well as the need to stockpile supplies for the war effort.[118] Inevitably, a number of proclamations were issued dealing with religion in a time of reformation, but not a remarkable number in view of the changes made.[119] In this modest use of proclamation, the Somerset practice was entirely in accord with that of the Cromwellian and Northumberland regimes. Finally, the royal minority probably accounts for the large number dealing with the king's private interests, a recent development but one which had become recognized procedure in Henry VIII's closing years.[120] Since the Somerset proclamations did not acquire a new purpose, the remarkably large numbers issued merely reflected the need and the willingness to use them and the frequency of this use.

A further distinctive feature of the Somerset proclamations concerned their penalties. As the table indicates, they were relatively harsh.[121] Compared with the practices of both the Cromwellian and Northumberland regimes, the Somerset government employed proclamations with remarkable frequency to impose the severe penalties of death and forfeiture of goods, chattels and lands. Noticeably, the harshness of the penalty stemmed from the degree of crisis which the proclamation had to meet. The death penalty, for example, was imposed only in 1549, in the period of five months stretching from mid-February to mid-July, a time of political and economic emergency.[122] In this respect, the Somerset

---

which allowed the prices to be fixed on a wide range of victuals; see Ferguson, *The Articulate Citizen and the English Renaissance*, pp. 297 and 354.

[116] See Russell, *Kett's Rebellion in Norfolk*, p. 58; Pocock, p. 14, and *SP Span.* 1547–9, p. 405.

[117] Five against nine.

[118] Eleven were issued.

[119] Ten against four for Northumberland and six for Cromwell.

[120] Twelve were issued in the reign of Henry VIII, eleven between 1533 and 1545. Seven were issued during the protectorate.

[121] Table 6.3, p. 152, and G. R. Elton, 'The Good Duke', *Historical Journal* 12 (1969), p. 706.

[122] Three in the space of a few days in July; two in the space of a few days in April.

government's use of proclamations closely resembled that of the Cromwellian regime; in each case savage proclamations were the product of critical circumstances. In Somerset's case, however, the rigour of the penalty seemed more apposite to the offence. Piracy, as a source of international discord, was without question a major hazard, particularly when good relations with the emperor were felt to be of vital importance. In the circumstances, extending the penalties for piracy to its abettors made sense.[123] Furthermore, when the lack of military discipline in the north seemed to threaten the whole policy towards Scotland, the extension of the statutory death penalty for indiscipline in that theatre of war, was realistic and inevitable.[124] In both cases a desperate situation can be held responsible for the harshness of the proclamation. Similarly, in view of the currency crisis, the proclamation extending the death penalty for counterfeiting to traffickers in counterfeited coin was not wilful and wayward, but directly relevant to a critical contemporary problem.[125] The remaining 'death penalty' proclamations all related to insurgency.[126] In each case, given the offence and the inadequacy of the law,[127] severity by proclamation was the only policy.

There was nothing questionable about the Somerset government's use of proclamation to impose the death penalty; nor to impose the penalty of extreme forfeiture. The penalty of extreme forfeiture in most cases accompanied the death penalty, and therefore was not misused. The one exception, an undeniably harsh proclamation threatening perpetual imprisonment and the forfeiture of lands, goods and chattels for assaulting the king's officers, was no innovation but a repeat of a proclamation first issued in 1538.[128] Noticeably, the Somerset proclamations resorted less frequently to the lesser forfeiture of goods and chattels, but this was no indication of their greater severity since the use of this penalty by the Cromwellian and Northumberland governments seemed out of keeping with the offence. Forfeiture of goods and chattels for regrating and forestalling corn, which both Cromwell and Northumberland imposed by proclamation, seemed unnaturally harsh,[129] as it did when a Cromwellian proclamation imposed it for importing books in English for sale in England, for publishing the scriptures in English without permission and, with the death penalty, for disputing the sacrament of the altar.[130] Moreover, when Cromwell resorted to the extreme forfeiture, in both cases the penalty appeared too rigorous for the offence. One was the proclamation, reissued by Somerset for the assault of officers; the other, made in the invasion scare of 1539, imposed death and forfeiture of lands, goods and chattels for conveying ships out of the realm without licence.[131] In Somerset's case, the harshness of the penalty related to circumstance, the nature of the offence and a body of statutory law which happened to fall short of present needs.

123 Hughes and Larkin, 323.

124 *Ibid.*, 325.

125 *Ibid.*, 326.

126 *Ibid.*, 333, 336, 341 and 342.

127 Until the enactment of 3/4 Edward VI, c. 5, and particularly after the repeal act, the government lacked a means of action in the law against riots which were not against the Crown or realm but against specific matters such as enclosures, rabbit warrens, dovecots, and livestock.

128 See Hughes and Larkin, 179 and 288.

129 *Ibid.*, 151 and 365.

130 *Ibid.*, 186.

131 *Ibid.*, 179 and 190.

It did not express a new concept of the use to which proclamations could be put or reveal that any liberty was being taken with the law.

A second important feature of the penalties imposed by the Somerset proclamations—obscured by the general statistical impression—was their relative mildness in certain matters. Compared, for example with that of the Cromwellian regime, the Somerset government's censorship of discussion and publication by proclamation was light, although far from gentle and permissive. The Somerset and Northumberland proclamations went no further than to commit offenders to prison, while those of the Cromwellian regime imposed the penalties of imprisonment, death and the forfeiture of goods and chattels, even prescribing capital punishment for recanted heretics who failed to leave the realm.[132] Compared with the Northumberland government, the Somerset regime proclaimed remarkably mild penalties for contravening the prohibited export of victuals and other commodities. Three of the seven Somerset proclamations which performed this function, imposed no more than the statutory penalty of forfeiture of the goods in question and threatened the king's indignation.[133] The remainder, in a customary manner, ordered the forfeiture of the illicit cargo and imprisonment.[134] In contrast, one of the Northumberland proclamations ordered the forfeiture of the cargo, the ships involved, and the goods and chattels not only of the exporters, but also of those who aided them and even of those consenting to the offence.[135] The other two Northumberland proclamations which related to this offence imposed the more normal forfeiture and imprisonment, and, in one case, a fine as well.[136] In the period 1534–40 only one proclamation placed a prohibition upon exports. It ordered imprisonment, and the heavy forfeiture of double the value of the illicit cargo—penalties Somerset also proclaimed, without the fine, for the illicit export of wool.[137] For leather, one of the commodities of the Cromwellian proclamation, the equivalent Somerset proclamation only threatened the king's indignation. For tallow, the other commodity of the Cromwellian proclamation, the Somerset proclamations only authorized the normal forfeiture of illicit cargo and imprisonment.[138] This evidence does not show the Somerset government to be remarkably mild in its proclaimed penalties, but it does demonstrate that, in his use of proclamations, Somerset was not in every respect prone to unusual harshness, and confirms the impression that when circumstances permitted it, his government had a normal attitude towards the penalties proclamations could legitimately impose.

A notable feature of the Somerset proclamations is the lack of those which might be labelled as suspect because of their penalties. Other than the adopted Cromwellian proclamation for the assault of the king's officers, only one stands out as unnaturally harsh—a proclamation regulating the manufacture of woollens.[139]

---

[132] *Ibid.*, 371 and 374; *ibid.*, 296, 299, 303, 313, 344; *ibid.*, 155 and 186.

[133] *Ibid.*, 304, 306 and 310.

[134] *Ibid.*, 295, 315, 319 and 345.

[135] *Ibid.*, 365.

[136] *Ibid.*, 357 and 361.

[137] *Ibid.*, 184 and 345.

[138] *Ibid.*, 310; *ibid.*, 304, 315 and 319.

[139] *Ibid.*, 328. At the same time, proclamation 336 which threatened offenders for taking the law

It imposed the pain of imprisonment, which was clearly thought excessive since the next session of parliament enacted the regulations of the proclamation almost verbatim, but amended the penalty to forfeiture and fine.[140] In the matter of penalties, the Somerset government seems to have used proclamations without autocratic intention and, except for this one slip, without autocratic mishap.

The final features of the Somerset proclamations sprang from the concern to make them work, a concern epitomized in the proclamation act and intensified by their importance as an instrument of government and by their chronic ineffectiveness. Basically Somerset had two solutions. Neither involved the creation of any new apparatus of government, the harnessing of the existing common-law machinery for the enforcement of proclamations, or the introduction of any startling innovation. The first solution was to offer rewards to cooperative subjects, the reward being expressed in the proclamation, and consisting of a payment by the Crown rather than the moiety of a forfeit as with an informer action. The second solution was to issue, in extreme circumstances, blood-curdling threats which aimed to enforce the royal will with a prospect of terror, a procedure which casts doubt on the validity of accepting penalties at their face value. Neither solution was entirely untried. Proclamations *quoad terrorem populi* had been employed in the past, and were later declared valid in Mary's reign by the opinion of the judges.[141] Rewards had also been offered earlier by proclamation.[142] The Somerset proclamations distinguished themselves by the frequency with which they promised rewards and issued terrible threats.[143] These practices did not express a new attitude towards proclamations. They derived from a desire to make them work, not to make them work with a new purpose.

The Somerset government's concern for enforcement seems responsible for the more dubious proclamations of the protectorate. While some of the suspect proclamations resulted from Somerset's difficulties with his colleagues, and others stemmed from the need to cope with emergencies, the rest were attempts to remedy the normal ineffectiveness of proclamations in situations where they were unavoidable and their effectiveness was a vital necessity.

Three proclamations were particularly suspect in the matter of enforcement. One, although non-statutory, allowed complaint to be made in a court of common law and penalties to be imposed by it: an outrageous misuse of the common

---

into their own hands with the penalties for treason and rebellion, was severe in comparison with 3/4 Edward VI, c. 5, which defined such offences as felonies.

[140] 3/4 Edward VI, c. 2.

[141] Under Cromwell: probably, Hughes and Larkin, 151, 168, 186 and 190; under Somerset, *ibid.*, 333, 336, 339; under Northumberland, *ibid.*, 373 and 377. Also see Pollard, p. 64. For an intimation of Cromwell's attitude towards this aspect of proclamations, see his remarks to Norfolk in which he reported a decision to search for a statute upon which to ground a proclamation and, when found, to add to the proclamation 'politically certain things for the putting the king's subjects and other in more terror and fear' (R. B. Merriman, *Life and Letters of Thomas Cromwell* (Oxford, 1902), I, p. 410).

[142] E.g. Hughes and Larkin, 168.

[143] *Ibid.*, 281, 317, 337 and 339; and see n. 141 and below, pp. 157*f.*

law by the prerogative, with nothing to be said in its extenuation, except that it dealt with a matter of religion, which might have convinced the government that it had greater licence than usual.[144] The second also sought to employ the machinery of the common law for its enforcement, by means of an informer action. In dealing with a coinage matter and an emergency, the calling in of testons which an impoverished government urgently required for the purpose of raising revenue by means of debasement, the proclamation was well within the prerogative sphere and, except for its anomaly of allowing common-law in-former actions, performed a function quite beyond the scope of statute.[145] Essentially, it has to be condemned for its impracticability. The history of the proclamations act had revealed the unwillingness of informers to bring common-law actions against offences created by proclamation.[146] In view of this, it seemed highly unlikely that a proclamation without a statutory base would encourage them to act. These two proclamations stand alone. They suggest a lack of realism rather than a deliberate attempt to break with the past and to demote statute by placing the machinery of the common law at the disposal of the prerogative power.

The third proclamation differed from the other two. While they had authorized with dubious legitimacy the employment of the common-law courts for the en-forcement of proclamations, this appeared to suggest the possibility of dispensing with due process at law.[147] However, the terror which the proclamation was meant to instil has to be distinguished from its real meaning. This is made clear in the surviving correspondence between the council and Lord Russell, evidence which reveals the danger of divorcing proclamations from the situation in which they were issued, and of taking their threats literally.[148] The proclamation was issued in the thick of the western rising. It proclaimed the insurgents as rebels and traitors and the right of faithful subjects to take immediate possession of the rebels' goods and chattels, lands and tenements, fees and offices. The proclama-tion appeared completely unconstitutional since it seemed not to recognize the necessity of trial. But the basic purpose of the proclamation was not to override the common law, but to terminate insurrection by sowing discord among the rebels and encouraging them to disband, or at least to hinder insurrection by deterring the rebels from moving eastwards. The government had no thought of completely enforcing the proclamation. Issued in an emergency, it was essentially an empty threat aimed to provoke fear. It represented the use of the proclamation *quoad terrorem populi*. This became clear when Russell proceeded to confiscate the rebels' possessions and to distribute them summarily. In criticizing his action, the government revealed the real function of the proclamation.[149] Russell was told that the purpose was 'only to draw back and divide the force of the countries which were coming against you'. In amplification, the government referred not

---

144 *Ibid.*, 292.
145 *Ibid.*, 332.
146 See above, p. 139.
147 Hughes and Larkin, 339.
148 See Pocock, pp. 24, 29, 32 *f*, 41 and 68 *ff*.
149 *Ibid.*, pp. 68 *ff*.

only to the wording of the proclamation, but also to the desperate situation in which Russell had reported to find himself, declaring that 'seeing your force was at that time very small, we thought this the best policy to stay the multitude from coming forwards.' It was intended, then, as a strategic ruse in a critical situation. The same correspondence also revealed the government's reverence for the common law and its belief that its proceedings were grounded upon it. In the letter of reproof, it first denied that 'the proclamation is any warrant to your gifts' and then asserted the common-law axiom: 'we do not think that any man should lose lands or goods before he be attainted of the crime which meriteth the punishment', claiming that the proclamation made this point clear by forbidding any grant 'otherwise than his majesty might lawfully dispose of the same'. As a parting declaration of the constitutional framework in which the government aimed to abide, it ruled: 'as in the king's majesty's grants and letters patent, so in all proclamations where any doubt is, the laws must declare and expound.'

Somerset and his colleagues did not seem to differ in their general attitude towards proclamations. Smith, Paget and Russell are known to have criticized particular proclamations of the Somerset government, but did so on the grounds of their insufficiency and ineffectiveness, not because they believed them to be unnecessary or illicit.[150] More criticism followed at Somerset's trial when two proclamations figured in the charges brought against him. Somerset was never accused by his contemporaries of wishing through proclamations to rule in a new way. One of these proclamations had been issued against the will of the other councillors, and stood rightly condemned as an expression of intolerable highhandedness; the other, a pardon which denied the victims of enclosure riots redress in the law, was objected to as an infringement of the law.[151] Further evidence of this conformity in attitude is provided by the proclamations of the Northumberland regime. Taking into account its practice of issuing compound proclamations,[152] and considering that some of the major reasons for using proclamations had disappeared with the declaration of peace in 1550 and the subsidence of peasant risings, and since the legislation of the third parliamentary session had helped to fill the gaps in the law which Somerset in 1549 could only paper over with proclamations,[153] it seems likely that the Northumberland government in its first two years made proclamations with a similar frequency to that of the Somerset government. This indicates that the Somerset regime's willingness to use proclamations did not spring from the protector's wilfulness. Only in 1552 did the proclamation policy appear to change since in that year very few proclamations were made, a fact which revealed the overriding role played by circumstance in determining their issue. Until then, the two regimes had pro-

---

[150] For Russell, see Pocock, p. 41; for Smith, see Ferguson, *op. cit.*, p. 297, and Tytler I, pp. 186 *ff*; and for Paget, see Strype II (2), pp. 431 *f*.

[151] Foxe VI, p. 291 (x): the proclamation was Hughes and Larkin, 327; Foxe VI, p. 291 (xiv): the proclamation was Hughes and Larkin, 340.

[152] See graph p. 130; e.g. Hughes and Larkin, 365, 366, 371 and 373. Somerset issued one: *ibid.*, 336. They were quite common earlier: e.g. *ibid.*, 163 and 186.

[153] Particularly, 3/4 Edward VI, cc. 5 and 17.

ceeded to make proclamations in large numbers in order to cope with emergency situations beyond the competence of statute: situations created by the accession, war, insurrection, currency disorder, rampant inflation and religious change. In 1552 the need disappeared with the absence of crisis. Improprieties were committed in the use of proclamations, but, as a rule, under the pressure of critical circumstances. Lapses into autocracy occurred because of desperation and incompetence, not intentionally and by design.

Somerset's attitudes towards the means of government resulted from the pressure of circumstance and the demands made by the rest of his government policy. Harried by the requirements of war, and the problems of carrying through a reformation, in a time of political weakness and economic crisis, Somerset predictably accepted the existing political system and acted to maintain the co-operation of the realm in the war against Scotland, to establish the true religion, and to stay in power. Governmental changes occurred in the turmoil of crisis and emergency, but not as a result of deliberate planning and cool choice and largely in response to the government's material needs. The only sphere of government in which the Somerset regime did plan and apply a novel approach, without having its actions essentially directed by circumstance, lay in Ireland. For this reason, the novelty of the regime's effective plans for government change derived, like its foreign policy, from a preoccupation with military garrisons, not from a desire to transform the polity of England.

Conclusion

Underlying the policy of the Somerset regime was the Scottish war. Because of the war, the course it took and the pressures it exerted, the government's policy as a whole acquired much of its character. The war determined the nature of the regime's domestic as well as its foreign concerns. It strongly influenced the evolution of the government's social programme, largely by preventing the government from proceeding against inflation with a monetary solution; it determined the government's treatment of peasant rebellion in 1549 when the tactics employed against the rebels owed much to Somerset's initial wish not to be diverted from his Scottish plans. It had a decisive effect upon the religious settlement since the Scottish war made it essential not to antagonize Emperor Charles V, and thus Somerset had to proceed with caution and ambiguity rather than in accordance with his religious beliefs. For the government the Scottish war had priority over other concerns. This not only influenced the nature of these concerns but also gave the policy as a whole a certain unity and coherence.

The standard interpretation of the government's policy stressed the importance of Somerset's appreciation of progressive ideas such as national consolidation, religious toleration, political liberalism, and the redistribution of wealth. But there is no good evidence to suggest that Somerset subscribed to these ideas. Moreover, the area of policy determined by ideas, as opposed to necessary expedients, was largely confined to the establishment of garrisons in Scotland and Ireland, and this was only the use of what had become an unfamiliar device for realizing a traditional aim. The garrisons gave the government's policy a certain distinction, but so did Somerset's persistence with them after changing circumstances had rendered them useless. Similarly, Somerset's social programme is characterized by the use of enclosure commissions in 1548 and 1549, but particularly because he persisted with them in spite of the evidence of their ineffectiveness. Somerset thus impressed himself upon the policy of the regime because of his preoccupation with garrisons and enclosure commissions, not because he was promoting principles alien to the period. He also made his mark because of his keen wish to appear a virtuous and dynamic ruler, and because of his tendency to offer clemency before using force as a means of getting his way, a tactic he used to deal with his brother, peasant rebels, offenders against the agrarian laws, religious dissidents and the Scots. Somerset failed because he was prone to *idées fixes*, not because he was an idealist or too magnanimous.

His personality rather than his political thinking produced a policy which was distinct from that of other Tudor governments. Somerset's basic aims—the garrisoning of Scotland, religious reform, the control of inflation and maintaining the security of the state—were far from strange to his contemporaries. His political and social beliefs and assumptions were, for the most part, shared by the rest of the government. In fact, much of the regime's policy was a joint responsibility, not something attributable to Somerset alone. In addition, the policy was moulded by circumstance. The policy of Edward VI's other government differed from Somerset's not only on account of Somerset's downfall but also because the war ended in 1550, the harvest failed in 1549, 1550 and 1551 and the cloth trade slumped in 1551 and 1552.

Essentially, Somerset struggled to uphold conventional values, principles and aims, handicapped by a difficult personality and by critical circumstances, some of which like the Scottish war and the peasant risings were largely his responsibility, while others, such as the minority, inflation, religious schism and the exhaustion of the country after the wars of Henry VIII, were not. The specific character of the regime's policy sprang from the difficulties in which the government was placed both because of Somerset's inflexible personality, and because of these circumstances. This was the making of the government's policy. Absent were unfamiliar principles or extraordinary personal qualities. Somerset was very much a man of his time. 'The good duke' was merely a reputation which he desired and gained and which affected the appearance of the regime's social programme. It did not determine the basic substance of his government's policy.

Index

M